Daughters
and Rebels

BY JESSICA MITFORD

Daughters and Rebels
The American Way of Death
The Trial of Dr. Spock
Cruel and Unusual Punishment
A Fine Old Conflict
Poison Penmanship

Daughters and Rebels

AN AUTOBIOGRAPHY

Jessica Mitford

AN OWL BOOK

HOLT, RINEHART AND WINSTON
New York

Published by Holt, Rinehart and Winston,
383 Madison Avenue, New York, New York 10017.
Published simultaneously in Canada by Holt, Rinehart
and Winston of Canada, Limited.

Library of Congress Cataloging in Publication Data
Mitford, Jessica, 1917–
Daughters and rebels.
1. Mitford, Jessica, 1917–   .   2. England—Biography.
3. England—Social life and customs—20th century.   I. Title.
CT788.M56A3   1980   942.083'092'4 [B]   81–47450   AACR2
ISBN 0–03–059683–1

First published in hardcover by
Houghton Mifflin Company in 1960.

First Owl Book Edition—1981

Printed in the United States of America
1 3 5 7 9 10 8 6 4 2

to Constancia Romilly
(The Donk)

Prologue

FAMILY SOUVENIRS have an almost universal fascination. In most homes there exist, put away in attics or on top shelves, a row of Baby's first shoes, Brother's prize-winning essay in the school paper, Sister's wedding veil, fading telegrams of congratulations on this, that and the other. Most houses, too, bear scars imprinted by those who have lived in them — the still-visible BB gun shots fired by an unsteady childish hand, the hole in the fireplace rug suffered when a party got too gay.

After the onset of middle age these trophies begin to hold considerable interest, for it is then that they bring back in startling relief forgotten events, memories completely buried under a mountain of thousands upon thousands of days gone by. When I first revisited my mother's house in 1955, at the age of thirty-eight, after an absence of nineteen years, I too fell under the spell of the past. The tangible evidences of this past are, it is true, somewhat different from those found in the average English home.

In the windows, still to be seen, are swastikas carved into the glass with a diamond ring, and for every swastika a carefully delineated hammer and sickle. They were put there by my sister Unity and myself when we were children. Hanging on the walls are framed pictures and poems done by Unity when she was quite small — queer, imaginative, interesting work, some on a tiny scale of microscopic detail, some huge and magnificent. The Hons' Cupboard, where Debo and I spent much of our time, still has the same distinctive, stuffy smell and enchanting promise of complete privacy from the Grown-ups.

There are shelves of family books in the drawing room: *Memories* by Lord Redesdale, Grandfather's depressingly huge autobiography; *Writings of a Rebel,* a privately printed volume of letters to *The Times* by Uncle Geoff; Esmond Romilly's *Out of Bounds* and *Boadilla;* a couple of books by Sir Oswald Mosley; an impressive shelf of Nancy's books, both in English and in translation.

The most fascinating of all are my mother's voluminous scrapbooks, dozens of them, huge tomes, each arranged carefully in some sort of order either of subject matter or of period. One is devoted entirely to newspaper clippings about the family: "Whenever I see the words 'Peer's Daughter' in a headline," she once commented rather sadly, "I know it's going to be something about one of you children." Another is a collection of her children's wedding photographs. Diana's wedding to Bryan Guinness, by far the grandest, takes up most of the book, and the sepia photos themselves are so huge that they hardly fit the immense pages. There is pose after pose, Diana close-up, Diana standing by the fireplace, Diana full face, Diana three-quarter face, all with the same pure, bridal expression. Then comes Nancy's wedding, with ten little page-boys in white satin, some of them bundled up against the cold in cashmere shawls. Pam and Debo seem to have been short-changed, for there are many fewer photos of their weddings, Pam's having taken place in a registry office and Debo's in the middle of the war. Somewhere buried in this wedding scrap-book is a rather fuzzy snapshot, labeled "Decca's Wedding," of my husband and myself, sitting together looking self-consciously defiant on the edge of an unmade bed in a hotel bed-room. "I'm sorry about it, Little D., but it's the only one there was, you know," my mother said gently.

Looking backward is not much in my nature, but, once having looked, I decided to set down what I saw. I suppose this is the place to mention that inaccuracies and distortions there are bound to be, as always when relying entirely on recollection; yet for an account such as this there are no other sources but one's own, sometimes unreliable, memory.

Daughters
and Rebels

I

THE COTSWOLD COUNTRY, old and quaint, ridden with ghosts and legends, is today very much on the tourist route. After "doing" Oxford, it seems a shame not to travel on another twenty miles or so to see some of the historic villages with the picturesque names — Stow-on-the-Wold, Chipping Norton, Minster Lovell, Burford. The villages themselves have responded prettily to all this attention. Burford has, indeed, become a sort of minor Stratford-on-Avon, its ancient inns carefully made up to combine modern comfort with a Tudor air. You can even get Coca-Cola there, though it may be served at room temperature, and the little shops are full of Souvenirs of Historic Burford, bearing the unobtrusive legend *Made in Japan.*

For some reason Swinbrook, only three miles away, seems to have escaped the tourist trade, and has remained as I remember it more than thirty years ago. In the tiny village post office the same four kinds of sweets — toffee, acid drops, Edinburgh Rock and butterscotch — are still displayed in the same four large cut-glass jars ranged in the window. Hanging in the back of the shop, as they have hung for two generations, are bright framed prints of contrasting Victorian beauties, one a golden-haired, delicate young lady with luminous blue eyes, her soft white shoulders draped in a pre-Raphaelite something, the other a roguishly pretty gypsy maiden whose incredibly thick black hair falls in great round curls. As a child, I always thought them amazingly like Nancy and Diana, my older sisters. Next to these, the unnaturally pink and white faces of King George V and Queen Mary still gaze benignly at the world.

The only other public buildings are a one-room schoolhouse and the church. Around these a dozen gray stone cottages lie huddled like Cotswold sheep, quiet and timeless. Inside the church, the rows of varnished oak pews — contributed by my father after the first World War, out of the proceeds of a successful bet on the Grand National — still seem to strike a too modern note in contrast to the medieval flagstones, buttresses, pillars and arches. The Redesdale coat of arms, bearing its blandly self-assured motto, "God Careth For Us," which hangs above the family pews, still looks a little too shiny and contemporary beside the crumbling gray stone memorials to an earlier Swinbrook family, whose statues have lain stiffly in place for four hundred years.

Two miles up the hill from Swinbrook village stands a large rectangular gray structure of three stories. Its style is neither "modern" nor "traditional" nor simulated antique; it bears rather the utilitarian look of frankly institutional architecture. It could be a small barracks, a girls' boarding school, a private lunatic asylum, or, in America, a country club. There has been more than a suspicion of all of these functions in its short history. It is actually Swinbrook House, built by my father to satisfy the needs, as then seen, of a family with seven children. We moved there in 1926, when I was nine years old.

Swinbrook had many aspects of a fortress or citadel of medieval times. From the point of view of the inmates it was self-contained in the sense that it was neither necessary, nor generally possible, to leave the premises for any of the normal human pursuits. Schoolroom with governess for education, riding stables and tennis court for exercise, seven of us children for mutual human companionship, the village church for spiritual consolation, our bedrooms for hospital wards even when operations were necessary — all were provided, either in the house itself or within easy walking distance. From the point of view of outsiders entry, in the rather unlikely event that they might seek it, was an impossibility. According to my father, outsiders included not only Huns, Frogs, Americans, blacks and all other foreigners, but also other people's children, the majority of my older sisters' acquaintances, almost all young men — in fact, the whole teeming population of the earth's surface, except for some, though not all, of our relations and a very few tweeded, red-faced country neighbors to whom my father had for some reason taken a liking.

In a way, he was not "prejudiced" in the modern sense. Since the thirties, this term has come to mean the focussing of passionate hatred against a selected race or creed, Negro, Oriental, or Jew; the word "discrimination" has even become almost synonymous with prejudice. My father did not "discriminate"; in fact, he was in general unaware of distinctions between different kinds of foreigners. When one of our cousins married an Argentinian of pure Spanish descent, he commented, "I hear that Robin's married a black."

Unceasing tug-of-war was waged with Farve by Nancy, Pam and Diana, the three grown-up daughters, to be allowed to have their friends to stay. Since my mother rather enjoyed having visitors she was often an ally, and these battles were frequently won. My brother Tom's friends — portly, blond young men known by Nancy as "the Fat Fairs" — were an exception; they were always allowed.

For the three younger children, Unity, Debo and me, the

company of one another was thought to be amply sufficient. Except for very rare visits from cousins, the three of us were brought up in complete isolation from our contemporaries. My mother thought the company of other children unnecessary and overstimulating. Nevertheless, there had been a time when we had been taken on rare occasions to birthday parties or Easter egg hunts at the homes of neighboring county families.

Even this limited social life came to an abrupt halt, never to be renewed, when I was nine — and I inadvertently caused its cessation. I was enrolled in a dancing class which met weekly, rotating among various neighbors' houses. Little girls in organdy dresses and cashmere shawls, accompanied by starched nannies, were delivered by their chauffeurs at the appointed place to await the teacher, who came out from Oxford by bus. One fateful afternoon the teacher was an hour late, and I took the opportunity to lead the other children up to the roof, there to impart some delightful information that had just come my way concerning the conception and birth of babies. "And — even the King and Queen do it!" I added impressively. The telling was a great success, particularly as I couldn't help making up a few embellishments as I went along. They begged to hear more, and swore solemnly on the Bible never to repeat a word to a living soul. Several weeks later my mother sent for me. Her face was like thunder; one look, and I knew what must have happened. In the dreadful scolding that followed, I learned that one of the little girls had wakened night after night with screaming nightmares. She had grown pale and thin, and seemed on the verge of a mental crisis. Finally, her governess had pried the truth out of her, and had found out about the horrifying session on the roof. (Luckily for me, she did not reveal that I had brought the King and Queen into it.) Just retribution quickly followed. My participation in the dancing class was abruptly terminated;

it was clear to everyone, even to me, that I couldn't be considered fit company for nice children after that. The enormity of my ill-advised act, the scope and enduring quality of its impact, was such that years later, when I was a debutante of seventeen, I learned from an older cousin that two young men of the neighborhood were still forbidden to associate with me.

Unity, Debo and I were thrown much on our own resources. As a lost tribe, separated from its fellow men, gradually develops distinctive characteristics of language, behavior, outlook, so we developed idiosyncrasies that would no doubt have made us seem a little eccentric to other children our age. Even for England, in those far-off days of the middle twenties, ours was not exactly a conventional upbringing. Our accomplishments, hobbies and amusements took distinctly unusual forms. Thus, at an age when other children would be occupied with dolls, group sports, piano lessons or ballet, Debo spent silent hours in the chicken house learning to do an exact imitation of the look of pained concentration that comes over a hen's face when it is laying an egg, and each morning she methodically checked over and listed in a notebook the stillbirths reported in the vital statistics columns of the *Times*. I amused myself by giving my father daily Palsy Practice, which consisted of gently shaking his hand while he was drinking his tea: "In a few years, when you're really old, you'll probably have palsy. I must give you a little practice now, before you actually get it, so that you won't be dropping things all the time."

Unity and I made up a complete language called Boudledidge, unintelligible to any but ourselves, into which we translated various dirty songs (for safe singing in front of the Grownups) and large chunks of the *Oxford Book of English Verse*. Debo and I organized the Society of Hons, of which she and I were the officers and only members. Proceedings were conducted in Honnish, the official language of the society, a sort of mixture of North of England and American accents. Contrary to a recent historian's account of the origin of the Hons the name derived, not from the fact that Debo and I were Honorables, but from the Hens which played so large a part in our lives. These hens were in fact the mainspring of our personal economy. We kept dozens of them, my mother supplying their food and in turn buying the eggs from us — a sort of benevolent variation of the share-cropping system. (The H of Hon, of course, is pronounced, as in Hen.)

The main activity of the Hons was to plan the outwitting and defeat of the Horrible Counter-Hons, of which Tom was the chief representative. "Death to the Horrible Counter-Hons!" was our slogan as we chased him all over the house with homemade spears. We developed and played endlessly a Honnish game called "Hure, Hare, Hure, Commencement" (of unbearable pain), a contest to see who could best stand being pinched really hard. "Hure, Hare, Hure" was a refinement on an earlier sport known as "slowly working away." Slowly working consisted of unobtrusively taking the hand of an elder, usually Tom, when he was reading a book. Very gently at first, and with infinite patience, one would scratch away at one spot. The goal was to draw blood before the victim noticed what was happening. "Hure, Hare, Hure," on the other hand, required the active co-operation of two players. The first player pinched the arm of the second, increasing the pressure while slowly and rhythmically chanting "Hure, Hare, Hure, Commencement" four times. The player who could endure in silence till the fourth time was the winner. We thought it a marvelous game, and were constantly begging Tom, who was reading law, to look into the possibilities of copyrighting it so that we could exploit it commercially — a royalty to be paid to the Hons' Treasury each time it was played.

Tom, our only brother, occupied a rather special place in family life. We called him Tuddemy, partly because it was the Boudledidge translation of Tom, partly because we thought it rhymed with adultery. "Only one brother and six sisters! How you must love him. How spoilt he must be," strangers would say. "Love him! You mean *loathe* him," was the standard Honnish answer. Debo, asked by a census taker what her family consisted of, replied furiously, "Three Giants, three Dwarfs and one Brute." The Giants were Nancy, Diana and Unity, all exceptionally tall; the Dwarfs Pam, Debo and me; the Brute, poor Tuddemy. My mother has to this day a cardboard badge on which is carefully lettered: "League against Tom. Head: Nancy."

In fact, the anti-Tuddemy campaign, which raged throughout childhood, was merely the curious Honnish mirror-world expression of our devotion to him. For years, he was the only member of the family to be "on speakers" with all the others.

In spite of frequent alliances of brief duration for Boudledidge or Honnish pursuits, or for the purpose of defeating some common enemy — generally a governess — relations between Unity, Debo and me were uneasy, tinged with mutual resentment. We were like ill-assorted animals tied to a common tethering post.

Occasionally Unity and I united in the forbidden sport of "teasing Debo." The teasing had to be done well out of earshot of my father, as Debo was his prime favorite, and fearful consequences could follow if we made her cry. She was an extraordinarily softhearted child, and it was easy to make her huge blue eyes brim with tears — known as "welling" in family circles.

Unity invented a tragic story involving a Pekingese puppy. "The telephone bell rang," it went. "Grandpa got up from his seat and went to answer it. 'Lill ill!' he cried . . ." Lill was on her deathbed, a victim of consumption. Her dying request was that Grandpa should care for her poor little Peking-ese. However, in all the excitement of the funeral, the peke was forgotten, and was found several days later beside his mistress's grave, dead of starvation and a broken heart.

This story never failed to send Debo into paroxysms of grief, no matter how often it was retold. Naturally, we were severely punished for telling it. Months of allowance would be confiscated, and often we were sent to bed as well. A more borderline case would be merely to say, in tones fraught with tragedy, "THE TELEPHONE BELL RANG," in which case Debo howled as loudly as if we had told the story to its bitter end.

Odd pursuits, indeed, and little wonder that my mother's continual refrain was, "You're very silly children."

My mother personally arranged and supervised our educa-tion, and taught us our lessons herself until we reached the age of eight or nine. Thereafter we entered the schoolroom, presided over by a fast-moving series of governesses. No doubt, educators all over the world were at that time debating the theories of John Dewey versus those of the traditionalists; no doubt thousands were somewhere flocking to lectures on the new "Child Psychology." If the fight for equal education for women raged somewhere as a part of the twentieth century struggle for equal rights, no hint of these controversies reached us at Swinbrook. Tom, of course, had been sent away to school at the age of eight, and thence to Eton; but my mother felt that school for girls was unnecessary, probably harmful, and certainly too expensive. She prided herself that she was able to finance our entire education out of the pro-ceeds of her chicken farm, which, after paying all expenses, including the wages of the chicken man, whose name was appropriately "Lay," netted something like one hundred and twenty pounds a year, about the right amount for a governess's annual wage in those days.

Lessons with Muv in the drawing room still stand out for me far more clearly than anything I learned later from the governesses. (The name Muv, set down in black and white, may convey the image of a petite, cozier-than-Mummy mother surrounded by children whom she refers to as "my brood." The name Farve may likewise conjure up the picture of a pallier-than-Daddy father. Not to me. In my earliest memory of them Muv and Farve were actually as tall as the sky and as large as the Marble Arch, and were somewhat more powerful than King and Parliament rolled into one.)

Muv taught English history from a large illustrated book called *Our Island Story,* with a beautiful picture of Queen Victoria as its frontispiece. "See, England and all our Empire possessions are a lovely pink on the map," she explained. "Germany is a hideous mud-colored brown." The illustrations, the text, and Muv's interpretative comments created a series of vivid scenes: Queen Boadicea, fearlessly riding at the head of her army . . . the poor little Princes in the Tower . . . Charlemagne, claimed by Grandfather as our ancestor . . . hateful, drab Cromwell . . . Charles I, Martyred King . . . the heroic Empire Builders, bravely quelling the black hordes of Africa for the glory of England . . . the wicked Indians of the Black Hole of Calcutta . . . the Americans, who had been expelled from the Empire for causing trouble, and who no longer had the right to be a pretty pink on the map . . . the Filthy Huns, who killed Uncle Clem in the war . . . the Russian Bolshies, who shot down the Czar's dogs in cold blood (and, as a matter of fact, the little Czarevitch and Czarevnas, only their fate didn't seem quite so sad as that of the poor innocent dogs) . . . the good so good, and the bad so bad; history as taught by Muv was on the whole very clear to me.

Muv had invented a method of teaching which obviated the necessity for examinations. We simply read the passage to be mastered, then closed the book and related whatever portion of the text we happened to retain. "I always think a child only needs to remember the part that seems important to her," she would explain vaguely. Sometimes it didn't work very well. "Now, Little D., I've read you a whole chapter. Tell me what you remember of it." "I'm afraid I don't remember anything." "Come now, Little D., can't you remember a single word?" "Very well then — THE." Fatal sentence! For years after I could be reduced to tears by sisters and cousins teasing in chorus, "Very well, then — THE."

I graduated to the schoolroom when I was nine. Our schoolroom at Swinbrook, big and airy, with bay windows, a small coal fireplace and chintz-covered furniture, was on the second floor, next to the governess's bedroom. It was separated from the visitors' rooms and my parents' rooms by a green baize door. Here we spent most of our time. We had lunch, and sometimes dinner, downstairs with the grownups except when there were visitors, in which case meals were sent up and we ate in the unenthralling company of the governess, fretfully wondering what delicious things they were having downstairs.

Unity — Bobo to the rest of the family but Boud to me — was the only other schoolroom-age child; Debo was only six, still having lessons with Muv, and otherwise in the nursery under the jurisdiction of Nanny. Nancy and Pam were long since grown up, Tom had gone to live abroad for a bit, and Diana was in Paris, restlessly poised between schoolroom and first London season.

Boud was a huge, outsize child of twelve. She reminded me of the expression "great girl" in Victorian children's books. "Oh dear, poor Boud, she is rather enormous," Muv complained when the semi-annual boxes of children's clothes arrived on approval from Daniel Neal's in London, to be tried on and invariably, in Boud's case, sent back for a larger size. Nancy gave her the blunt nickname of Hideous, but Boud wasn't really hideous. Her immense, baleful blue eyes, large, clumsy limbs, dead straight tow-colored hair, sometimes in neat pigtails but more often flowing loose, gave her the appearance of a shaggy Viking or Little John. She was the bane of governesses, few of whom could stand up for long to her relentless misbehavior, and as a result we never had the same one for any length of time. They came and left in bewildering succession, and each replacement brought with her a new slant on the sum total of human knowledge.

Miss Whitey taught us to repeat, "A-squared-minus-B-squared-equals-A-squared-minus-2-AB-plus-B-squared," but she did not stay long enough to explain why that should be. Boud found out that she had a deadly fear of snakes, and left Enid, her pet grass snake, neatly wrapped around the W.C. chain one morning. We breathlessly awaited the result, which was not long in coming. Miss Whitey locked herself in, there was shortly an earsplitting shriek followed by a thud. The unconscious woman was ultimately released with the aid of crowbars, and Boud was duly scolded and told to keep Enid in her box thereafter. Miss Whitey was succeeded by Miss Broadmoor, who taught us to say *mensa, mensa, mensam* all the way through. Nancy, even in those early days preoccupied with U and non-U usage, made up a poem illustrative of the main "refainments" of Miss Broadmoor's speech: "Ay huff a löft, and öft, as ay lay on may ayderdown so söft (tossing from sade to sade with may nasty cöff) ay ayther think of the loft, or of the w-h-h-h-h-eat in the tröff of the löft." We couldn't resist reciting it each morning as lesson time drew near. Latin lessons came to an end after Miss Broadmoor left. Miss McMurray grew beans on bits of wet flannel and taught the names of different parts of these growing beans — plumule, radical, embryo.

She was soon followed by Miss Bunting, whose main contribution to our education was to teach a little mild shoplifting. Miss Bunting was a dear little round giggly woman, shaped like a Toby Jug, with a carefree and unorthodox approach to life that we found most attractive. Boud towered over her, and sometimes scooped her up and put her, squealing, on the schoolroom piano.

We made occasional trips to Oxford. "Like to try a little jiggery-pokery, children?" Miss Bunting suggested. There were two main methods: the shopping bag method, in which an accomplice was needed, was used for the larger items. The accomplice undertook to distract the shop lady while the lifter, or Jiggery-Poker in Miss Bunting's idiom, stuffed her bag with books, underclothes or boxes of chocolates, depending on the wares of the particular store. The dropped hanky method was suitable for lipsticks or small pieces of jewelry. Miss Bunting in her governessy beige coat and gloves, Boud and I in matching panama straw hats, would strut haughtily past the deferential salespeople to seek the safety of Fuller's Tea Room, where we would gleefully take stock of the day's haul over cups of steaming hot chocolate.

Miss Bunting was very relaxed about lessons. Only when we heard my mother's distinctive tread approaching the schoolroom did she signal us to buckle down to work. She knew nothing and cared less about algebra, Latin or the parts of the bean, and needless to say we liked her much better than any of her predecessors. We did all we could to make life tolerably attractive for her, with the result that she stayed on for some years.

2

PARTICIPATION in public life at Swinbrook revolved around the church, the Conservative Party and the House of Lords. My parents took a benevolent if erratic interest in all three, and they tried from time to time to involve us children in such civic responsibilities as might be suitable to our age.

My mother was a staunch supporter of Conservative Party activities. Although she was never particularly enthusiastic about our local Member of Parliament ("such a *dull* little creature," she would say sadly), Muv campaigned faithfully at each election. Crowds of placid villagers were assembled on the lawn at Swinbrook House to be harangued by our uncles on the merits of the Conservative Party, and later to be fed thick meat sandwiches, pound cake and cups of nice strong tea. Our family always had its booth at the annual Oxfordshire Conservative Fete, where we sold eggs, vegetables from the kitchen garden, and quantities of cut flowers. Debo and I, dressed in our expensive Wendy frocks, were allowed to parade around selling bouquets. Debo hated these occasions because the grownups always cooed over her: "Oh, doesn't Debo look *sweet!*" "Well, Decca's sweet too," was her furious rejoinder.

At election time, sporting blue rosettes, symbol of the Party, we often accompanied Muv to do canvassing. Our car was decorated with Tory blue ribbons, and if we should pass a car flaunting the red badge of Socialism, we were allowed to lean out of the window and shout at the occupants: "Down with the horrible Counter-Honnish Labor Party!"

The canvassing consisted of visiting the villagers in Swinbrook and neighboring communities, and, after exacting a promise from each one to vote Conservative, arranging to have them driven to the polls by our chauffeur. Labor Party supporters were virtually unknown in Swinbrook. Only once was a red rosette seen in the village. It was worn by our gamekeeper's son — to the bitter shame and humiliation of his family, who banished him from their house for this act of disloyalty. It was rumored that he went to work in a factory in Glasgow, and there became mixed up with the trade unions.

The General Strike of 1926 provided enormous excitement. There was a thrilling feeling of crisis in the air. The grownups, unnaturally grave, pored over the daily national bulletin that replaced the newspapers. I managed to smuggle my pet lamb, Miranda, into my bedroom at night to prevent her from being shot down by the Bolshies. Everyone was pressed into service for the emergency. Nancy and Pam, then in their early twenties, established a canteen in an old barn on the highway, about two miles from our house, in which they took alternate shifts serving tea, hot soup and sandwiches to the scabbing lorry drivers. After lessons, Boud and I with our governess, and Debo with Nanny would toil up the hill to help, Miranda strictly at heel in case a Bolshie should jump out of the hedges.

Since lorries keep going all night (a fact none of us had realized before), it was necessary to start the first shift very early in the morning, before sunrise. Pam was detailed for this first shift; she was easily the best at running the canteen, as she was interested in home economics and knew how to make the tea and sandwiches and how to wash the cups. Nancy was known to be hopeless at this sort of thing, and moaned sadly when called on for anything more than handing round the sandwiches: "Oh darling, you know I don't know how to take things out of ovens, one's poor hands . . . besides, I do so hate getting up early."

One morning, about five o'clock, Pam was alone at the canteen as usual when a filthy tramp lurched in from the eerie pre-dawn darkness. Dressed in a ragged suit and worker's cap, his face grimy and hideously scarred, he was a terrifying sight. "Can I 'ave a cup 'o tea, miss?" he leered at Pam, thrusting his dreadful face close to hers, winking with his horribly bright green eyes. Pam nervously started to pour the tea, but he nimbly stepped round the counter. "Can I 'ave a kiss, Miss?" and he put his arm round her waist. Pam, thoroughly terrified, let out a fearful shriek, and in her mad haste to get away from him fell and sprained her ankle. The tramp turned out to be Nancy in disguise. All in all, we were rather sad when the General Strike came to an end and life returned to dull normalcy.

Rather to my mother's disappointment, Farve's interest in politics was much more sporadic than her own. On very rare occasions he lumbered into his London clothes and with much heavy breathing prepared for the trip — always considered a tremendously arduous journey, although it was actually only eighty miles — to sit in the House of Lords. But he only went if the matter being debated presented really burning issues, such as whether peeresses in their own right should be granted permission to sit as equals with Their Lordships. On this occasion Farve roused himself to go and vote against their being admitted; Nancy maintained that the real reason for his opposition to seating the peeresses was that there is only one

W.C. in the House of Lords, and he was afraid they might get in the habit of using it.

Farve's deepest ire, however, was reserved for a proposal to reform the House of Lords by limiting its powers. The Lords who sponsored this measure did so out of a fear that unless such a course was taken, a future Labor Government might abolish the House altogether. Farve angrily opposed this tricky political maneuver. His speech was widely quoted in the press: "May I remind your Lordships that denial of the hereditary principle is a direct blow at the Crown? Such a denial is, indeed, a blow at the very foundation of the Christian faith." To Farve's annoyance, even the Conservative press poked fun at this concept, and the labor press had a field day with it. "What *did* you mean to say?" we asked, and he patiently explained that just as Jesus became God because he was the Son of God, so the oldest son of a Lord should inherit his father's title and prerogatives. Nancy pretended to be surprised at this explanation: "Oh, I thought you meant it would be a blow at the Christian faith because the Lord's son would lose the right to choose the clergyman."

The right to hire and fire the clergy was one which my father would have been loath to relinquish. He had the "living" at Swinbrook, which meant that if the incumbent vicar died or left the parish it became Farve's responsibility to interview and choose among prospective replacements. Shortly after we moved to Swinbrook such choice was made necessary by the death of the Reverend Foster, the parish clergyman. Debo and I managed to eavesdrop on at least one of the interviews that followed. A pallid young man in regulation dog collar was admitted by the parlormaid. "Would you come this way, sir? His Lordship's in the Closing Room," she explained. My father's study had once been known by the more usual terms for such rooms — library, business room, smoking room — but I pointed out to Farve that since he spent virtually his entire life within its walls, one day, inevitably, his old eyes would close there, never to open again. Thus it came to be called the Closing Room, even by the servants. The Closing Room was a pleasant enough place to spend time in if one was not there under duress; it was lined from floor to ceiling with thousands of books amassed by Grandfather, and there was a lot of comfortable leather-covered furniture and a huge gramophone — but the idea of being summoned for an interview with Farve filled us with vicarious terror.

"Oh, poor thing! There he goes. He's for it," Debo whispered from our hiding place under the stairs. We heard Farve explaining that he would personally choose the hymns to be sung at Sunday service. "None of those damn complicated foreign tunes. I'll give you a list of what's wanted: 'Holy, Holy, Holy,' 'Rock of Ages,' 'All Things Bright and Beautiful,' and the like." He went on to say that the sermon must never take longer than ten minutes. There was little danger of running overtime, as Farve made a practice of setting his stop watch and signaling two minutes before the allotted time was up.

"Do you go in for smells and lace?" he suddenly roared at the astonished applicant. "Er?" Questioning sounds could be heard through the walls of the Closing Room. "Incense, choir robes and all that Popish nonense! You know what I'm driving at!" Debo and I squirmed in sympathy.

The poor vicar who was finally selected must often have wished for a softer berth. For one thing, church attendance was an inflexible rule for the whole Mitford family. Every Sunday morning, rain or shine, we stumped off down the hill with Nanny, governess, Boud's goat, her pet snake Enid, Miranda, several dogs, and my pet dove. Some of the graves in Swinbrook churchyard were conveniently surrounded by high railings for better preservation and privacy. These made good cages for the assorted animals, whose loud yelps, cooing and

baaing blended nicely with the lusty voices of the village choir
and effectively drowned out most of the ten-minute sermon. If
Tom was at home, Debo, Boud and I amused ourselves during
the service by trying to "make him blither" — a Honnish expression for an unwilling or suppressed giggle. The best moment for this occurred during the reading of the Ten Com-
mandments. Ranged in the family pew, prayerbooks open,
we'd wait for the signal: "Thou shalt not commit adultery,"
then nudge all down the row to where poor Tom was sitting,
desperately trying to suffocate the giggles. We were sure
he led a glamorous life of sin abroad and in his London
flat, and needed emphasis on this particular Command-
ment.

My mother was hard to pin down in theological discussions.
"Do you believe in Heaven and Hell?" I asked. "Well, one
always hopes there'll be some sort of afterlife. I'd like to see
Uncle Clem again one day, and Cicely, she was such a good
friend of mine . . ." She seemed to envisage the afterlife as a
pleasant afternoon gathering where anyone might drop in.
"But if you don't believe in the miracles and things, what's the
point of having to go to church every Sunday?" "Well, Little
D., after all it *is* the Church of England, we have to support
it, don't you see."

The support took various forms. When Muv remembered she
invited the Vicar and his wife for Sunday luncheon: "Poor
things, they always look so hungry, I rather wonder if they
get *quite* enough to eat." Her vagueness about church procedure must have caused the Vicar some uneasy moments. Once
he came to the house to ask her if she would contribute some
money to help purchase the bier. "Certainly, how much is
needed?" Muv asked. The vicar opined that five pounds
would do nicely. "Five pounds? But who on earth is going
to drink all that beer?"

Muv often took me with her to visit the village women in

Swinbrook with small gifts of charity. Their poverty worried me and filled me with uneasiness. They lived in ancient, tiny cottages, pathetically decorated with pictures of the Royal Family and little china ornaments. The smell of centuries of overcooked cabbage and strong tea lurked in the very walls. The women were old, and usually toothless, at thirty. Many had goiters, wens, crooked backs and other deformities associated with generations of poverty. Could these poor creatures be people, like us? What did they think about, what sort of jokes did they think funny, what did they talk about at meals? How did they fill their days? Why were they so poor?

On the long walk home after one such visit, a brilliant thought suddenly occurred to me.

"I say, wouldn't it be a good idea if all the money in England could be divided up equally among everybody? Then there wouldn't be any really poor people."

"Well, that's what the Socialists want to do," Muv explained. I was abashed to learn that the counter-Honnish Socialists had already thought of my good idea, but pursued the subject nevertheless.

"Why couldn't it be done?"

"Because it wouldn't be fair, darling. You wouldn't like it if you saved up all your pocket money and Debo spent hers, and I made you give up half your savings to Debo, would you?" I immediately saw the point. My idea was pretty hopeless after all.

Shortly after this I was taken to a Conservative Party campaign meeting in the village. Uncle Geoff made the speech. "The trouble with the Labor Party is that they want everyone to be *poor*," he said, "but we want everyone to be *rich*." I had never heard this ancient cliché before, and it struck me as a penetratingly original thought of enduring significance. It was several years before I gave any more thought to Socialist ideas.

3

GROWING UP in the English countryside seemed an interminable process. Freezing winter gave way to frosty spring, which in turn merged into chilly summer — but nothing ever, ever happened. The lyrical, soft beauty of changing seasons in the Cotswolds literally left us cold. "Oh, to be in England Now that April's there," or, "Fair daffodils, we weep to see you haste away so soon . . ." The words were evocative enough, but I was not much of an April noticer or daffodil fancier. It never occurred to me to be happy with my lot. Knowing few children of my age with whom to compare notes, I envied the children of literature to whom interesting things were always happening: "Oliver Twist was so *lucky* to live in a fascinating orphanage!"

Nevertheless, there were occasional diversions. Sometimes we went up to London to stay at our mews in Rutland Gate for Christmas shopping (or shoplifting, depending on whether we were accompanied by Nanny or by Miss Bunting), and sometimes, when Swinbrook was let for a few months, a full-scale migration, Nanny, governess, maids, dogs, Enid, Miranda, dove and all of us, went to my mother's house on the outskirts of High Wycombe. But these small excursions only served to emphasize the dullness of life at Swinbrook.

We were as though caught in a timeproofed corner of the world, foster children, if not exactly of silence, at least of slow time. The very landscape, cluttered up with history, was disconcertingly filled with evidence of the changelessness of things. The main road to Oxford, built by Julius Caesar two thousand years ago, had been altered only by modern surfacing for the convenience of motorists; Roman coins, thrown up by the plow as though carelessly dropped only yesterday, were to be had for the gathering. As part of our lessons we kept Century Notebooks, a page for each century, in which we listed by date the main battles, reigns of kings and queens, scientific inventions. Human history seemed so depressingly short as one turned the pages. The French Revolution only two pages back, and flip! here we are at the twenty-first century, all of us dead and buried — but what will there be to show for it? "Precious little, if we're going to be stuck at Swinbrook for the rest of our lives," I mused sadly.

The great golden goal of every childhood — being a Grownup — seemed impossibly far away. There were for us no intermediate goals to fill the great, dull gap; no graduation from one stage of education to the next; no adolescent "first parties" to look forward to. You were a child, living within all the bounds and restrictions of childhood, from birth until you reached the age of seventeen or eighteen, depending on where your birthday fell in relation to the London season. Life broke down to an endless series of unconnected details, the days punctuated by lessons, meals and walks, the weeks by occasional visits from relations or the older children's friends, the months and years by the unexpected and unplanned for. . . .

Uncles and aunts frequently came to stay. Since my father

was one of nine children, and my mother one of four, an avuncular network extended over the length and breadth of England, from the Scottish border to London. Very occasionally an aunt or uncle would earn permanent banishment from my father's sight, never again to be mentioned in his presence, because of some offense such as getting divorced or marrying a foreigner, but these were the exceptions.

Aunts fell roughly into two categories. There were the married ones, mothers of large families, managers of large staffs of servants, chivvyers of children. These indomitable women of rugged feature and iron hair, seasoned tweed suit and roughened skin, would seek one out on the coldest, sleetiest day in one's refuge by the Closing Room fire. Armed with a good stout walking stick, such an aunt would rap one smartly on the behind: "Reading? In this stuffy house? Come on, come on, get out of doors for a lovely walk, you lazy little thing." Nanny hinted they might be driven by a force beyond their control — the physical and psychological torments of menopause; for when one commented, "I wonder why Aunt —— is so perfectly bloody," she always answered significantly, "It's just her *age,* darling." (According to Nanny, a person's age was at the core of most personality problems, and she would make the same rejoinder to any of our complaints about behavior, whether of a three-year-old cousin, an adolescent sister, or a grandmother: "You must remember, darling, she's just at that *age.*")

There was also the Maiden Aunt, a gentler, wispier type, who lived alone in a small London flat with one maid. The status of the Maiden Aunt had remained generally unchanged since Victorian days. She subsisted on an allowance carefully designed to provide minimum necessaries, a sum considered sufficient but not excessive for Unmarried Daughters and Younger Sons of peers. Whereas the Younger Sons were free to supplement their incomes by going into a profession, the Armed Services, Empire Building or even Trade, such avenues were firmly closed to the Unmarried Daughters, who as time went on sank into the twilight state of aunthood.

The Maiden Aunt was often surrounded by an aura of legend, the more mysterious because those of her generation who, like my mother, knew the facts could never be prevailed upon to reveal the full story. The hints that Muv occasionally dropped only deepened the mystery, making it the more disturbing. "Why didn't she ever marry?" Muv's face would cloud with disapproval at the impertinence of such curiosity about another's private life. "Well, darling, it's none of your business, but, if you must know, something awful happened to her teeth when she was a young girl." "What *sort* of awful thing?" "I think it's called pyorrhea. Anyway, they started to fall out, and for many months she managed to hold them in with bits of bread, but it didn't work . . . now run along, that's all I'm going to tell you." The horror of it! I could never again look at that particular aunt without visualizing a young girl with a glorious Edwardian hairdo, panic-stricken, alone in her room trying to shore up her ruined teeth.

To yet another aunt an even stranger misfortune had occurred. At her first ball, a young man had stepped on her foot. She was laid up for some time, and by the time she recovered it was too late for marriage. "Can't a person get married even though toothless and footless?" I asked Muv, but she merely frowned and changed the subject.

Uncle Tommy, my father's brother, lived only a few miles from us, and therefore we saw more of him than any of the others. A retired Navy captain with bright pink face and snowy hair, he seemed to me like an exaggerated picture of a seafaring uncle out of a story. One of Nancy's young men friends once made the mistake of saying in my father's hearing,

"Darling, your uncle is *easily* the most *beautiful* man I've ever seen in my whole life," which sent Farve into a furious passion and us children into fits of laughter.

Uncle Tommy presided as magistrate at the local police court, and in this capacity doled out his own ideas of justice to the local citizenry. He was particularly proud of having given a three months' jail sentence to a woman driver who accidentally ran her car into a cow on a dark night: "Clap 'em in the brig! That's one way of keeping these damn women off the road."

As magistrate, his duties would include witnessing a hanging if one should occur in the county of Oxfordshire. Somebody mentioned that it was possible for magistrates to avoid this responsibility by paying a fee to a professional witness. "Pay someone to go to the theater?" roared Uncle Tommy, "I should say not."

He was fond of regaling us with stories of his seafaring days, and claimed to have tasted human flesh in the form of black babies served up in a stew in southern U.S. ports. I found his stories disgusting and unfunny. Once I was sent to bed for expressing the wish that he had been caught by cannibals to be boiled up into a tasty soup.

My mother's relations were very different from the Mitfords. Her brother, Uncle Geoff, who often came to stay at Swinbrook, was a small, spare man with thoughtful blue eyes and a rather silent manner. Compared to Uncle Tommy, he was an intellectual of the highest order, and indeed his vitriolic pen belied his mild demeanor. He spent most of his waking hours composing letters to the *Times* and other publications in which he outlined his own particular theory of the development of English history. In Uncle Geoff's view, the greatness of England had risen and waned over the centuries in direct proportion to the use of natural manure, or compost, in fertilizing the soil. The Black Death of 1348 was caused by gradual loss of the humus fertility found under forest trees. The rise of the Elizabethans two centuries later was attributable to the widespread use of sheep manure.

Many of Uncle Geoff's letters-to-the-editor have fortunately been preserved in a privately printed volume called *Writings of a Rebel*. Of the collection, one letter best sums up his views on the relationship between manure and freedom. He wrote,

> Collating old records shows that our greatness rises and falls with the living fertility of our soil. And now, many years of exhausted and chemically murdered soil, and of devitalized food from it, has softened our bodies, and still worse, softened our national character. It is an actual fact that character is largely a product of the soil. Many years of murdered food from deadened soil has made us too tame. Chemicals have had their poisonous day. It is now the worm's turn to re-form the manhood of England. The only way to regain our punch, our character, our lost virtues, and with them the freedom natural to islanders, is to subsoil and compost our land so as to allow moulds, bacteria, and earthworms to re-make living soil to nourish Englishmen's bodies and spirits.

The law requiring pasteurization of milk in England was a particular target of Uncle Geoff's. Fond of alliteration, he dubbed it the "Murdered Milk Measure," and established the Liberty Restoration League, with headquarters at his house in London, for the specific purpose of organizing a counter-offensive. "Freedom, not Doctordom!" was the League's proud slogan. A subsidiary, but nevertheless important, activity of the League was advocacy of a return to the "unsplit, slowly smoked bloater" and bread made with "English stone-ground flour, yeast, milk, sea salt, and raw cane sugar."

Wherever he went, Uncle Geoff carried stacks of copies of

his letters to the *Times* and *Spectator,* together with printed directions for preparing unsplit, slowly smoked bloaters and homemade bread. My mother gave wholehearted support to his ideas on health, to which she added a few of her own. In defiance of the law, she refused to allow any of us to be vaccinated ("pumping disgusting dead germs into the Good Body!"). Not only were we strictly forbidden to eat any canned food, but adherence to Mosaic diet laws was enforced as rigidly as in any orthodox Jewish household. Pork, shellfish, rabbit were proscribed for schoolroom fare on the grounds that Moses had considered these foods unhealthy for consumption by the Israelites, and because my mother had a theory that Jews never got cancer.

Not being of an age to appreciate eccentricity, I was merely bored by the uncles. Nor did I particularly relish the idea of following in the footsteps of either the married or the unmarried aunts. The conversation and mode of life of the older generation filled me with an uneasy restlessness and a strong desire to escape to other realms.

I longed passionately to go to school. The warm, bright vision of living away from home with girls my own age, learning all sorts of fascinating things, dominated my thoughts for years. But no arguments I could advance would move my mother on this point. Besides, she had heard them all before; the older children, with the exception of Pam, had all in turn begged to go. Pam was the only one of the older four who had consistently loved living at home in the country. As a child she had wanted to be a horse, and spent long hours practicing to be one, realistically pawing the ground, tossing her head and neighing.

"I want to go to a university when I grow up," I insisted.

"Well, darling, when you grow up you can do whatever you like."

"But you can't go to the university unless you've passed the exams, and how can I possibly learn enough to pass with a stupid old governess?"

"That's a very rude way to talk. If you went to school you'd probably hate it. The fact is children always want to do something different from what they are doing. Childhood is a very unhappy time of life; I know I was always miserable as a child. You'll be all right when you're eighteen."

This, then, was life: a Gustave Doré mountain, steep, dark and arduous on the way up, thorny, toe-stubbing — but the other side, after reaching the sunlit peak of eighteen, would be easy traveling, pleasure-filled . . . it sounded right, but would one ever reach the peak?

Yet two things did happen in the latter years of the twenties. True they took place in that bright other world of the Grownups, and we in the schoolroom were mere spectators, to be dragged unwillingly away or shooed out of the drawing room at the most exciting moments. Nevertheless, we were not unaffected. These events, which at least lifted life temporarily from the drab and unchanging, were the publication of Nancy's first novel and Diana's marriage to Bryan Guinness.

For months Nancy had sat giggling helplessly by the drawing-room fire, her curiously triangular green eyes flashing with amusement, while her thin pen flew along the lines of a child's exercise book. Sometimes she read bits aloud to us. "You *can't* publish that under your own name," my mother insisted, scandalized, for not only did thinly disguised aunts, uncles and family friends people the pages of *Highland Fling,* but there, larger than life size, felicitously named "General Murgatroyd," was Farve. But Nancy did publish it under her own name, and the Burford Lending Library even arranged a special display in their window, with a hand-lettered sign: "Nancy Mitford, Local Authoress."

The General was portrayed as an ardent organizer of shooting parties, a man of violent temper, terror of housemaids and gamekeepers, who spent most of his time inveighing against the Huns and growling at various languid, aesthetic young men in pastel silk shirts who kept popping up at unexpected moments. My father's peculiar argot — "Damn sewer!" "Stinks to merry hell!" — his loathing of anything or anyone who smacked of the literary or the artistic, were drawn to the life.

Thus Farve became — almost overnight — more a character of fiction than of real life, an almost legendary figure, even to us. In subsequent years Nancy continued to perfect the process of capturing him and imprisoning him between the covers of novels, sometimes as General Murgatroyd, later as the terrifying Uncle Matthew of *Pursuit of Love.* So successful was she that even the obituary writer of the *Times,* describing my father shortly after his death in 1958, betrayed a certain confusion as to whether he was writing about the Rt. Hon. David Bertram Ogilvy Freeman-Mitford or "the explosive, forthright Uncle Matthew . . ."

In spite of the brief row that flared when Nancy insisted on publishing *Highland Fling* under her own name, it became evident that my parents, and even the uncles and aunts, were actually quite proud of having an author in the family. They cited an earlier Miss Mitford — Mary Mitford, author of a minor Victorian novel after the style of *Cranford.* They remarked that such talent often skips a generation, and pointed to *Memories,* by Lord Redesdale, Grandfather's monstrously boring two-volume history of his life.

As for Farve, he rather loved being General Murgatroyd. Now that he had been classified, so to speak, his Murgatroyd-ish aspects began to lose some of their dread, even to take on some of the qualities of raw material for fiction. Actually, by the time I was out of the nursery the terrifying old fires had burned down somewhat, and Farve was considerably mellower than when the others were growing up.

The childhood trials of Nancy, Pam, Tom and Diana had already receded into legend. There was the awful time when they had rashly invited a distinguished German scientist to tea, and Farve had gone into such a furious rage at the idea of having a "bloody Hun" in the house that they were forced to telephone the professor and explain that it would be better if he didn't come. "No one spoke for a week," the story ended. And even I dimly remembered the hushed pall that hung over the house, meals eaten day after day in tearful silence, when Nancy at the age of twenty had her hair shingled. Nancy using lipstick, Nancy playing the newly fashionable ukelele, Nancy wearing trousers, Nancy smoking a cigarette — she had broken ground for all of us, but only at terrific cost in violent scenes followed by silence and tears.

Outsiders suffered even worse. When Nancy was two, a doctor was called in to treat a badly infected foot. He determined that it required lancing, and anesthetized Nancy with a chloroform-soaked handkerchief. Farve, always in attendance at operations — he even supervised the birth of each of his children — noticed that Nancy appeared to have stopped breathing. "What did you do then?" we asked at this point in the story. "I seized the doctor by the neck and shook him like a rat." Nancy survived, but whether the hapless doctor ever recovered we never knew.

Now that Farve was General Murgatroyd we all entered into the spirit of the thing. I developed the theory that he was a throwback to an earlier state of mankind, a missing link between the apes and Homo sapiens. My mother confiscated my allowance for calling him "the Old Subhuman," but he didn't really mind.

"Come on, dear, I want to measure your cranium to see how

far it corresponds to the measurements of the Piltdown Man."

"Well, all right . . . but what are you going to do with the measurements?"

"Turn them over to Science, of course. How would you prefer to be catalogued? Would you like to be known as the Swinbrook Man, the Rutland Gate Man or the High Wycombe Man?"

The languid young aesthetes of *Highland Fling* also turned up frequently in real life, imported by Nancy, as visitors at Swinbrook. Most of these had the effect on Farve of driving him into a Murgatroydish rage; to one or two he took an unaccountable liking. Which was the worse fate — to be loathed or liked — was somewhat of a toss-up, since to remain in good odor required such substantial sacrifices as taking part in weekend shooting parties and being down for breakfast promptly at eight o'clock.

"Brains for breakfast, Mark!" Farve roared genially at one of his capriciously chosen favorites who, to maintain status, had staggered uncertainly into the dining room, looking haggard and drooping, on the dot of eight. The standard aesthete's breakfast was a *cachet faivre,* nearest thing to a tranquilizer in those days, and a glass of orange juice or China tea, taken at about noon.

Poor Mark turned a delicate shade of chartreuse, excused himself, and was heard violently retching in the nearest W.C. This incident, too, passed in its turn into part of the mythology of Farve. To celebrate it Debo and I promptly made up a Honnish song, a sort of signature tune for Mark, to be sung whenever he came to Swinbrook, with the lugubrious chorus: "Brains for Breakfast, Mark! Brains for Breakfast, Mark! Oh, the damn sewer! Oh, the damn sewer!"

The oddly chosen battleground of Nancy's generation was that of the Athletes versus the Aesthetes — sometimes called the Hearties and the Arties — and the newspapers were full of accounts of pitched warfare staged at Oxford University between these opposing forces.

The Athletes, of course, were direct ideological descendants of past patriots, winners of wars on the playing fields of Eton, Old School Tie men and their horsy-set women.

The Aesthetes laid claim to a more exotic heritage . . . the Romantics, the England of Oscar Wilde, the France of Baudelaire and Verlaine. Most of the Aesthetes were vaguely pro-Socialist, pro-pacifist and (horrors!) opposed to shooting, hunting and fishing on the grounds that these hallowed blood sports were cruel and sadistic. They gaily toppled the old, uncomplicated household gods — England, Home and Glory, the Divine Right of Kings (and hence of the House of Lords), the axiomatic superiority of the English over all other races; they sacrilegiously called the Boer War, in which Farve was "thrice wounded," according to Debrett's Peerage, "the Bore War"; they paraphrased Blake's "England's green and pleasant land" to "England's green, unpleasant land."

On weekends they would swoop down from Oxford or London in merry hordes, to be greeted with solid disapproval by my mother and furious glares by my father.

Boud, Debo and I were on the whole carefully insulated from Nancy's friends, as my mother considered them a totally bad influence. "*What* a set!" she always said when some of their more outrageous ideas were expounded by Nancy. They talked in the jargon of their day: "Darling, too too divine, too utterly sickmaking, how shamemaking!" Fascinated, I would hang around the drawing room as much as I dared, until my presence was noticed and I was chased back up to the schoolroom. Sometimes, if I was lucky, I would be brought in by Nancy and Diana to "show off" with a translation into Boudledidge of some minor English poet, or to play a hand of Hure, Hare, Hure, Commencement. A high point in my life came when Evelyn Waugh, a writer feller and one of the main Swinbrook sewers, promised me that he would immortalize Miranda by substituting the word "sheepish" for the standard "divine" in his forthcoming book, *Vile Bodies*. I was on tenterhooks until the book was actually printed for fear he might go back on his word. But there it was, in black and white: "He left his perfectly sheepish house in Hertford Street . . ." With Miss Bunting's help I lifted an extra copy from the Oxford bookshop, and hung it proudly on a tree in Miranda's field.

Since I had no educational yardstick by which to judge ideas and intellect, and was isolated in a world where Muv's and Farve's views of life were the only ones I'd ever had a chance to hear — the only ones, indeed, that I'd thought existed — the irreverent outpourings of these attractive, stimulating people made the most profound impression on me. I filched "forbidden" books I'd heard them discussing — Aldous Huxley, D. H. Lawrence, André Gide — and surreptitiously read them by flashlight under the bedclothes. Weird, undreamed-of horizons began to open up on every side, dozens of possible variations of a non-Swinbrook outlook.

Nancy became a devotee of new trends in art. We rather assumed that at least a partial reason for this interest was to "tease the Old Subhuman" — and tease him it did, most effectively. The sculpture of Jacob Epstein ("damned Hun!" as Farve inaccurately called him), the works of Picasso ("filthy sewer!") in turn produced fascinating rows downstairs of which we in the schoolroom heard only small repercussions. The culmination was reached when Nancy brought home a print of Stanley Spencer's "Resurrection." This work, with its portrayal of oddly elongated people in modern dress easing themselves out of their graves, provoked Farve to one of his classic rages, shaking the household from top to bottom.

His fury was redoubled when Nancy announced her intention to move to London and study art at the Slade School.

As usual, we got only the echoes of the titanic rows going on downstairs. We came down for meals that were eaten in dead silence, and returned to the schoolroom to hear the occasional tantalizingly muffled thunder of my father's voice. Muv must have interceded, for Nancy finally won her point and went to live in a furnished bed-sitting room in Kensington. I watched her action with immense interest, and was terribly disappointed when she came home after about a month.

"How *could* you! If I ever got away to a bedsitter I'd never come back."

"Oh darling, but you should have seen it. After about a week, it was knee-deep in underclothes. I literally had to wade through them. No one to put them away."

"Well, I think you're very weak-minded. You wouldn't catch me knuckling under because of a little thing like underclothes."

Dimly, through the eyes of childhood, I glimpsed another world; a world of London bed-sitters, art students, writers ... a world of new and different ideas ... a world from which Swinbrook would seem as antiquated as a feudal stronghold. A marvelous idea flashed into my mind — one of those ideas to be cherished, polished, perfected until it can become a reality. I decided to run away from home. Not yet — I knew a twelve-year-old would hardly have a chance to survive for long without being discovered and returned to the family — but one day, when I had worked out a thoroughly satisfactory plan, and had saved enough money to support myself for a while. I wrote immediately to Drummond's Bank; in a couple of days I had their answer.

"Dear Madam, We respectfully beg leave to acknowledge receipt of ten shillings as initial deposit in your Running Away Account. Passbook Number —— enclosed. We remain, dear Madam, your obedient servants ..."

I triumphantly flashed the letter around the family. "Look!

And fancy Drummond's being my obedient servants! What bliss!"

Muv only said vaguely, "Well, darling, you'll have to save up a nice lot, you have no idea how expensive living in London is these days." But she had other things on her mind: Diana had just become engaged to be married.

4

DIANA, youngest of the four grown-up Mitfords, had traditionally been my Favorite Sister. There were seven years between us in age, so we had just missed each other in the schoolroom; Diana had been sent to do lessons in Paris at about the time my schoolroom days began. Boud, Debo, and I were too uncomfortably close in age for friendship. We got dreadfully in each other's way in the fierce and competitive struggle to grow up. Boud, three years older than I, hated being classified with me and Debo as "the little ones"; I in turn tearfully resented being lumped with Debo, two years my junior, as "the Babies." Nancy was too sharp-tongued and sarcastic to be anyone's Favorite Sister for long. She might suddenly turn her penetrating emerald eyes in one's direction and say, "Run along up to the schoolroom, we've all had quite enough of you," or, if one had taken particular trouble to do one's hair in ringlets, she was apt to remark, "You look like the oldest and ugliest of the Brontë sisters today." Pam, now she had abandoned hope of becoming a horse, was too stolidly immersed in country life, devoid of the restless, unformulated longing for change that, in one form or other, gripped the rest of us. But Diana had the necessary qualities for a Favorite Sister. She was bored and rebellious, all right, a follower in Nancy's footsteps. If not an initiator of jokes, she was at least a roarer at them, and inclined to take an interest in me.

My mother's choice of names for her children seemed, in some cases, to have been inspired with a certain amount of second sight. Nancy had been named after the Nancys of seafaring ballads, and her thick, dark curly hair, worn (after the ill-fated shingling) in a very short upsweep, her tall, fashionably boyish figure and her penchant for the exotic did give her something of the aspect of an elegant pirate's moll. Boud, christened Unity Valkyrie — a very odd, and therefore obviously prophetic, choice of names for a girl born four days after the outbreak of war with Germany — began at an early age to run true to form and to take on the appearance of a flaxen-haired war maiden. Diana looked like a *Vogue* cover artist's conception of the goddess of the chase, with her tall, rather athletic figure, large blond head, a perfection of feature more modern than Grecian.

Diana was the one who patiently tried to teach me to ride. Day after day we sallied forth in our jodhpurs, she on her gray mare, I on my rough little pony Joey; day after day she patiently picked me up from my spills in the stubble field. "Do try to hang on this time, darling. You know how cross Muv will be if you break your arm again." (Two Arms Broken before Ten was my proud childhood boast. "Poor Little D., she doesn't seem to have bounce," Muv would sigh.) Diana helped me with my piano practice, and encouraged me to learn French. She also egged me on in my favorite role — that of "court jester" when there were visitors at Swinbrook. "Come on, Decca, do 'I'm Sex Appeal Sarah' in Boudledidge," and eyes rolling wildly in the approved Boudledidge grimace

I'd sing:

> *Eem dzegs abbidle Dzeedldra,*
> *Me buddldy grads beedldra*
> *Idge deedem ee abeedldron ge dzdedge.*

Diana would translate, looking carefully around to make sure the parents weren't in hearing distance:

> *I'm Sex Appeal Sarah,*
> *My body grows barer*
> *Each time I appear on the stage.*

Inevitably, when Diana became engaged to Bryan Guinness during her first London season, I was violently partisan to "her side." That there were "sides" regarding this event was part of the family pattern of struggle. At Swinbrook, any change — a haircut, the acquisition of a new dog, the introduction of a new friend — was bound to cause a passionate flare-up, followed by an uneasy period of strife before truce was finally achieved.

To become engaged was the most daring, inflammatory act yet attempted by any of us, one that inevitably signaled a call to arms. It was axiomatic that my father disliked all young men, and that months of hostilities would precede any marriage that any of us might contemplate.

Boud, Debo and I, though excluded as usual from the raging arguments downstairs, managed to get a lot of secondhand information about the engagement, to which we added our own speculations. Bryan seemed to possess many desirable qualities. He was young, a few years older than Diana, handsome, rather intellectual but hadn't gone too far in that direction — he was as yet neither a writer nor an artist — liked riding, was obviously madly in love with Diana . . . Nevertheless, the grown-up relations lined up solidly behind Farve in opposition to the marriage. Aunts and uncles noted with clucking disapproval that Diana was only eighteen — "barely out of the schoolroom." We gathered that Muv's main objection centered on the fact that Bryan was "so *frightfully* rich." "It's probably really because Bryan's family made their money in trade," I suggested to Debo. "They don't like the idea of poor Diana being advertised on posters. 'Guinness Is Good For You,' you know."

In point of fact, the richness of the Guinnesses *may* have had something to do with my mother's opposition. She herself had a strong feeling for the virtue of economy — a virtue hardly likely to be fostered in an eighteen-year-old bride suddenly in command of one of the large fortunes in England. Muv was forever fending off a slightly mythical wolf from our door by the practice of various rather oddly chosen economies. She worked out the cost of washing and ironing an average of nine napkins, three meals a day, 365 days a year, found it staggering, and eliminated napkins from the dining room table forever. Paper ones would, of course, have been unthinkable, and individual napkin rings too disgusting for words. To her annoyance, the *Daily Express* ran the story of our napkinless meals under the headline "Penny Pinching Peeress." Muv made sporadic efforts to interest us in the subject of household economy, and once offered a prize of half a crown to the child who could produce the best budget for a young couple living on £500 a year; but Nancy ruined the contest by starting her list of expenditures with "Flowers . . . £490."

Diana's method of attaining her objective, perhaps the only one that could have succeeded short of elopement, was to sulk for an entire winter. She stayed in her bedroom a great deal of the time, and came down to the drawing room only to sit in stubborn silence, looking vacantly out of the window. This strategy for getting one's own way was not entirely unknown to us. Some years earlier Debo had successfully pined away for a Pekingese, causing suspension of an ironclad family rule that no one under the age of ten could own a dog.

"I wonder if Diana is actually pining away, or if she's just practicing being frightfully rich," I said to Debo.

The sight of Diana pining — or practicing, whichever she was doing — filled me, as nothing else quite had, with a consciousness of the monotony of Swinbrook, its remoteness from anything exciting. As prisoners confined to their cells manage to communicate to each other their restless, intolerable anxieties, creating the conditions for a mass riot, so Diana managed to communicate boredom. In sympathy I brooded over my Running Away Account, dispatching every possible shilling or penny I could scrape up to Messrs. Drummond's.

Diana made slow but sure progress in her campaign to be allowed to marry Bryan, and after a few months my parents reluctantly withdrew their objections.

Meanwhile, owing to a bit of luck, I was able to register an unexpected increase in my Running Away Account that winter. An extraordinarily acute pain seized me one morning in the middle of breakfast. Never having had a stomach ache before, I knew at once that it must be appendicitis. "Poor Little D., I expect you ate too much," Muv said sympathetically. "If you really have an awful pain, I expect we should call the doctor," but she went off for her daily inspection of the chickens. The pain kept on hurting, so I telephoned Dr. Cheattle in Burford. "Would you mind coming over to take out my appendix?" I asked him. He arrived in a surprisingly short time. Muv came back from the chickens, and she and Nanny at Dr. Cheattle's direction covered all the

nursery furniture with white sheets. Farve was summoned
from the Closing Room to assume his usual self-appointed role
of supervisor at the operation. Dr. Cheattle covered my face
with a chloroform-soaked handkerchief.

An unusually understanding doctor, Dr. Cheattle presented
me with the appendix, fixed up in a jar of alcohol, as soon
as I awoke from the anesthetic. Debo hung around enviously.
"You *are* so lucky to have a dear little appendix in a bottle,"
she said. It was no trouble at all to relieve her of a pound
she'd been saving since last birthday. A couple of weeks later
Nanny flushed the appendix down the W.C. "Nasty thing,
and besides it's beginning to smell." Debo wailed bitterly,
but the pound was safely deposited with Drummond's.

Operations were about the only form of medical treatment
"allowed" by my mother. She permitted them on the grounds
that they had biblical sanction in the passage, "if thine eye
offend thee, pluck it out." Appendectomy was, in those days,
supposed to be followed by weeks of complete bed rest, but
my mother surreptitiously made me walk round the room as
soon as the anesthetic had worn off and Dr. Cheattle was
safely out of the way. She had a complete mistrust of doctors
and all their works. Dr. Cheattle was summoned only on
rare occasion, and even then his instructions were never
followed. As soon as he was out of sight, Muv quickly poured
all the medicine down the drain. "Horrid stuff! The Good
Body will throw off the illness if left to itself."

Muv considered me to be living proof of her health theories.
I had the doctor five times as a child — more than all the
other children put together — and each visit presented a new
challenge for pitting the Good Body theory against prevalent
medical practices, a new opportunity to outwit the long-suffer-
ing Dr. Cheattle. He would arrive with his little black bag
containing pills, bottles of chloroform, splints and bandages.

The examination generally took place in the drawing room where parents, sisters, uncles and aunts and anyone else who happened to be present could closely observe and check on his every move.

The first time I broke my arm, Dr. Cheattle put me to sleep on the drawing room sofa with the usual chloroform-soaked handkerchief, and set the bone with an elaborate arrangement of bandages and slings. He told my mother to leave the dressing undisturbed until his next call. However, that night Muv took off all the bandages and made me do exercises with the broken arm "to prevent it from growing stiff." As she was unable to get the bandages to look the same after that, she canceled Dr. Cheattle's second visit for fear he might be upset by her disregard of his instructions. Rather surprisingly, the Good Body triumphed as Muv had confidently predicted; the arm not only healed by itself, but even became interestingly double-jointed, to the envy of Debo and Boud.

Dr. Cheattle prescribed a starvation diet, nothing but sips of water, for a case of typhoid fever when I was five. He explained that typhoid perforated the sufferer's stomach, and any food would fall through, causing certain death; but Muv smuggled me bits of chocolate and bread and butter under the very eyes of the trained nurse, and once more the Good Body pulled me through.

Possibly my mother's total war on the germ theory of illness, together with my rash enlightment of the dancing class girls, had contributed to our complete isolation from all other children. The "County" families had been thoroughly shocked when, at the height of my typhoid bout and in defiance of the doctor's recommendations, Nancy's "coming out" ball had been held as scheduled in the germ-infested house. Afterwards, Muv triumphantly pointed to the fact that none of the guests had come down with the fever: "If you're going to have it, you'll have it, and that's all there is to it. Obviously, Little D.'s typhoid wasn't caused by germs, there weren't any other cases for miles around." Illnesses, no matter how catching they were generally supposed to be, were never allowed to interfere with family plans. We were taken, covered with chicken-pox scabs or choking with whooping cough, to weddings, birthday parties, Christmas gatherings, to the great annoyance of the other mothers. "This silly germ theory is something quite new," Muv said placidly. "The truth is doctors don't have any idea what really causes illnesses, they're always inventing some new theory."

All in all, the appendicitis was well worth while; I now had a lovely eight-inch scar in addition to my double-jointed arm and an extra pound toward running away, and the nice long convalescence created a pleasant change from daily routine.

Shortly after my recovery we all went up to London, well in advance of Diana's wedding.

5

THE WEST END of London was in those days partitioned into a number of distinct residential districts, with nothing haphazard or fortuitous about them. The precise character of each seemed as fixed as if it had been determined by some immutable Law of the Universe. The very rich and fashionable lived in Mayfair, Belgravia, Park Lane; the artistic, literary and bohemian gravitated toward Chelsea or even Bloomsbury; Hampstead, Hammersmith and St. John's Wood were middle class; while the substantial London houses of run-of-the-mill squires, knights, baronets and barons were found in Kensington, Paddington, Marylebone and Pimlico.

We were in the last category. Our huge, seven-story house at 26 Rutland Gate in Kensington reflected comfort and serviceability rather than elegance. There was even a passenger lift which my father had installed and of which he was immensely proud.

Rutland Gate is a fairly short cul-de-sac facing Hyde Park, its entrance marked by dirty white Victorian pillars. Down the middle is a large fenced-in square garden, to which each resident of the Gate has a key. It is a grassless garden, filled

with sad-looking shrubs and bright, grimy tulip beds.
White-uniformed nannies assemble there in the long summer
evenings to sit on the green iron park benches, rocking infants in baby carriages and cautioning toddlers, "Don't
touch anything, darling, it's so nasty and dirty in this garden."

We used the house in Rutland Gate only occasionally for
the London season. Most of the time it was either let or
stood unoccupied; then, very, very rarely, one or two of us
were allowed to stay for a few days with Nanny in the
Mews, a tiny flat, formerly chauffeur's quarters, at the back
of the house over the garage. We considered this a tremendous treat. Life in the Mews had the quality of camping
out. There was no cook there so Nanny did the cooking, and
she sometimes let us help her prepare unfamiliar delicacies
whose recipes she dug up somewhere out of her memory: prune
whip, tripe and onions, bread pudding. Even having one's bath
was an adventure at the Mews. The bathroom, with its
ancient claw-foot tub, was dominated by a big, round, evil-
smelling water heater called the Amberley. Lighting it was
an action fraught with danger. It entailed turning a small,
stiff handle and poking a lighted taper through a little trap
door, producing a loud and terrifying pop. After this you
had to judge exactly when the water would be hot enough
for a bath, but not hot enough for the Amberley to blow up.
None of us ever knew when that point might be reached.
It seems likely, on looking back, that the Amberley people
may have provided, unknown to us, some sort of safety mechanism in case one forgot and left it burning. If this was
so, we never guessed it, and each bath was a rather anxious
experience.

A move up to the big house at Rutland Gate was a very
different matter, resembling the evacuation of a small army.
For days before, and after the actual journey tension filled the

air and a special sort of cold, restrained anger, brought on
by the myriad details that have to be attended to in a move,
seemed to settle into the very marrow of the Grownups till
the last suitcase had been unpacked. The sharply spoken
words, "Don't be ridiculous!" were sufficient warning to me
that the subject of bringing Miranda up to London had best
be dropped. "The dear thing *would* so love it. She's never
been to London . . ." but the words froze at the sight of
Muv's face.

Mountains of suitcases, great wax-paper mounds of homemade bread to last till the next baking, Debo half dead from
carsickness being lugged out of the car — and we were there.
The sleeping furniture seemed to come slowly back to life
as the dust sheets were removed one by one; familiar objects,
half forgotten since the last time we stayed in London, were
exposed to view to be examined and fingered. A huge gold
vase, covered with ornate tracery, stood on the sideboard
in the dining room. "How did we get that?" "Don't you
remember darling, it was given to Great-Great-Grandfather by
the Irish; they were so *extremely* grateful to him for helping
to put down one of their rebellions."

Staying in London was always a delightful experience, but
the year Diana was married the thrilling wedding preparations lent a special, Midas touch. The excitement of it!
Debo and I could hardly bear it. There were endless fittings
of our gold and cream-colored bridesmaids' dresses, parcels
of wedding presents arriving by every post to be unpacked
and pawed over, lists of delicious food for the reception to be
studied. Debo and I breathed in an unaccustomed, luxurious
atmosphere of satin, lace, tissue paper, crepe de Chine
trousseau underclothes, pigskin luggage, with the promise of
lobster mousse and wedding cake in the immediate offing.
Boud, huger than ever and in the extreme throes of adoles-

cence, stood gloweringly aloof, and could only be persuaded with difficulty to try on her enormous bridesmaid's dress.

Nanny did her best to keep us out of the way. There were the usual London outings: visits to Mme. Tussaud's Wax Works, the Zoo, the Victoria and Albert Museum, or, when all else failed, a nice walk up to the Albert Memorial in Kensington Gardens. When we tired of these diversions, or if Nanny was too busy to take us anywhere, we spent our time in the square garden at a new Honnish activity: escaping from white slavers.

Miss Bunting had first introduced us to this fascinating subject. During a geography lesson on the major industries of South America, the subject of Buenos Aires had come up, and she explained that the capital of Argentine was mainly noted as a distribution center for white slaves. In fact, a friend of a friend of a friend of hers had had a rather unnerving experience as a result of going to a London cinema alone. An innocuous-looking old lady sat beside her and gave her a morphine injection, and the poor friend's friend's friend had next been heard of in Buenos Aires.

Since Debo and I were not allowed to go beyond the entrance to Rutland Gate alone, and had often been cautioned by Muv "never to speak to anyone not in uniform," our contribution to the fight against the white slave traffic was of necessity somewhat limited. However, we carried on as best we could under the circumstances.

There was one white slaver in particular who lived a few houses from us in Rutland Gate. Every morning, as we were walking our dogs, he hurried past us in his bowler hat and black suit, carrying a furled umbrella; and he always said "Good morning." Since he was not in uniform and we had never been introduced to him, his greeting was proof enough that he must be a Slaver. "Don't answer him, Debo, or you'll wake up in Buenos Aires and be distributed," I warned her. "And don't run — that only excites them." Every evening at six he came striding back down Rutland Gate, and with a preoccupied smile — probably thinking over some of his distribution problems in Buenos Aires — he said "Good evening." We walked firmly ahead, never quickening our step, never looking in his direction. But our reaction was one of undisguised annoyance when we learned that he was only a friend of Nancy's, a highly respectable married stockbroker, who greeted us because he knew we were Nancy's little sisters. "Very Counter-Honnish of Nancy, and besides he may be just pretending to stock-broke," Debo and I agreed. Nancy, in turn, spread the story all over London, and the poor stockbroker became known in London society as "The White Slaver," a nickname he probably carries to this day.

At last the longed-for day of the wedding rolled around; but Debo and I were in bed with scarlet fever and high temperatures. "I don't think it would hurt them to get up, just for the service, and then they could go right back to bed afterwards," Muv said. But Bryan's family put all their feet down in concert and with great firmness. Even Diana felt that the appearance of our bright red faces might cast a certain pall over the occasion and cause some unfavorable comment among the wedding guests. We raged and fumed at our bad luck, and were hardly consoled with tidbits sent up from the feast and with reading the lengthy accounts of the ceremony which appeared in the society papers.

Diana and Bryan went abroad for their honeymoon. They sent us huge boxes of expensive French chocolates, filled with a special sort of dark truffle, the memory of which, to this day, recreates for me the early days of their marriage.

After they returned to England, Debo and I were allowed

to go and stay with them in the country with Nanny. The visit was not altogether a success. It was preceded by long arguments with my mother, who was very reluctant to let us go; Diana and Bryan were definitely part of "What-a-set," more so even than Nancy, and Muv feared that the company of their unsuitable friends might have a disastrously over-stimulating effect on us.

The visit, when it finally came off, fell short of my expectations. To be sure, the Guinnesses' house was as beautiful and as luxuriously comfortable as I had expected. They even had a swimming pool, an extraordinary innovation for those days. Debo and I made Diana take us through all the newly decorated rooms: "How much did that cost? And those curtains? How much a yard was the wallpaper?" We were intensely curious about how the frightfully rich spent their money. The unsuitable friends, on the other hand, were a disappointment. Perhaps they were inhibited by Debo's and my presence; in any event, the scintillating, improper conversation to which I had so eagerly looked forward never quite came off.

Diana seemed different since her marriage. She was now a Beauty with a capital B. Photographs of her stared from the covers of the society weeklies with great regularity; her portrait was painted by a dozen artists. Her face always seemed to come out looking the same — large, calm, gazing rather vacantly into space; and she seemed to be getting like that in real life, too. Debo and I thought she was becoming "affected." She had almost given up laughing or frowning, and developed a permanent expression for all occasions not unlike that of Mona Lisa. Her eyes, already about half as big again as most people's, remained in a wide stare, her mouth slightly open, relaxed but not set, chin medium high. She once unbent to explain to us that if you keep your face in a relaxed and beautiful expression when you are young, you are less likely to suffer the normal ravages of age. I tried the beautiful expression a few times, but on me it didn't seem to work, and only succeeded in provoking remarks from Nanny: "What's the matter, darling, aren't you feeling well?"

Diana's manner toward me had changed too. She became uniformly, and annoyingly, kind and gentle, treating me with a brand of restrained patience usually reserved for animals, babies or half-wits. I felt she must be developing a Beautiful Character to go with her face. This made me uncomfortable in her presence. Regretfully, I demoted her from Favorite Sister; Nancy's astringent if often cutting behavior was more varied and interesting, and therefore more palatable, Boud's unregenerate sullenness more real.

We saw little of Diana and Bryan after that visit, though we followed their goings on in the society columns of the newspapers. There were "baby parties" at which guests arrived dressed as infants in prams or on hired donkeys, some even accompanied by reluctant nannies borrowed for the evening. There were treasure hunts in which each guest was given a list of items he must retrieve; a lamppost, a St. Bernard dog, a policeman, a duck from St. James's Park. The newspapers dubbed the participants the Bright Young People, and railed at these sons and daughters of the rich for fiddling while Rome burned.

Sometimes the Bright Young People joined forces with the Aesthetes. Diana and Bryan sponsored an art exhibit at one of the fashionable West End galleries. The pictures, by a "newly discovered" artist, Bruno Hat, were ultramodern. They ranged in style from Cubism to the brand-new Surrealism. Some were merely canvases with pieces of wool, cork or glass fragments stuck to them. The exhibit was widely advertised, and attracted critics from all the newspapers, who arrived

to examine and appraise these examples of a new art. Bruno
Hat, a Pole who spoke no English, sat in a wheel chair in
one corner, his bearded face muffled in a scarf, murmuring
unintelligible sounds when addressed.

Next day's papers, from the most respectable to the purely
sensational, carried lengthy and serious critical evaluations of
the Bruno Hat exhibit. But finally the secret leaked out;
Bruno Hat was none other than Bryan Howard, a friend of
the Guinnesses, in heavy disguise. The whole exhibit had
been arranged as a hoax. My mother disapproved: "Mislead-
ing all those poor people. Very naughty of Diana," but we
thought it immensely funny and very clever of the Guinnesses
to have hoodwinked even the art critics.

6

AFTER DIANA'S WEDDING the familiar atmosphere of solid, unchanging monotony once more settled over us at Swinbrook — a suffocating sense of the permanence of one's surroundings, family, and way of life. It affected the three of us left in the schoolroom in different ways. Boud endured in baleful silence. She induced my mother to let her have a private sitting room on the top floor, known as the D.F.D., or Draw ing Room From Drawing Room, to which she withdrew with paintbox and art materials to create fantasies of her own. Debo, who loved Swinbrook and never pined for London or Abroad, was no problem. She threw herself vigorously into country activities. She was an excellent rider, lived for the Saturday hunts, and spent hours with the chickens or picking fleas off her dachshund Jacob.

To me, at the discontent age of thirteen, the unvarying sameness of life had suddenly become unbearable. The only mitigating factor was the presence of Tuddemy, at home from time to time studying for his exams. Sometimes he let me read passages from great musty law tomes, and devise from what I had read possible exam questions with which to test him.

Perhaps, although he was ten years older than I, he still remembered the discomfort of adolescence, and believed the best cure to be hard work, for he made me tackle Milton, Balzac, Boswell's *Life of Johnson* — books I should never have read without his prodding.

I guiltily realized that outward circumstances were not altogether responsible for my obscure *malaise,* because objectively life was extremely varied. In fact, now we were all growing older, my mother was always planning activities for our amusement. We were taken to Switzerland for the winter sports, to Sweden to visit the beautiful cities and beaches, to the seaside for summer holidays. Yet even these excursions, much as I always looked forward to them, never came up to expectations. It was as though I were a figurine traveling inside one of those little glass spheres in which an artificial snowstorm arises when the sphere is shaken — and no matter where I was, in a train, a boat, a foreign hotel, there was no escape outside the glass. Invisible boundaries kept me boxed in from the real life of other people going on all around — there were rules against talking to strangers, seeing a film unless Muv had seen and approved it first, going anywhere without a grownup; there was the company of my own family exclusively; there was, above all, the crushing realization of my own limitations.

The Bible asserts glibly, "When I was a child, I spake as a child, I understood as a child, I thought as a child; but when I became a man, I put away childish things" — as though it were that easy, with never a word about the uneasy transition, the restless search for one's own personality, the longing, not only for independence, but for that particular kind of independence which one dimly feels will come with self-knowledge.

I measured myself against people in the world of books,

mentally trying them on for size as a woman glancing through a fashion magazine visualizes herself in each outfit. Yet even my new-found bosom fell far short of the bosoms of literature! It just added to my general tubbiness. "Look at Decca's Budding Bust," Boud and Debo chanted derisively — but alas! there was no waist to go with it. Rather than the "snowy hills, blue veined" of Elizabethan poets, the effect was more that of a plateau, especially when I was done up in the "stays" that Nanny thought good for growing girls, and wearing a sat-out tweed suit.

A thirteen-year-old is a kaleidoscope of different personalities, if not in most ways a mere figment of her own imagination. At that age, what and who you are depends largely on what book you happen to be reading at the moment. You are the yellow-haired, skinny little heroine of *The Secret Garden,* slowly adjusting to the rigorous disciplines of English country life after being pampered by your devoted Indian ayah. You are a Brontë sister — not Anne, not Charlotte, more likely Emily — pouring out your wild genius on the lonely moor. You are Elizabeth Barrett Browning on her sickbed, great luminous eyes staring from an emaciated face, the helpless victim of a narrow-minded, vengeful father — but your iron will is capable of triumphing over his petty tyranny in the end. You are Jane Eyre, painfully thin and pale of face but steadfast in spirit, able to withstand the cruelty of the hateful Reeds and in the end, after their downfall, to forgive them. For a day or two you might be a tall, serious, dark-eyed sixth-form prefect out of one of Angela Brazil's school stories, adored by the smaller girls, and, though full of human little faults, pride and joy of the headmistress. Sometimes you are even Clara Bow, the "It" girl, stirring thousands with your warm beauty and throaty voice; or the mysterious Swedish spellbinder, Greta Garbo.

But then, when you catch sight of yourself in the mirror, you realize sadly that while all these people are extremely thin, you are plump and healthy; that while some are exceptionally beautiful and some fascinatingly ugly, you are medium pretty. (Annoyingly enough, Debo had the looks to be almost any heroine, tragic or romantic, she would want to choose. She had the right figure for it, beautifully thin and long-legged, the pallor, the huge eyes, the straight yellow hair — she could have had her pick, from Joan of Arc to National Velvet to Anna Karenina — but since she hardly ever read anything but *Sporting Life* she obviously didn't realize what she was missing.)

It suddenly occurs to you that the hundreds of people you see in the course of a day in London — men with umbrellas and raincoats flapping in the wind, ladies hurrying along with bundles in the gray rain — are as real as yourself each with his own individuality, with a past, even a childhood in his background. Heretofore people outside the immediate family were two-dimensional, half-men and -women, part of the scenery. With the dawning of self-consciousness, the discovery of other people's reality — more than fifty million in England alone! — is one you can grasp from time to time, only to find it eluding you again, its vastness proving too much for you to handle.

You discover suffering — not just your own suffering, which you know is largely of your own making, nor the childhood sufferings over *Black Beauty, David Copperfield,* Blake's little chimney sweeps — but you catch disturbing, vivid glimpses of the real meaning of poverty, hunger, cold, cruelty.

The train journey to London led through miles and miles of immense buildings of flats, surrounded on all sides by lines of washing hung out in the filthy London air. Sometimes groups of white-faced, ragged children could be seen from the train, or gaunt young women in men's caps wheeling pallid babies. The newspapers from time to time carried stories of hardship cases — a whole family living in one room, children who had died of cold in the winter, old people living on pensions who couldn't afford sugar in their tea.

What could be done about it all? I fretted and fumed at my inability to discover a solution. Nanny thought it would be nice if we joined an organization called the Sunbeams. The idea was that a rich child would be given the address of a poor child, they would correspond, and the rich child would send old clothes or toys from time to time. Nancy had once belonged when she was little, but she had lost the address of her Sunbeam and had addressed her letter, "Tommy Jones, The Slums, London," much to the fury of Nanny, who didn't think that was at all nice. I enthusiastically signed up.

My Sunbeam was a girl a year older than I named Rose Dickson. I spent hours packing up old jerseys and skirts into exciting-looking parcels, and spent all my pocket money on presents for Rose. I imagined that my letters, which consisted of a highly romanticized account of life at Swinbrook, must bring great rays of joy into her otherwise drab existence. True, I made myself out to be a sort of cross between Little Lord Fauntleroy and Sarah in *The Little Princess*. My unsuccessful daily bouts with scrubby little Joey, who usually managed to throw me, became transformed into fearless gallops through woods and copses on my thoroughbred. My spaniel Tray came through as a great mastiff of unusual intelligence and sensitivity, faithful and gentle with his mistress, but a dangerous brute indeed if crossed by a stranger.

Rose seemed to like the letters. Hers to me were in an extremely flowery style and strictly phonetic spelling, and I found them fascinating. She was one of six children, and she described in heartrending detail the miserable, overcrowded conditions in which they lived—all six of them in two beds in one tiny room.

I began to be obsessed with the idea that we must at all costs get Rose away from London. I begged my mother to let her come for a visit. "I really don't think that would do, Little D.," Muv said gently. "Think of how dreadfully *uncomfortable* she'd feel." After weeks of campaigning on my part, my mother hit on an idea. She would engage Rose, now fourteen and out of school, as a Between Maid, or Tweeny.

I was overjoyed by her decision, and wrote off immediately to Rose. "It's like a fairy tile come true!" Rose said in her reply, full of profuse thanks. "I'm afraid being a Tweeny isn't really much like a fairy tale," my mother commented, but of course I didn't believe her. On the contrary, I thought it a very apt simile for one about to be plucked from the London slums and wafted to a beautiful country house. I tried to imagine what Rose would look like; probably mere skin and bones, with huge, soulful brown eyes.

At last the day of her arrival dawned, and I was allowed to go to the station with the chauffeur to meet her. To my surprise she was quite fat, but she had the pasty, drawn look of sunless London children. After greeting each other we became completely tongue-tied, and sat in silence for the whole drive home. The eloquence that had marked our correspondence was unaccountably and painfully missing. I was relieved when we got to Swinbrook and Rose was handed over to Annie, the head housemaid, to be instructed in the duties of a Tweeny.

I didn't see much of her after that. Once or twice I passed her on the upstairs landing, carrying slop pails and dusters, looking different in her uniform. Two days after her arrival, my mother broke the sad news to me. Annie had reported that Rose cried herself to sleep every night, and refused to eat. Annie guessed that she was suffering tortures of home-sickness. When she was asked if she would like to go home, she brightened up for the first time since her arrival, and my mother arranged to send her back to London on the next train.

The whole episode worried and puzzled me a great deal. Was it my fault? Should I have anticipated that Rose would miss her family? Homesickness was not only unknown to me —I couldn't even imagine what it must feel like. My few visits away from home alone, to cousins' houses during Nanny's two-week annual holiday, had all seemed to me outstanding events, great treats to be cherished in the memory. Could being a Tweeny have had something to do with Rose's un-happiness? I looked up the duties of a Tweeny in Mrs. Beeton's *Book of Household Management,* and read: "The Between Maid is, perhaps, the only one of her class deserving of com-miseration; her life is a solitary one, and in some places her work is never done ..." Perhaps that had been the trouble ...

As the months and years dragged slowly by, like the watched pot that never boils, the sad and embarrassing memory of Rose gradually receded, to be replaced much later by new and more revolutionary notions of how to solve the world's ills. Meanwhile, something so exciting happened in my life that it left no room for regrets or self-searching. Debo and I were at last sent to school for a few months — the fulfillment of my dearest wish.

We were staying at Old Mill Cottage at the time, since both the other houses were let. "From Batsford Mansion to Asthall Manor to Swinbrook House to Old Mill Cottage" was our slogan to describe the decline of the family fortunes from Grandfather's day. The cottage was a delightful little house on the outskirts of High Wycombe, and Oakdale was a private day school for girls, attended mostly by the daughters of merchants, doctors and business people in the town. Debo hated it so bitterly that Muv, fearful of another onset of pining, allowed her to leave. "The headmistress kissed me goodbye! Beastly old Lesbian," she announced furiously. "Oh, darling, that's extremely naughty, you're not to say words like that, and I *do* think it's a bit unfair, she was probably only trying to be nice."

I, on the other hand, gloried in every minute of school for the few months I was there. The clatter of hundreds of girls rushing through the corridors, the unfamiliar business of competing in lessons, the huge smelly meals in an enormous dining room with an endless choice of people to talk to, the vast pleasure of "showing off" and baiting the mistresses in front of the other pupils — even the irrational rules against whistling in the corridors or putting your feet up on your desk — it all went to my head like wine.

I quickly made "best friends" with another girl in my form. Her name was Viola Smythe, and actually I only rather liked her, but she adored me with a doglike subservience. We decided to start a club; I would be the Head of it, and Viola the Subhead. We drew up elaborate rules, the most important of which was that we would meet every Saturday at the house of one of the members. The first meeting was to be at my house. I asked my mother if I could have some girls to tea the following Saturday.

"To *tea*? Oh no darling, of course not. If you have them to tea they'll invite you to tea with them, and you wouldn't be able to go. You see, I don't know any of their mothers."

No use arguing, or pressing for a reason. This sort of discussion always produced a cold, grim anger in the Grownups, like that caused by making jokes about God or talking about sex. The explanation of *why* Viola couldn't be invited was not one that could be brought out into the open. The very phrase, "unsuitable companions," was itself unsuitable for utterance. Gone was the Victorian frankness of earlier days on these knotty questions: "Is she *one of us,* dear child?" Grandmother used to ask, to place the station in life of a person under discussion. My mother would join mildly in our amusement at the outrageous question. Class was a delicate matter, a subject for intuition rather than conversation, one of those "borderline" subjects, deeply felt but never discussed.

It was also a complicated matter. My parents would have been not so much shocked as blankly uncomprehending if anyone had accused them of "being snobbish." Snobbishness was, surely, by definition a purely middle class attribute, finding expression in an unhealthy desire to rise above one's station, to ease oneself in where one wasn't wanted, and in turn to look down superciliously on those below one in the social scale. My parents would not have dreamed of looking down on anyone; they preferred to look straight ahead, caring not at all if this tended to limit their vision. Neither were they social climbers, for they rather disliked really "smart" society.

The Lower Orders were much less of a problem than the middle class Viola Smythes. As the old hymn put it so succinctly, "All things bright and beautiful, all creatures great and small, All things wise and wonderful, the Lord God made them all. The rich man in his castle, the poor man at his gate, God made them high or lowly, And order'd their estate . . . " Whereas the Smythes of this world, so uncomfortably perched between, represented "the haunting danger of the *bourgeois.*"

In my parents' view of history, upper class, middle class and working class were destined to travel forever harmoniously down the ages on parallel tracks which could never meet or cross. Yet collisions did occur; there had been a nasty smash-up in Russia, another was threatening in Germany, and in that year of 1931 there were growing signs of upheaval in England itself.

7

MAJOR STORMS were brewing beyond the confines of the fortress. Unemployment was rising alarmingly throughout England. Hunger marches, at first small demonstrations, later involving populations of whole areas, were reported in the papers. Police and strikers fought in the streets from London to Birmingham, from Glasgow to Leeds. Great population centers were designated "distressed areas" by the Government — which meant areas where there was no prospect of improvement in the employment situation. The Family Means Test, under which the dole could be denied any unemployed worker whose relatives still held jobs, was the subject of violent protest by the Communists, who gradually succeeded in swinging most of the labor movement into the fight.

The younger generation was highly political. They accused the elder statesmen of the Allied countries of sowing the seeds of a new and more horrible world war through the Versailles Treaty, the systematic crushing of Germany, the demands made on the defeated enemy for impossible war reparations.

Old concepts of patriotism, flag-waving, jingoism were under violent attack by the young writers. The creed of pacifism, born of a determination to escape the horrors of a new world war, swept the youth. Students organized demonstrations against the Officers Training Corps.

The Oxford Union vowed: "Under no circumstances will we fight for King and Country." This action by a small handful of Oxford undergraduates produced electrifying results. The Oxford Pledge, as it came to be known, was taken up as a rallying cry by youth of all countries. We read of student meetings in France, Germany, far-off America, where the Oxford Union's message was discussed and adopted. The Pledge became the subject of editorials in every newspaper, and of a raging debate in the letter columns. It seemed as though every retired colonel in England must have roused himself from country torpor to put pen to paper in defense of King and Empire against the incredible pronouncement. The left-wing press hailed the Pledge as a blow to the armaments race, and called for its adoption by every trade union, every church, every youth group.

Within the fortress, we viewed these events as through a glass darkly — or perhaps, more accurately, as seen in the crazy mirror of a fun house. Uncle Geoff saw the economic crisis as the inevitable consequence of years of murdered soil, brought about by generations of chemical fertilization. He attributed the growing pacifist movement to spinelessness caused by Murdered Milk fed to helpless babies in their nurseries throughout the land. My mother felt that the crisis had been caused by the institution of unemployment benefits, which had removed all incentive, and by the eight-hour day, which dictated to freeborn Englishmen how many hours they could work. Parents and uncles alike agreed that the young pacifists of the Oxford Union would benefit greatly from a good horsewhipping. Aunts warned that the London Season, with its debutante balls and court presentations, might even in our generation become a thing of the past.

I responded, like many another of my generation, by becoming first a convinced pacifist, then quickly graduating to socialist ideas.

When I was fourteen I read *Cry Havoc,* Beverly Nichol's indictment of war. It pictured in vivid detail the horrors of bombing raids in the first world war, and pleaded eloquently for total, world-wide disarmament. *Cry Havoc* made immediate appeal to young people throughout England; it was a best seller overnight. I was enormously impressed with the originality and force of its arguments. A whole new world had opened up for me. Pacifist literature led directly to the left-wing press, of which I became an avid reader. I even grudgingly used up a little of my Running Away money to send for books and pamphlets explaining socialism.

I discovered that Human Nature was not, as I had always supposed, a fixed and unalterable entity, that wars are not caused by a natural urge in men to fight, that ownership of land and factories is not necessarily the natural reward of greater wisdom and energy. I read about great movements in England and other countries to divest the rich of their wealth and to transfer ownership of land and factories to the workers.

I felt as though I had suddenly stumbled on the solution to a vast puzzle which I had been clumsily trying to solve for years. Like many another suddenly confronted for the first time with a rational explanation of society, I was bursting with excitement about it. I longed to meet some flesh-and-blood exponents of this new philosophy. Nancy and her pro-labor friends were disappointing. When they discussed politics they seemed to support socialism, but as far as I could see they never really did anything about it. I felt they didn't take anything very seriously. They tore down old standards on every hand, they jibed and satirized and talked fast and long, but that seemed to be about all.

"Why don't you campaign for the Labor Party?" I asked Nancy.

"Oh, darling, you know how it would upset the Poor Old Revereds . . . besides, think of the *dreadful* boredom . . ."

"There you go, being weak-minded again, just like you were about the bed-sitter and your underclothes. A drawing room pink, that's what you are."

I knew I could expect little success in converting the rest of the family. Boud was away at boarding school, where she had been sent despite my cries of "unfair!" when Debo and I were at Oakdale day school, and Debo, now aged eleven, was not specially interested in the class struggle.

However, I did begin to see the family in a new light.

"Farve, d'you realize that as well as being a Subhuman you're a Feudal Remnant?"

"You're not to call Farve a remnant, Little D., that's very rude," Muv intervened.

"Not so rude; there's even a Lord Remnant next to Farve in the Peerage, I just looked him up. Lord Remnant probably realizes he is one, that's why he chose that title. Anyway, Muv, don't you realize *you* are an Enemy of the Working Class yourself?"

Muv was genuinely stung.

"I'm *not* an enemy of the working class! I think some of them are perfectly sweet!" she retorted angrily. I could almost see the visions of perfectly sweet nannies, grooms, gamekeepers, that the phrase must have conjured up in her mind. I decided to keep my new ideas to myself for a while; there was little hope they would take root in this distinctly unfertile soil.

Nevertheless, a new dimension was added to my Running-Away plans. I knew now what I was running away from, and what I should be running to.

8

ALTHOUGH Boud and I had fought and quarreled unremittingly throughout childhood, by the time she was eighteen and I was fifteen we had, surprisingly, become great friends. Boud had grown from a giant-sized schoolgirl into a huge and rather alarming debutante. Almost six feet tall, with a thick blond mane of hair, she towered over her fellows at the various debutante functions like a big Santa Claus among the Christmas dolls. Her rather overpowering personality matched her size. In the schoolroom, she had hastened the departure of many a governess, and had in fact achieved something of a record as easily the most unmanageable of all of us. She had been expelled from school, according to her version, "simply for saying one word," when she had been called on to recite before the assembled school, board of trustees and parents. The word was "rot," which she had added to the line, "A garden is a lovesome thing, God wot." She had perfected a method of making my father fly into a rage by the simple expedient of glowering at him in a certain way at mealtimes. She would sit silently stowing away quantities of mashed potatoes, her eyes fixed on Farve with a somber, brooding glare. He would glare back, trying to make Boud drop her gaze, but she invariably won out. Crashing his fists on the table he would roar: "Stop looking at me, damn you!" I envied her this accomplishment, at the same time pointing out that she was taking unfair advantage of my father's subhuman aspects: "Poor Farve, he's like a lion, not able to stand being fixed by the Human Eye."

Boud had always had a flair for a certain baroque style of decorative art. In a sort of original variation of *collage*, she had created huge canvases depicting historical scenes: Hannibal crossing the Alps, with a background of clay mountains, the silver trappings of Hannibal and his army picked out in tinfoil; Noah's Ark, with bits of real fur pasted on the animals. As a debutante, she began to apply this talent to her selection of clothes. She shone like an enormous peacock in flashing sham jewels, bought at a theatrical costumer's, and immense brocade evening dresses. To my mother's consternation she bought a sham tiara, resplendent with rubies, emeralds and pearls, and insisted on wearing it to dances. She was generally out to shock — to *"épater les bourgeois,"* as my mother disapprovingly put it — and in this she succeeded. Boud's dissatisfaction with life mirrored my own. I applauded her outrages, roared when she stole some writing paper from Buckingham Palace and wrote to all her friends on it, cheered when she took her pet rat to dances.

The Bright Young People had faded from the London scene a couple of years before, as their transatlantic counterparts, the Flaming Youth, had no doubt disappeared from the American scene with the passing of the twenties. The London season had reverted to its usual stodgy pattern, an endless succession of luncheons, dances, dinners, the "emerging" (usually newspaper-engineered) of the most popular debs of the season, a few scandals, a few engagements ...

Boud's efforts to brighten up the social scene gained few

adherents. Perhaps if she had been in a position to try that sort of thing in, say, 1926, it might have caught on. But the debutantes of 1932 just weren't in the mood. As a result, Boud was considered a little eccentric by her contemporaries.

Boud, in turn, was a bored and restless participant in the ritual of "coming out." She was casting about for something more exciting, more intriguing than the London season offered — something proscribed by the parents, something amazing, shocking . . .

Diana's house seemed like a good beginning, for we had been forbidden to visit her when, after a few years of marriage, she and Bryan were divorced. As usual, we in the school-room had been excluded from the dreadful row which followed their separation. We knew only that unutterable shame and disgrace had been brought by Diana on the family, that according to the Reverends the chances of any of the rest of us ever getting married were now very greatly reduced, as no respectable young man would wish to have much to do with the sisters of a divorcee. Needless to say, all this only made Diana more glamorous in our eyes.

Debo and I saw nothing of Diana for over a year, but for Boud it was a different matter. Freed from schoolroom, governess and daily walks, she could now come and go as she pleased, and unknown to the Reverends she made many a surreptitious visit to Diana's. There she met Sir Oswald Mosley, whom Diana later married. Mosley's political career had led him through the Conservative Party, the Labor Party and the New Party, an abortive venture that had lasted only about a year in spite of heavy backing by Lord Rothermere and the *Daily Mail*. He was now busily engaged in organizing the British Union of Fascists, which Boud immediately joined.

"Don't you *long* to join too, Decca, it's *such* fun," she begged, waving her brand-new black shirt at me.

"Shouldn't think of it. I hate the beastly Fascists. If you're going to be one, I'm going to be a Communist, so there."

In fact, this declaration was something more than a mere automatic taking of opposite sides to Boud: the little I knew about the Fascists repelled me — their racism, supermilitarism, brutality. I took out a subscription to the *Daily Worker,* bought volumes of Communist literature and literature that I supposed to be Communist, rigged up some homemade hammer and sickle flags. My Communist library was a catholic one indeed, and many of the authors would no doubt have been amazed to find themselves included. It contained not only works by Lenin, Stalin, Palme Dutt, but also those of writers whom I had heard referred to by the Older Generation as "bolshevik" — Bertrand Russell, Laski, the Webbs, Bernard Shaw. I got John and Lytton Strachey mixed up and plowed gamely through several of Lytton's biographies before discovering my mistake. The result of all this was that I greatly increased my knowledge of modern English literature and progressive thought, and the more I read the more fascinated I became with the enormous new vistas of thought and action that opened up on every side.

Boud and I both avoided the company of the Grownups at this time as much as we could. At Swinbrook, we lived in the D.F.D. except for mealtimes. We divided it down the middle, and Boud decorated her side with fascist insignia of all kinds — the Italian *fasces,* a bundle of sticks bound with rope; photographs of Mussolini framed in passe-partout; photographs of Mosley trying to look like Mussolini; the new German swastika; a record collection of Nazi and Italian youth songs. My side was fixed up with my Communist library, a small bust of Lenin purchased for a shilling in a second hand shop, a file of *Daily Workers.* Sometimes we would barricade with chairs and stage pitched battles, throwing books and records until Nanny came to tell us to stop the noise.

Yet Boud and I often teamed up together against the Grown-ups in our own very peculiar version of the United Front. Once we were left in charge of my mother's produce stall at the Conservative Fete. "Look at all this money!" I said to Boud. "It does seem a shame to think of the beastly old Conservatives getting it all. I think I'll send about £5 of it to the *Daily Worker* for their fund drive." Boud insisted that she was going to take, shilling for shilling, an equal amount for the British Union of Fascists. There wasn't much time for argument about it as my mother was expected back any minute; quickly we pocketed £5 apiece, which we dispatched that night to the respective offices. I have often wondered since what the *Daily Worker* people must have thought when they read the note accompanying the contribution: "£5 dona-tion from the Annual Conservative Fete of Oxfordshire."

The endless schoolroom talk of "What are we going to do when we grow up?" changed in tone. "I'm going to Germany to meet Hitler," Boud announced. "I'm going to run away and be a Communist," I countered. Debo stated confidently that she was going to marry a duke and become a duchess. "One day he'll come along, The duke I love . . ." she hummed dreamily. Of course none of us doubted for a minute that we should reach the objectives we had set for ourselves; but perhaps seldom have childhood predictions materialized with greater accuracy.

Although Boud's interest in fascism had at first been kept a secret from the Grownups, it soon leaked out. She begged to be allowed to go to Germany. "But, darling, I thought you didn't like Abroad," my mother said. (Boud had always refused to learn French because she thought it an affected language, and France was somehow synonymous with Abroad to us.)

It was the year of Hitler's accession to power. Boud's announced intention was to go to Germany, learn German, and meet the Führer. My parents put up much less opposition than might have been expected. Perhaps the thought of another London season of sham tiaras and tame rats let loose in ballrooms was a bit more than my mother could contemplate with any pleasure. Boud was allowed to go.

Within six months, she came home for a brief visit, having accomplished both her objectives. She already spoke fairly fluent German, and had met not only Hitler, but Himmler, Goering, Goebbels, and others of the Nazi leaders. "How on earth did you actually manage to get to know them?" we asked in some amazement. Boud explained that it had been fairly simple; she had reserved a nightly table in the Osteria Bavaria Restaurant, where they often went. Evening after evening she sat and stared at them, until finally a flunky was sent over to find out who she was. On learning that she was an English fraülein, an admirer of the Nazis, and a member of the British Union of Fascists, Hitler invited her to join them at their table. Thereafter she became one of their circle, saw them constantly in Munich, accompanied them to meetings, rallies, the Olympic games.

"As I thought! Hitler's just another subhuman, like The Poor Old Male, and you subdued him with the power of the human eye," I said bitterly.

But Boud wouldn't be teased about her devotion to the Nazis. She was completely and utterly sold on them. The Nazi salute — *"Heil Hitler!"* with hand upraised — became her standard greeting to everyone, family, friends, the astonished postmistress in Swinbrook Village. Her collection of Nazi trophies and paraphernalia now overflowed our little sitting room — bundles of Streicher's anti-Semitic paper, *Der Stürmer;* an autographed copy of *Mein Kampf;* the works of

Houston Stuart Chamberlain, a nineteenth century forerunner of fascist ideologists, albums of photographs of Nazi leaders.

About this time the ban on Diana was lifted, and she again became a visitor at Swinbrook. Family relationships took a sudden turn, and Boud and Diana, formerly far from friendly, became thick as thieves.

Diana accompanied Boud to Germany and was also admitted to the Nazi inner circle. Their activities soon reached the newspapers, and a columnist reported that Hitler had declared them to be "perfect specimens of Aryan womanhood."

The press made much of the prophetic nature of Boud's Christian names — Unity Valkyrie.

My parents first looked on Boud's new-found interest as rather a joke. Conservative opinion of Hitler at that time ranged from outright disapproval of him as a dangerous lower class demagogue to a grudging sympathy for his aims and methods — after all, had he not decisively crushed the German Communist Party and destroyed the labor unions in a surprisingly short time? Thus the words "that feller Hitler" on the lips of countless English squires could be expressed in tones equally of derision or of admiration. Indeed, with Hitler's rise to power the concept of "filthy Huns" had mysteriously been completely discarded.

Boud and Diana begged the Revereds to go with them to Germany and see for themselves. "Farve is really one of Nature's fascists. He'd simply *love* the Führer," they insisted. Before long they prevailed. Muv and Farve were given a royal time in Germany. They were lent a chauffeur-driven Mercedes-Benz and shown all the gaudy trappings of the new regime, and they returned full of praise for what they had seen.

Family reactions to their conversion were varied. Boud was naturally delighted. For the first time, she now became a favorite with my father and was on excellent terms with

Muv. Nancy said spitefully that the Revereds had been won over by simple flattery, having been treated as important people for the first time in their lives by the Nazis, who had a completely distorted idea of the amount of influence wielded in English politics by obscure country aristocrats. Tom was amused but aloof. I hardened my resolution to run away and to cast my lot with the anti-fascists.

I still loved Boud for her huge, glittering personality, for her rare brand of eccentricity, for a kind of loyalty to me which she preserved in spite of our now very real differences of outlook. When I thought about it, I had a sad and uneasy feeling that we were somehow being swept apart by a huge tidal wave over which we had no control; that from the distance a freezing shadow was approaching which would one day engulf us. Sometimes we even talked of what would happen in a revolutionary situation. We both agreed we'd simply have to be prepared to fight on opposite sides, and even tried to picture what it would be like if one day one of us had to give the order for the other's execution.

9

FORTRESS ASPECTS of life at home now came to the forefront
with a vengeance, virtually drowning out all others. I was
in headlong opposition to everything the family stood for and
it was on the whole a very lonely opposition.

I did at last have a "best friend" of my own age, my first
cousin Idden Farrer. We had a great deal in common, for
Idden also longed to escape from home. She had held fast to
her childhood ambition to be an actress, and was now going
through a series of stormy scenes with her parents. Unlike
me, she had loathed the thought of boarding school as a child,
but had been forced to go by her parents. "You see?" my
mother pointed out triumphantly. "Children are simply never
satisfied." I thought it would have been truer to say that
grownups have their ways of finding out what children
would like to do, and then seeing that they are made to do the
exact opposite.

Idden and her sister Robin often came to stay at Swinbrook,
when we would spend hours commiserating with each other
about the unfairness of life and the horridness of the older
generation. When we had children of our own, we decided,

we would try to fulfill their every desire. Mine would be sent to lovely schools where the entire store of mankind's knowledge would be spread before them for their enjoyment and instruction (I didn't know very much about schools in those days), and Idden's would be kept in her dressing room among the flowers sent by admirers and allowed to play with her make-up. They would never be made to go for walks, made to dress like their younger sisters, made to do anything, in fact. They would be allowed to wear high-heeled shoes as soon as they wanted, to read improper books and to see improper films, to make friends with anyone who took their fancy, whether or not we knew their parents. They would also be allowed to wear two-piece bathing suits. This was a particularly sore spot with Robin, a beautiful blonde a few years older than Idden and I. She had rashly worn such a bathing suit at a swimming party in the presence of my father, and had quickly been reduced to tears when he furiously roared at her before the assembled company, "I don't know why Robin finds it necessary to expose her very indifferent middle." Our children would never be roared at. We would love and cherish them, and tell them they had beautiful middles . . .

Being Grown Up was still an interminable one or two years off in the distance, and all my movements were subject to the restrictions of schoolroom life. The dead-endishness of the few hours of daily lessons weighed heavily. They could never now lead to college because I was too far behind girls my age who had been to proper schools, and the lessons seemed a complete waste of time.

I endlessly mulled over possible running away plans, discussing them at length with Idden. The Loch Ness monster was attracting attention in the newspapers about that time, and my mother was one of many who firmly believed in its existence. "After all," she would point out, "no bodies have ever been recovered from fishing boats wrecked on Loch Ness. What other explanation is there? Obviously the monster eats them." A practical possibility occurred: I could go to Loch Ness equipped with a complete change of clothing, leave a suicide note on the shore, together with the clothes I had been wearing, and escape to some Scotch town. No one would be surprised if a search failed to turn up my body, as all would assume it had been eaten by the monster. But after I had made good my escape, how should I live? At sixteen I had absolutely no training in anything, and virtually no education. Perhaps I could get a job as a maid in somebody's house . . . but Idden convinced me that I would never cut the mustard at this occupation. She reminded me of Nanny's constant complaints about my untidiness and failure to hang up my nightgown in the mornings, the only household task actually required of me. My greatest fear was of making an abortive attempt at running away, only to be ignominiously discovered and hauled back home to face greater strictness than ever.

There was no one with whom to share my socialist ideas. True, Nancy still seemed to veer in that direction occasionally. She wrote a book called *Wigs on the Green,* a satirical novel about Boud and the British Union of Fascists. In the book Boud was a huge eighteen-year-old called Eugenia, a member of the Union Jackshirts, who spent her time riding round the countryside and haranguing the villagers on the merits of the Leader. Nancy brought forth renewed accusations of "weakminded" on my part by holding up publication of the book for some time because of threats by Diana and Boud that they would never speak to her again if *Wigs on the Green* appeared in print.

In our London house, where there was no extra sitting room, I was allowed to use the disused ballroom for my Communist literature, and Nancy joined with the others in teasing me about being a "Ballroom Communist" — a cut below a "drawing room pink."

Rumors began to reach us about our second cousins, Giles and Esmond Romilly, who were at Wellington College, a military Public School. They had infuriated their parents and become the subject of family gossip by refusing to join the Officers Training Corps and announcing that they were pacifists. It was said that they had wrecked the school's Armistice Day observance by inserting pacifist leaflets in all the prayerbooks. The leaflets had fluttered out at the moment of the two minutes silence, causing a row of almost unimaginable proportions. Early in 1934 the activities of Esmond Romilly began to reach the press. The *Daily Mail* ran a two-column story under the headlines: RED MENACE IN PUBLIC SCHOOLS! MOSCOW ATTEMPTS TO CORRUPT BOYS. OFFICER'S SON SPONSORS EXTREMIST JOURNAL. SCOTLAND YARD INQUIRY. The extremist journal was titled *Out of Bounds,* published and edited by Esmond. The *Daily Mail* quoted from the magazine's statement of principles: *"Out of Bounds* will openly champion the forces of progress against the forces of reaction on every front, from compulsory military training to propagandist teaching." There was considerable discussion of the Romilly brothers in family circles. "Poor Nelly and Bertram! What have they done to deserve such dreadful sons? Those two deserve a good horsewhipping," the Grownups would chorus.

Shortly after the *Daily Mail* story appeared, the news broke that Esmond had run away from school. Newspapers variously headlined the story: MR. CHURCHILL'S 15-YEAR-OLD NEPHEW VANISHES; WINSTON'S 'RED' NEPHEW; COLONEL'S SON RUNS AWAY FROM SCHOOL; 'UNDER INFLUENCE OF LONDON COMMUNISTS' SAYS MOTHER. My admiration for Esmond was unbounded. Although we were second cousins, I had never met him. The closest we had come to meeting had been once years ago when I was about nine, and Debo and I had been sent with Nanny to stay with the Churchills for a few weeks during the summer. Giles was there, and I remembered one of the Nannies saying to another, "You should have been here last week when Esmond was here . . . ooh, he was a naughty boy, a holy terror!"

I wondered now if I could somehow arrange to meet him, but his whereabouts were apparently unknown even to his parents.

As the year dragged interminably by, at last a plan developed which seemed to offer some hopes of at least temporary alleviation of boredom, and perhaps even a measure of escape. My schoolroom days came to an end, and Idden and I were sent to Paris to stay with a French lady and perfect our knowledge of French at the Sorbonne.

My mother came with us to help us get settled. Always deeply suspicious of the French, she was in a furious rage against the whole nation from the moment of our arrival at the Gare du Nord, where our porter bravely tried to fight her down about the amount of his tip. My mother stood her ground, and much to the amusement of Idden and myself the porter went off grumbling in French, "You're the kind of Englishwoman who murdered Joan of Arc." Muv was most intensely annoyed by the admiring glances (and sometimes even pinches) which Idden and I excited as we strolled about Paris. No use to point out that, since the same sort of thing seemed to happen to every young woman in that romantic town, it was evidently simply a national way of expressing friendliness. She even threatened to take us straight back home if this sort of thing kept up. Idden and I were terrified she might carry out the threat, and we marched ahead, eyes front, to avoid giving the slightest encouragement to the young Parisian hopefuls.

Just before Muv left something happened which, had she been a little more observant, might easily have resulted in the cancellation of our plan to spend some months in Paris. One night Muv took us to a movie. I sat between her and Idden, and no sooner was the theater darkened than I became aware of a muted struggle taking place on Idden's side.

"What's the matter?" I whispered.

"The man next to me is stroking my leg!" Idden whispered back frantically. "You'd better tell Aunt Sydney; we must find other seats."

"Now, Idden, you know perfectly well that if we tell her she'll get simply furious and take us home to England. Besides, I specially want to see this film. You'll simply have to put up with it."

Poor Idden bravely struggled through the news, the cartoons, and the two-hour movie. I sympathetically solicited occasional bulletins:

"Where's his hand now?"

"Oh, Decca, this is *too* awful. Quite a bit above my knee."

"Well, stop shoving round so, I can't concentrate. Just push him away quietly, I'm afraid she'll hear."

By the time we left the theater, Idden's face was blazing red with embarrassment and indignation, but luckily my mother had remained blissfully unaware of what was going on.

We only really relaxed after Muv had left and the danger of being taken back to England receded. Madame ——, with whom we were staying as boarders, had put on an excellent front while Muv was still in Paris. She had promised to chaperon us at all times, to supervise our attendance at the Comédie-Française and the Opéra Comique, to see that we led an existence suitable to two young English schoolgirls. We in turn had promised to be good as gold, and to obey Madame in every respect. However, it soon became obvious, much to our joy, that Madame had no intention of accompanying us to the theater or indeed of supervising our activities in any respect. She was busy with her own life, consisting mainly of entertaining groups of middle-aged French ladies with *tilleuls, tisanes,* sweet port and little hard caraway seed cakes. She was frequently *souffrante,* when she would take to her bed and consume quantities of enormous black pills shaped like straw hats.

Idden and I were left much to our own devices. We loved our studies at the Sorbonne, where we were surrounded by students of all ages and nationalities; dark-skinned Spaniards who spoke in what Idden called a "cr-cr accent"; lumpy blond Germans; American ladies of uncertain age finishing up something they referred to as "units." In the afternoons the art appreciation master took us in groups to the Louvre, where he would point to the masterpieces with a long stick like a conductor's baton. *"Regardez la ligne, mademoiselle, et voilà les masses."* At night we attended the Comédie-Française, to be enchanted by the old-fashioned, stylized productions of classical drama and comedy. We took fullest advantage of Madame's negligence as a chaperon, and often, unknown to her, we would substitute the Grand Guignol, a night club, or even the Follies Bergères for the evenings we were supposed to be spending at the Opéra.

We struck up an acquaintance with two French students we'd met at the Sorbonne, jaunty, nattily dressed, bright-eyed young men in their early twenties. On Sundays they would take us driving in the Bois de Boulogne or to the nearby countryside. After the drives, we often returned to their flat for brief bouts of flirtation. We nicknamed them respectively "the Actor" and "the Speaker." Idden's was the Speaker, so called because while he addressed her in the most poetic terms of endearment — *"Ah! Que tu es belle, je t'adore, ma petite Idden"*

—he never tried to kiss her. Mine was the Actor, for his conversation consisted of the most trite observations, delivered between passionate kisses: *"Qu'il fait beau temps aujourd'hui, n'est-ce pas? J'espère que vous vous amusez bien à Paris, mademoiselle."* We got rather fed up with them after a few such experiences; Idden wished hers was more of an actor, while I wished mine could learn to be more verbally expressive and a trifle less ardent.

The most unlikely adventures seemed to lie round every corner in Paris, but somehow nothing important ever came of pursuing them. Nancy had provided me with a few introductions to intellectual old ladies who conducted weekly *jours,* or "at homes," where artists and writers would gather to partake of the same little caraway seed cakes, port and *tisane* served by our Madame to her cronies. I faithfully reported to these *jours,* hoping something interesting would happen, though I must have seemed like an odd fish out of water in my English jersey-and-skirt, and the people at the *jours* all seemed to me to be incredibly ancient. The conversation was tantalizingly above my head, about books, personalities, events of which I knew nothing, but which sounded somehow fascinating. If I could only catch on, find the key to what was being discussed! But I was content to sit unobtrusively listening while a new play was brilliantly dissected, a poet torn to shreds, an actress mimicked in that beautiful language so suited to such talk.

Once I was invited out to dinner by a middle-aged Frenchman whom I had met at a *jour.* I had to ask Madame's permission to go; she merely shrugged her shoulders, and said, *"Ma petite, il vous jetera sur un divan et il vous violera,"* but she let me go all the same. I couldn't help feeling that Madame must be exaggerating a bit. After all, surely people go out to dinner together in every country from time to time without such untoward results? For the occasion, I went to the Prix Unic and bought a very cheap, tight, shiny black satin coat and skirt and a very cheap frilly white georgette blouse. Thus rigged out in the trappings of sophistication, I felt uncomfortably as though I were wearing a heavy disguise of some sort.

The evening started out ordinarily enough. We went to the Bal Tabarin, and watched the gaudy burlesque show. I was desperately trying to tailor my conversation to match the clothes I was wearing, and pretended to understand the rapid-fire dirty jokes and innuendoes being delivered from the stage. On the whole, I felt my Woman of the World act was coming along quite nicely — warm but enigmatic, knowledgeable but hard to get, basically chaste, but capable of great depths of passion if aroused.

After an hour or so at the Bal Tabarin, my companion suggested we should go somewhere else; he offered to show me *"le vrai Paris."* Feeling a little flustered, I followed him to his car. We drove through the dark streets for some distance, finally arriving at what appeared to be an ordinary house in a row of dwellings. He rang the doorbell and spoke briefly to his chauffeur, who to my dismay drove off. We were admitted by a kindly-looking old French lady to a brightly lit empty drawing room. I felt all my new-found sophistication seeping out fast, and was hardly reassured when several naked girls appeared carrying champagne and glasses.

"This is one of the finest houses in Paris," my companion explained. "Wouldn't you like to see the rest of it?"

"Well, it's getting a little late, Madame will be expecting me home . . ." but having gone this far, I really was rather anxious to see over the place, and with mixed feelings followed the girl who was to guide us. We looked into a succession of rooms opening off a long corridor. Our guide explained that they were designed to cater to every imaginable preference. One was lined, floor to ceiling, with mirrors, another was full of statues and pictures of the Virgin Mary ("*pour les pygma-lionistes,*" she pointed out); yet another was a replica of a Pullman carriage, and our guide proudly showed how, by turning on a switch, the whole room could be made to shake and rumble like a real train, while artificial scenery appeared to move past the window. I was simply fascinated but at the same time feeling rather uneasy; how on earth was I going to get out of this?

An incongruous vision leapt into my mind — the shades of people at home suddenly transplanted into this setting. Nanny, wiggling her shoulders the way she always did if ruffled about something, saying, "Not at all a nice place, Jessica, I should think"; Muv, glowering angrily. Would she murmur something about the Good Body? There were certainly enough of those around.

The room "*pour les sadistes*" was the most amazing of all, and I did wish Idden could have been there to see it. It was decorated like a torture chamber, with racks, thumbscrews, whipping posts, realistic-looking plaster snails crawling over the rough stone walls. Two of the naked girls appeared and began to whip each other in a desultory sort of way.

"I really do think it's about time we were getting along," I said anxiously. I wondered whether the blood of Charlemagne, which Grandfather had so painstakingly proved was coursing through my veins, would come to the rescue in this pinch. A brief struggle followed, along the lines Madame had predicted, which I managed to win with a combination of physical dexterity and fast talk. My new satin suit was considerably the worse for wear by the time I finally got home, alone in a taxi — but I had quite a tale to tell Idden. We shuddered delightedly at the spine-chilling thought of what our parents would do if they knew how we were spending our time in Paris. But real escape seemed just as far off as it had in London.

The traditional "year abroad," and the delightful feeling of freedom engendered by it, were coming to an end. Now must follow, as inevitably as the sun rises, but never sets, on the British Empire, my first London season. There was no real alternative. College was out — impossible now to qualify. What was going to happen next? The season might turn out to be fun. After all, one was bound to meet literally hundreds of people; among them there must be a few kindred souls, a few people of my age also looking for a way out of their own particular fortresses. All the same, I had an uneasy feeling I wasn't going to enjoy it much, that I knew in advance what my new companions would be like, and that the only good thing to be said for the whole procedure was that at last I'd be a Grownup.

10

WE ARRIVED back in England to find that Esmond Romilly was in the news again. Using a left-wing Bloomsbury bookshop as his headquarters, he had established a sort of informal center for other boys who had run away or been expelled from public schools. With their help, he plotted the editing, production and distribution of *Out of Bounds*. The magazine was flourishing, after a fashion. Its "infant left-wing editor," as the newspapers sarcastically called Esmond, had succeeded in attracting support and financial contributions from numerous unlikely sources. Bernard Shaw had sent a check and his congratulations; the *New Statesman* had commended some of the articles; even some of the London dailies had treated the venture with a sort of spoofing sympathy.

Out of Bounds was in truth a rather remarkable production. Subtitled "Public Schools' Journal against Fascism, Militarism and Reaction," it ran to some fifty printed pages of editorial comment, articles, correspondence, book reviews.

"We attack not only the vast machinery of propaganda which forms the basis of Public Schools, and makes them so useful in the preservation of a vicious and obsolete form of society; we oppose not only the semi-compulsory nature of the

Officers' Training Corps, and the hypocritical stuff about character building — we oppose every one of the absurd restrictions, and petty rules and regulations . . ." Thus were the revolutionary goals of *Out of Bounds* set forth in a leading editorial.

Much of the material was contributed anonymously by boys still attending public schools in various parts of England. Political articles ranged from the general and historical ("Gangsters or Patriots: How Britain Built Her Empire," by Esmond Romilly) to a firsthand account of a meeting of the British Union of Fascists at Olympia signed "T.P., Rugby." The Rugby student related how he had started out for the meeting with "a considerable interest in both Fascism and Communism, but no definite leaning towards either," how he had been mistaken for a Communist, kicked down the steps and beaten up by armed blackshirts. He ended on the rueful note: "Do you wonder, then, that I sign myself, 'Yours faithfully, Anti-Fascist.' "

Sir Oswald Mosley's book, *The Greater Britain,* got short shrift in the book review section. It was dismissed curtly, and no doubt deservedly, as "a mass of fallacious jargon, absolute twaddle, untruthful as well as unsound."

Conversely, John Strachey's *The Menace of Fascism* received exuberantly enthusiastic endorsement: "From start to finish it is chock-full of extraordinarily important statements . . . a marvelous piece of writing . . . you must beg, borrow or steal, or if you are unsuccessful buy, a copy . . ."

The letters to the editor, many written in a style suspiciously similar to that of the editor himself, exploded with spirited controversy and expressed a most interesting variety of opinions as to the value of *Out of Bounds:*

"Never in my life have I read such unmitigated drivel . . . it is, without exception, the most futile magazine ever produced, and I think the best thing you could do is to fall under a tram ... it is rumoured that you were expelled from Wellington (and a damn good thing, too)." "Nothing quite like *Out of Bounds* has ever existed before. At last we have a paper which does not shrink from setting down the honest opinions of the average intelligent boy."

With a shrewd eye to circulation-building, the editor had included an article by his brother Giles Romilly, entitled "Morning Glory: Sex in Public Schools." The article dealt with the various degrees of homosexual romances which bound the life of the public schoolboy, and told from firsthand experience of the "wary and reticent" warnings doled out to the mystified twelve-year-old newcomers on their arrival at Wellington. According to Giles, official instruction was delivered by a master, who gathered the little innocents for the Straight Talk which would clarify once and for all any questions they might have about the Facts of Life as practised at Wellington: "Men! There are men here who will try to take advantage of a man because a man is a new man. That's all I have to say to you." A forthcoming article on the daring subject of co-education, a dirty word in Public School circles, was promised for a future issue.

A column entitled "Public School Notes," consisting of contributions secretly smuggled out by boys "on the inside," provided a roundup of political developments at different schools. This column, more than any other department of *Out of Bounds,* demonstrated the degree to which new ideas of pacifism and general revolt against the old order of things had trickled down among the secluded populations of the public schools. The spirit of guerrilla warfare against the Old School Tie came through with force:

ALDENHAM: The activities of the Christian Union have been considerably restricted ... ASHFORD HIGH SCHOOL: On May 24 leaflets were circulated in the School attacking the jingoistic celebrations on Empire Day . . . CHARTERHOUSE: Considerable protest has been raised in regard to an inscription on the east window of the Chapel: "Who Dies for England lives." CLIFTON: *Out of Bounds* may not be distributed inside the College . . . ETON: One hundred and twenty copies of *Out of Bounds* were sold here at the beginning of this term . . . FRIENDS SCHOOL, SAFFRON WALDON: At this "progressive" Quaker School, expulsion has been threatened to several members of the School for an offence known as "attitude of mind." HIGHGATE: A motion that "Pacifists should be sent to blazes" was heavily defeated at a recent debate. HAILEYBURY: At a debate on the subject of Fascism this term, approval for Fascism was defeated by 103 votes to 13. STOWE: A debate is to be held this term on the subject of "Fighting for the Empire." News has just come to hand that this debate has been banned by the Headmaster.

Distribution of the magazine presented enormous difficulties. As its front page proudly and starkly proclaimed, it was "BANNED in ALDENHAM, CHELTENHAM, IMPERIAL SERVICE COLLEGE, UPPINGHAM, WELLINGTON." In schools where there was no official ban, unofficial groups of public school patriots among the boys would see to it that copies were destroyed and suitable punishment meted out to *Out of Bounds* supporters. Esmond and his cohorts made frequent forays into Eton, Wellington, and other enemy strongholds, and were able to report sardonically: *"Out of Bounds was banned at Wellington last term. But 142 copies were sold."* In spite of duckings in school ponds and other forms of reprisal against its sales representatives, the magazine's circulation jumped from 1000 to 3000.

Rumors of these fascinating goings on reached us from time to time in London. I envied Esmond tremendously and longed to follow him, or at least to find some appropriate and dignified way of notifying him of my existence. But meanwhile preparations for my London season went inexorably ahead. Since I was the fifth girl in the family to make her debut, these preparations assumed a certain routinism. Dog-eared lists of people to invite to my coming-out dance were brought out and corrected by my mother with the help of older sisters:

"Let's see; little Johnny Forrester should be old enough by now to go to dances."

"Oh *really,* Muv, you are so vague, he's at least forty-five by now. Besides, I think he's been in India for the last ten years."

Nancy had been married a short time before, while I was in Paris, to Peter Rodd, and following the custom of the time she accompanied my mother and me to be presented at Buckingham Palace, she as a bride and I as a debutante. A hairdresser came to the house to arrange the regulation white ostrich feathers in our hair, and we set forth in a hired Daimler for the hours-long journey down the Mall, inching forward in an endless procession of debs and their mothers. Crowds of Londoners traditionally turned out to appraise the new debs; one would hear their comments as they peered through the car windows.

"Ow, ain't she a corker!"

"That one ain't much. Lookee 'ere, there's a beaut for ye!"

"Ain't the mother an old battleaxe!"

Clambering finally out of the car, we stumbled through the rainy dark into a brightly lit, crowded corridor, filled with bare shoulders and the musty smell of rented ostrich feathers. More hours of inching, this time through seeming miles of slightly overfed human flesh. Occasional gasps:

"I think I'm going to faint!"

"You *can't,* there isn't room."

The girl in front of me stops dead.

"Oh help!" in an agonized whisper, "I think my knickers are coming off," but she steps gracefully out of them and tucks them away in her evening bag.

Finally, the end of the road; a magnificent flunkey arranges our trains, another bawls out: "The Lady Redesdale. The Honorable Mrs. Peter Rodd. The Honorable Jessica Mitford." We are in the presence of what appear to be two large stuffed figures, nodding and smiling down from their thrones like wound-up toys. One more river to cross; the curtsies, one to each of the stuffed figures, then backing away without stumbling until one is out of the Presence.

The specific, English upper class version of the puberty rite is over. I am now a Grownup. Or am I? I surreptitiously cram several chocolates from the buffet into my little Victorian bouquet of flowers. After the presentation, we have an appointment at a photographer's to have our pictures taken in our court dresses. To my consternation, the chocolates tumble out all over the floor just as she is readying the camera ...

11

IN A WAY, I had been rather guiltily looking forward to being a debutante. Although the whole procedure was against my new-found principles, there did seem to be many interesting possibilities ahead. The idea of unlimited companionship of people my own age was in itself a very exciting prospect. Then, being at last "out" in that vague, undefined thing called "the world" . . . there was no telling what might happen. One might create a scandal by having an affair with some fascinating Older Married Man; one might even get married oneself. I told myself that I really was now, for all intents and purposes, out of the fortress; for was I not liberated from the schoolroom, free to roam London alone (at least in the daytime), free to study if I wanted to, perhaps at some intriguing stronghold of left-wing thought like the London School of Economics?

The day-to-day realities of the London season quickly dispelled most of these ideas. For one thing, there just wasn't time for anything except getting from one function to another — lunches, teas, the newly imported cocktail parties, dinners, dances — with all too little time to sleep in between. The lunches were usually all-girl affairs. "Fork luncheons" they were called. They consisted of buffet food, creamed stuff that could be eaten with a fork alone. The purpose of the fork lunches was to give the debutantes an opportunity to become acquainted with each other — an important enough function, since the girls and their mothers had firmly in hand the invitation lists to dinners, dances and weekend house parties. Conversation tended to be limited to a discussion of dances already held, dances to come, clothes already bought, clothes to be tried on, photographs taken for the society papers, photographs to be taken.

The dances were, of course, the main thing. These would take place at least nightly, five nights a week; sometimes there were as many as three in a single night. Endless successions of flower-banked ballrooms filled with very young men and women, resembling uniformly processed market produce at its approximate peak, with here and there an overripe or under-ripe exception . . . but the awful thing was that I could never remember any of their names. Easier would it be, I thought, to recognize the individual faces of sheep on an Australian ranch than to match names and faces among this monotonous sea of seemingly unvaried human beings. Smooth, fair, guileless faces, radiating the health bestowed by innumerable fresh-air-filled upbringings in innumerable country houses; straight or snub features bearing ample evidence of years of rather more than adequate protein and fat consumption; eyes blue to hazel, hair yellow to brown, height well above average for the human race as a whole — there really wasn't much to distinguish one from another. "Not Angles, but angels," Pope Gregory the Great is supposed to have commented at his first glimpse of the inhabitants of Albion's shore, and tediously angelic were the forms and faces of the hundreds of seventeen-to-twenty-one-year-old Anglo-Saxons who frequented the deb dances.

Conversation wasn't much of a clue to identity. After initial introduction one would stumble onto the dance floor in the arms of one of the Australian sheep. Opening gambits were generally restricted to two or three subjects: "D'you do much riding?" "Do you get up to Scotland much?" "Care for night clubs?" Since, in my case, a truthful reply to any of the three happened to be in the negative, keeping the conversation going usually proved to be uphill work. Often the first words would be the dreaded, "I say, we met last night at the so-and-sos', don't you remember?" (Oh Lord! Did we? Last night? What *could* his name be?), and hopelessly at a loss I'd have to answer lamely, "Oh yes, of course, good party, wasn't it?" My mother reproached me gently for my awful memory:

"You really *must* try to remember some of their names, darling, so naughty of you. I expect the trouble is you can't see very far, but you must get in the habit of recognizing people." I was, in fact, very shortsighted, but Muv would never have thought of taking me to an oculist about it for fear he might prescribe glasses, which she thought both hideous and expensive. She thought it quite awful that so many young people — and sometimes even children — had taken to wearing glasses. "The Good Body will eventually right it. You'll probably be able to see more as time goes on," she would comment vaguely.

The London season lasts for about three months in the summer; to me, it seemed to drag on forever. In the middle of it, I heard that Esmond Romilly had been sentenced to a six weeks term in a Remand Home for delinquent boys. He and Philip Toynbee, an eighteen-year-old runaway from Rugby, had shown up drunk at the Romillys' London house, and Esmond's mother had called the police. At the next day's court appearance she had told the judge that Esmond was uncontrollable, upon which the judge had decided to subject him to an appropriate discipline. I thought of making discreet inquiries on how one went about becoming a Prison Visitor, a form of Good Works I had heard of being practiced by elderly ladies with plenty of time on their hands, but was held back by my own feelings of inadequacy. What good could I possibly be to Esmond? Now I really was a Ballroom Communist with a vengeance. He would probably sneer at any efforts I might make to prove myself on his side.

Family reactions to Esmond's latest exploit were tempered this time by a certain amount of criticism of his mother for having lost her head and called the police, and for not standing by him at the trial. "That Nelly, she always was an hysterical woman," my mother said crossly. He was finally released, not to his parents' custody, but as the ward of an elderly cousin, Mrs. Dorothy Allhusen. We learned that he had gone to stay at her country house and was writing a book.

As the season drew to an end, it became cruelly evident that it had been a complete waste of time. I had made no real friends, had learned nothing, was no further advanced in planning my life. I cursed myself for not having the brains or ability to find my own way out of the deadly boredom that was enveloping me like a thick fog, out of the trivial, dull daily round of activities in which I found myself.

We returned to Swinbrook for an endless winter, broken only by an occasional invitation to a country houseparty or hunt ball.

Lucky Idden had succeeded in getting her parents to allow her to attend the Royal Academy of Drama and was living in London. I mounted a halfhearted campaign to be allowed to join her. "Now, little D., you know perfectly well you only want to go because Idden is going. You wouldn't have talent for acting." I felt this was true, but argued that acting wasn't very difficult and I could learn to do it. Another cousin,

Sarah Churchill, was learning; why couldn't I? "Well, you can't go, so there's no point in going on arguing about it."

I settled into a mood of unrelieved gloom, hating myself and everyone else, cross and bitter to sisters and parents alike.

12

THE FAMILY at Swinbrook had dwindled considerably. Nancy was living in London, Tom was abroad, Pam off doing something or other in the country, Boud lived now almost continuously in Germany. Debo and I were the only ones left at home, she still in the schoolroom doing lessons, I sitting around in the drawing room waiting for the next meal.

During that freezing, interminable winter two books were published which seemed to crystallize for me all the ideas I had been developing over the past few years. They were *The Brown Book of the Hitler Terror* and *Out of Bounds; The Education of Giles and Esmond Romilly*.

The *Brown Book* detailed and documented as much as was then known of the revolting cruelties to which the Jews were being subjected in Germany. It contained actual photographs of the bruised and bleeding victims of Nazi sadism, and related in horrifying detail how the new anti-Semitic laws were working out in practice. My parents maintained that the book was Communist-inspired, and that anyway the Jews had brought all this trouble on themselves, apparently by the mere fact of their existence. Boud and Diana, on their rare visits to Swinbrook, justified the atrocities as necessary to the survival of the Nazi regime. They produced a big autographed photo of one of their new-found friends — Julius Streicher, Gauleiter of Franconia, and one of the maddest of that group of madmen.

"Take that beastly filthy butcher out of here," I demanded furiously.

"But *darling!*" Diana drawled, opening her enormous blue eyes *"Streicher* is a *kitten!"*

Nancy as usual made a joke of the whole thing; she pretended to have discovered a Great-Grandmother Fish lurking somewhere in our family tree, and to Boud's and Diana's fury threatened to start the rumor that we were all one-sixteenth Jewish. I no longer found their antics rather funny. When they came to stay there were often bitter scenes, in which I felt hopelessly outnumbered and usually ended by going up to my room for a lonely cry.

One possibility occurred over and over again; I could pretend to have been suddenly converted to fascism, accompany Boud to Germany and meet the Führer face to face. As we were being introduced I would whip out a pistol and shoot him dead. Of course I should immediately be felled by Hitler's guards; but wouldn't it be worth it? The awful thing would be if I missed and still died in the attempt. Unfortunately my will to live was too strong for me actually to carry out this scheme, which would have been fully practical and might have changed the course of history. Years later, when the horrifying history of Hitler and his regime had been completely unfolded, leaving Europe half destroyed, I often bitterly regretted my lack of courage.

It was perhaps inevitable that the appearance at about this time of *Out of Bounds* should have made an enormously strong impression on me. The book created a considerable stir in the newspapers, and received almost uniformly favorable reviews, which I eagerly read and cut out. Even the *Daily Mail,* originator of the Red Menace story, admitted that *Out of Bounds* "shows that the two young iconoclasts lack neither brains nor literary ability." The *Times Literary Supplement* praised its "simplicity of wording and appositeness of phrase"; the *Observer* commented on its "considerable intelligence, modesty, and tolerance, a series of clear, humorous, and lively pictures of schools, boys, masters and parents." The *New Statesman* and the *Spectator* gave it unqualified approval. Overnight, the book became a minor best seller.

For the first time I got the full story — between the covers of a book, not in unsatisfactory, piecemeal fashion from newspapers and gossip — of the Romilly brothers' revolt against school, family, tradition. A very intriguing story it was.

Out of Bounds was written in two sections. The first, by Giles, began with his experiences at Seacliffe prep school, where both boys spent their childhood years. In very entertaining fashion Giles depicted the daily routine followed at this archaic institution, the customs and traditions, the quirks of masters and pupils. Understandably, methods of punishment evidently still painfully fresh in the mind of the young author were treated in vivid detail. It read like something out of Dickens. There was one master, for instance, whose peculiar way of enforcing discipline was to "pull our ears very hard and pinch our noses between an enormous pair of wooden compasses." Another master, "if he saw a boy making a nuisance of himself would take him by the short hairs, and just gently rock him to and fro; it was exceedingly painful." Yet another "would push back his chair, take hold of the boy round the stomach and pull him across his knee; he would then turn up his shorts and give him several terrific smacks on the bare thigh."

Esmond's part of *Out of Bounds* fascinated me particularly because it revealed so many almost exact parallels with my own life. Like me, he had been intensely partisan in politics on the Conservative side as a small child; "Not only was I a Tory," he wrote, "but I was also something far more romantic, a Jacobite. I worked out on a piece of paper during a geography hour that King George was an imposter, as Prince Rupprecht of Bavaria had a superior claim to the throne. When writing out the Kings and Queens on a genealogical table, instead of 'Old Pretender' and 'Young Pretender,' I would write 'James III' and 'Charles III.'" Called upon to attack the Russians in a debate at Seacliffe on "whether the Five Year Plan was a menace to civilization," Esmond had written to his uncle, Winston Churchill, for help in the way of facts and figures: "Churchill had replied that he was too busy to give me much information, but that the great point to stress was that the Russians murdered millions of women and children." How similar to my own views on the Russian revolution at about the same age!

At Seacliffe, Esmond had been treated to an analysis of England's three major political parties much like that given us at Swinbrook by Uncle Geoff: "Just before the 1929 General Election, Mr. Lancaster gave us a brief talk on the issues between the three political parties. The Conservatives, he said, were for leaving things much as they were, and putting Britain first. The Liberals were for building new roads; and the Socialists for taking everyone's money away, and landing the country in a mess."

Esmond's abrupt conversion to Communist ideas had come about in a way very similar to my own. He wrote: "I had a violent antipathy to Conservatism, as I saw it in my relations. I hated militarism, as this meant the O.T.C., and I had read a good deal of pacifist literature. Like many people, I mixed up pacifism with Communism. While I was in London at the beginning of the Easter holidays in 1933, before crossing to Dieppe, a street seller sold me a copy of the *Daily Worker*. I was excited and intrigued, and gave an order to have a copy sent each day to Dieppe while I was there. Though I did not learn much Communism, I learned that there was another world as well as the one in which I lived." That other world! And now Esmond was launched in it, I envied him with all my heart.

There were other parallels. While I was being teased about being a Ballroom Communist, Giles and Esmond were the object of similar barbs: "My uncle [Winston Churchill] thought it a great joke when Giles was considered to be a 'Red'; at that time I was still an ardent Jacobite. 'The Red Rose and the White Rose,' he used to call us."

Nanny and my mother had often pointed out to me that if I was really a Communist, I should be more considerate of those members of the working class who happened to be at hand: "Little D., I should think a Communist would be much tidier, and not make so much extra work for the servants," Muv would say. Apparently, Esmond had the same problem with his parents: "It must be remembered that all this time I was living in a conventional Conservative world. The conflict between this world and the one that centered for me round my Communist friends was bound to arise for a schoolboy taking an interest in the politics of the Left. My parents saw the absurdity of my position without trying to help. Usually, in fact, they elaborately drew and overdrew the contradiction for me. If I was a Communist, they would say, surely I should be working with my fellow men. As a start, it would be suggested that I should do a little housework, the practical proposal being that I should make the beds and clean the boots and shoes."

Reading *Out of Bounds,* I almost felt as though I knew Esmond. Rebellious, certainly — the "holy terror" of Chartwell days grown older; but he was also much more than that. He emerged as a person of unlimited resourcefulness, with that extra degree of good humor which comes from absolute self-confidence in all situations, fearless, indestructible...

There was a photograph of the Romilly brothers in *Out of Bounds,* which I pored over endlessly. I had seen other pictures of Esmond in the papers from time to time, but these had been for the most part unsatisfactory "candid" shots, revealing little of his personality. In the *Out of Bounds* frontispiece Giles was seated, looking out at the world with a faintly sardonic expression playing round his eyes. Esmond was standing, looking rather stern, his thick eyebrows slightly knit, forehead partly obscured by a thatch of hair, his rounded features slightly familiar because of resemblance to the Churchill children.

My copy of *Out of Bounds* was enshrined in an honored place among my Communist literature, and I resumed my ill-tempered brooding.

13

MY MOTHER was not particularly prone to worrying about her children. These were the simple days of family upbringing, before ideas of modern psychology had taken hold, saddling parents with the additional uneasy and frustrating burden of the unknowable; or, if such ideas were beginning to circulate in some advanced quarters, at least they had not trickled down to Swinbrook House.

Girls were to be trained, by precept and example, in the normal virtues, which included chastity, thrift, kindness to animals, considerateness of servants, and common sense. They were in general to be educated to the level of a good knowledge of English and French, simple arithmetic, and anything else they could pick up along the way, and were to acquire enough knowledge of cooking and household management to enable them to run a large or small staff of servants after marriage. If to this training nature should see fit to add those concrete and universally prized assets of beauty, charm and wit, so much the better.

The end goals of this education were marriage for love and not for money (but, it went without saying, within the confines of one's own class, and save for very exceptional cases one's own nationality and religion); the establishment of a wholesome and well-run household; and service to community and country, the specific character and extent of such service to be determined by one's interests and one's husband's particular station in life.

Pursuing these ends for the six of us, my mother had spent endless time, energy, and the proceeds of her chicken farm; but it was becoming rather apparent by this year of 1935 that not all of us were turning out quite according to plan. Pam, it is true, had shown interest and ability in English countryside affairs, was proficient in household management and had even worked for a time managing a farm. True to her childhood love for horses, she eventually married a jockey named Derek Jackson, and to this day retains a firm of solicitors called Withers. Nancy was happily married at last, though definitely part of "What-a-set." Peter Rodd, her husband, liked to affect the role of a bit of a reprobate. The blow of Diana's divorce had been weathered, but she was still eyed with disapproval by most of the Older Generation. Boud's extremist activities were something no one could do much about, even if they wanted to, and no doubt the thought of trying to deflect that iron will from its chosen direction into calmer and more appropriate channels was too much even for my mother.

While my mother philosophically accepted the fact that these four were, for good or ill, pretty much launched and set on their respective courses, I was still thoroughly underfoot. What is so accurately described as "The Difficult Age" was, in my case, lasting rather too long for comfort, and there were as yet no signs of my pulling out of it. My mother never sought discussion with me about the causes of my impossible moodiness. For one thing, this would have been considered an invasion of privacy; for another, whenever the subject of my frame of

mind was even obliquely approached it would produce tearful recriminations on my part about not having been allowed
to go to school. My Ballroom Communism was considered a
very harmless joke. I didn't talk about it much any more because the whole subject was becoming too painful and too
serious to me.

That "girls are usually restless and unhappy until they
marry" and that "they really only settle down after marriage"
were concepts strongly rooted in my mother's view of life.
She would have rightly rejected the idea that these opinions
had anything remotely in common with a cruder concept, "She
needs a man." In her view, the whole point of marriage was
that it gave you something to do, a *façon d'être,* a house to run,
a routine to follow; it provided the satisfying and constructive
framework upon which a life and a future could be built.

Not only was I making no progress in this direction, I had
not even established a circle of friends or a milieu which
might eventually lead there. Clearly, I needed a change of air,
that tried and true remedy for all physical or emotional ail-
ments. Wheels were set in motion for Muv, Boud, Debo and
me to embark on a Mediterranean cruise in the spring of 1936.

Naturally, we were all delighted at the idea. I even enter-
tained the sneaking hope that it might provide a good running-away opportunity — possibly love-at-first-sight with some
Sicilian peasant, Greek shepherd, or swarthy African . . .

The cruise my mother had selected was a semi-educational
affair. Most of our fellow passengers were students from Eton
and other public schools, and university people. There was
a Church of England canon on hand to give lectures about
Moorish art, Greek philosophy and other subjects. There
were also a number of miscellaneous people, like ourselves
bound for a few weeks of sunshine and quick culture, among
them a redheaded peer of the realm called Lord Strathmilton.

I wrote to Nancy, tongue in cheek and mindful of my mother's probable intention in taking us on the cruise: "There is a Lord on board." She wrote back:

> There is a Lord on board,
> A Lord on board, poor Decca roared,
> But the Lord on board is a bit of a fraud
> 'Cause the Lord on board has a wife called Maud,
> There is a Lord on board ...

This was the first time in some years that Boud, Debo and I had been anywhere together, and unfortunately, from my mother's point of view, the situation brought forth all of our family "oddness" in full force. When bridge tournaments were announced, Debo and I insisted on pressing for a "Hure, Hare, Hure, Commencement" tournament to determine the pain threshold of our fellow passengers. Following a lecture on democracy by the Canon, Boud formally demanded, and received, the floor to eulogize the glories of Nazi dictatorship.

We "borderlined" continually, this time seeing how far we could go in shocking my mother and the other people on the cruise. Debo and I pretended to be madly in love with Lord Strathmilton; "Strathmilton, Red, come to bed," we would bluntly chant, just out of his hearing. Our family sat at the purser's table, and mealtimes provided an ideal opportunity for such borderlining.

"He's such a nice little Scotchman," my mother said. "Really you children *might* try to be better behaved. What *must* he think of you?" But her efforts to restrain only spurred us on to further outrages. After a day in Gibraltar where we had been shown the fortifications, Debo said loudly at dinner: "Did you see the cannon's balls today, Decca?" The three of us exploded in giggles, and great kickings under the table ensued. My mother tried to foresee, and to forestall, probable trends of conversation. At Algiers, she cautioned us: "Now, you silly children, you are NOT to go on about White Slavers, really you seem to have that sort of thing on the brain."

But the real test of her control came at Constantinople. There we were conducted through the palace, where one of the "sights" was the last remaining eunuch, a tiny wizened old man with a face like a dried apple and a high squeaky, grumbly voice. That night, Muv told me to summon Boud and Debo to the cabin; there was something very serious she wanted to discuss with us. From her stonily solemn face and tone of voice, I could only assume that she had heard some bad news from home — perhaps a death in the family — and my heart pounded with real fear as I went in search of the others. When we were all assembled, Muv announced in her very gravest tones, "Now, children, YOU ARE NOT TO MENTION THAT EUNUCH AT DINNER."

We howled and screamed with laughter, and, although we would not have dared actually to disobey, kept referring all through dinner to the "you know what" with knowing looks and suppressed mirth.

But in spite of all the giggling and teasing, an underlying bitterness was growing up between me and Boud. This flared into the open toward the end of the trip, when we stopped at a port in the south of Spain and were taken in cars to see the Alhambra. Boud insisted on wearing her swastika brooch. The cruise party cars pulled up in the glaring white square in Granada, and curious Spaniards came forward in little groups to get a better view of the tourists. Their friendly interest quickly turned to rage when they saw Boud's swastika. She was surrounded by a hostile crowd, shouting at her, clawing at her clothes, trying to tear off the hated symbol. Other cruise members hustled us back into the car, and we started the long, miserable journey back to the ship. On the way

back Boud and I had a furious quarrel which ended in a
fist fight and hair-pulling match, and my mother crossly sent
us to the cabin as soon as we boarded the cruise ship.

Lying disconsolately on the bunk, I reviewed in my mind
alternative courses of action I might have taken. Had I
muffed an ideal opportunity to run? Could I have slipped
away in that hot, sunny town with its attractively unfamiliar
garlicky smell, to lose myself in that lively dark-faced crowd, to
merge with them and cast my life with theirs? Not likely, I
though sadly. Visions of British consuls and local police hot
on my trail immediately came to mind, and I had to admit it
wouldn't have required much sleuthing on their part to track
me down in my white linen cruise suit, panama hat, new brown
Oxfords, and complete ignorance of the Spanish language . . .

14

WE LIVED in London for several months after the cruise, Swinbrook having been let for most of that year.

Round the piano after dinner, where we often gathered to sing to my mother's playing, such old favorites as "Grace Darling," "The Last Rose of Summer," "I'll Sing Thee Songs of Araby," and "I Dreamt I Dwelt in Marble Halls" had been replaced. The drawing room now rang to the strains of the "Horst Wessel Lied," "Deutschland über Alles," "Die Wacht am Rhein." Boud and I had learned rival words to many of the same tunes, and while her huge voice blared forth the latest hymn of praise for the Führer — "Und jeder S. A. Mann ruft mutig: Heil Hitler! Wir stürzen den jüdischen Thron!" I countered, trying rather ineffectually to drown her out: "And every propeller is roaring Red Front! Defending the U.S.S.R."

We were preoccupied with politics. Daily battles over possession of the latest editions of the papers were commonplace. The six o'clock ritual of listening to the BBC News now frequently was the signal for renewal of hostilities with Boud, if she happened to be at home, or, failing that, with my parents.

It was certainly a year for news. Ominous as the first menacing quivers before a major earthquake, as the first unnaturally heavy raindrops that herald a great thunderstorm, events of 1936 forecast the shape of things to come for the next decade. Fascism was on the offensive everywhere. In the spring, Ethiopia fell to the Italians and Hitler marched into the Rhineland. British Tories stood nervously by, those in power saying as little as possible. Stanley Baldwin, the Prime Minister, quietest of them all, earned himself the nickname "Old Sealed Lips." Others in positions of lesser influence hoped out loud that it imght be possible to sick Hitler onto Russia before further embarrassing onslaughts were made in the direction of Western Europe. Lloyd George warned that the overthrow of Nazism might result in the greater threat of a Communist Germany. The *Daily Mail,* heretofore despised by my parents as one of the more horrid examples of the Yellow Press, suddenly began to mirror their views editorially:

"The sturdy young Nazis of Germany are Europe's guardians against the Communist danger. Once Germany has acquired the additional territory she needs in Western Russia, the problem of the Polish Corridor could be settled without difficulty."

Winston Churchill, long since out of the Government and a thorn in the side of his Party, thundered: "Are we a rabble fleeing before forces we cannot resist?"

My mother said Winston was a dangerous man, good thing he had so little following among the Conservatives. The Communists, often joined by Labor spokesmen and liberals of all parties, campaigned loudly for collective security with the Soviet Union against the Hitler menace.

In July Franco launched his attack on the Spanish Popular Front government. Now melodious, unfamiliar names of Spanish towns filled the news (mispronounced, however, in the BBC tradition of diction, as though they had been English names): Malaga, Cueva, Badajoz, Casablanca; and with every name a new fascist offensive was recorded. Believed at first to be an insignificant rebellion by a few disgruntled Army generals, the civil war fast assumed sinister proportions. "The proving ground for a second World War," some of the more farsighted political writers called it. It was first rumored, soon confirmed, that Italian and German troops and planes were being poured into Spain.

Sides were chosen up throughout the family. Nancy and Peter Rodd were strongly pro-Loyalist; Peter even talked in a desultory way of joining up with the newly formed International Brigade. He rather fancied himself in the role of Soldier of Fortune, and claimed to have spent much of his youth organizing revolutions in various South American countries. The aunts and uncles were mildly, the Revereds strongly, Diana and Boud violently, pro-Franco. They announced that the Führer had proclaimed Franco to be an "honorary Aryan," a title already conferred on Mussolini and the Emperor of Japan. "So — I suppose the Moorish mercenaries are Honorary Honorary Honorary Aryans?"

For me, the war in Spain inevitably now became my major preoccupation. My thoughts centered obsessively on ways of getting there; I mulled over and discarded endless plans. Yet it must be possible. The Loch Ness monster idea now seemed incredibly childish and pointless. It would have been doomed to failure, I clearly saw. But I was older now, and my Running-Away Account had reached quite adequate proportions — I had almost fifty pounds. I cut pictures of women guerrillas out of the papers, determined, steady-looking women, wiry, bright-eyed, gaunt-faced, some middle-aged, some almost little girls. How to take my place at their side? I considered asking Peter Rodd for advice. But no, he would probably make a great joke of it and the Revereds would soon find out. The now familiar stab of envy shot through me when I overheard a cousin telling my mother:

"Poor Nelly, she does have a time with those boys of hers. Of course, Esmond has always been the most troublesome of the two. She was telling me the other day, sometimes she fears for his mind. Now he's gone off to fight in Spain; he joined up with the Reds . . ."

Something closer to home, seemingly more foreboding, more threatening to the established order, than any of these rows abroad dominated the thoughts and conversation of London society. Now the British monarchy itself was threatened — and, of all things, by an American woman with the unlikely and extraordinarily unprepossessing name of Wallis Simpson.

"Her Christian name can't *really* be Wallis. The papers must have got it wrong. You know how inaccurate they are about everything."

"Children! You are not to mention that dreadful woman in front of the servants. And I don't want you to bring any of those American magazines into this house."

In fact, uncensored copies of *Time* Magazine, the first publication to take notice of the scandal, were hard to come by. Only those lucky enough to know someone who received a subscription direct from America were able to follow the progress of the shocking affair week by week. All reference to it had been neatly scissored out of the newsstand copies.

Peter Nevile, a recent acquaintance of mine, kept me supplied with the latest uncensored issues of *Time*. Peter was a tall, lanky young man with a carefully cultivated American accent; he had once been in the States for a few weeks and had become a great devotee of everything transatlantic. His great fascination for me lay, not so much in his rather disreputable appearance and odd way of talking, as in the fact that he was a friend of both the Romilly brothers, an ardent pro-

Loyalist, and a great admirer of Esmond. The latter was evidently Peter's political mentor, and since he was unavailable for consultation, Peter tried to conjecture what his course of action would be in the political crisis that now gripped England over the King and Mrs. Simpson. A showdown was approaching; Mrs. Simpson was granted a divorce, and simultaneously it was rumored that Baldwin and the Archbishop of Canterbury were bringing enormous pressure on the King to choose between Wally and the Throne. I didn't specially care one way or the other what the outcome might be. The romantic aspects seemed to me intensely dull; two middle-aged people with nothing in particular to recommend them, a good deal less interesting than the average film star — besides, Edward had recently shown signs of being impressed with the Hitler regime.

But Peter insisted: "Now's the time for action! A demonstration in front of Buckingham Palace — that'd be just the thing."

"How do we go about getting the demonstration organized?"

"We'll start from Hyde Park, Sunday afternoon — we won't need too many people, because once we start marching thousands will join us. Can't you visualize the scene? 'Down with Baldwin!' will be their cry. The papers tomorrow will be full of pictures and stories about this great throng. Like wildfire, news of our demonstration will reach the provinces. Next day the Tory Government will fall . . . "

Peter's enthusiasm was infectious. Could it be possible that he and I together could so simply bring about the downfall of the Conservatives? Why not? I specially liked the idea of the news "spreading like wildfire to the provinces," a way of referring to the English countryside that wouldn't have occurred to me, yet it sounded so right in the context — like something out of a history book.

I met Peter at the designated spot in Hyde Park the fol-

lowing Sunday. He had prevailed on a few others to participate in the demonstration, and we held aloft our homemade
banners painted with such slogans as "Edward's right, Baldwin's wrong," "Baldwin — Resign!" "Long Live Edward!"
I had an uncomfortable feeling that somehow all this was a
form of Royalism, and an even more uncomfortable feeling that
my parents might find out that I had been in the demonstration.

We were an oddly assorted little group. Peter had gathered
a few young men in polo-necked sweaters, a few society girls,
a few unpublished poets. After hanging around for about an
hour or so waiting for others to show up, stamping our feet
to keep warm in the chilly winter air, we marched toward
Buckingham Palace. Rather to my surprise we actually did
attract, if not the thousands that Peter had expected, about
fifty of the curious who fell into line behind us. We stood
outside the palace shouting, "We Want Edward!" A few additional passers-by stopped to gawk.

"See, this thing is catching on," Peter whispered excitedly.
But after about half an hour, when it became apparent that
Edward would not appear and some of us were getting rather
cold, I suggested moving the demonstration to No. 10 Downing Street.

"It would seem politically sound; besides, the walk will
warm us up," I urged.

Peter thought it an excellent suggestion. He turned to his
followers. "To Downing Street!" he cried, rallying them with
an authoritative wave, and he started to lead the way back
up Constitution Hill. Murmurs of doubt were soon heard among
the demonstrators: "I don't think this is the right way to
Downing Street, is it?"

Finally we had to stop a mounted policeman.

"Could you tell us the way to Downing Street, my good

man?" Peter asked, in as offhand a manner as he could muster. The officer reined his horse and saluted respectfully.

"Certainly, sir, yes, sir, I'm afraid you're headed in the wrong direction." With gloved hand he pointed out the correct route. Undaunted, Peter turned in the opposite direction and repeated his rallying gesture. "To Downing Street!" he cried once more, and again we obediently followed. But when we got there Downing Street was blocked off. "Typical Ruling Class trick!" said Peter, though I privately thought it looked as though routine street repairs were under way. The demonstrators, murmuring that it was time for tea, gradually dispersed.

The experience made me lose faith in Peter as a political leader; at least he might have taken the trouble to ascertain the way to Downing Street in advance, so that we wouldn't have had to ask a policeman, traditional Enemy of the Working Class. Besides, the provinces remained disturbingly calm and unshaken by our effort, and the Tory Government, far from falling, won the day soon after when Edward abdicated in deference to their wishes.

However, Peter remained my one contact with the pro-Loyalists, and I hung on to him for all I was worth. I consulted him about ways and means of getting to Spain, and he readily arranged for me to meet Giles Romilly.

We met in Lyons Corner House near Marble Arch, that huge, anonymous acre of tearoom where you are hardly likely to run into anyone you know. I should have recognized Giles anywhere. He sat slightly hunched over his tea, gazing round him with that quizzical expression, critically amused at the world, which I had looked at so often in the frontispiece of *Out of Bounds*. He told me he was thinking of going to Spain soon to join the International Brigade.

"That's what I want to do, couldn't you fix it up for me?"

I asked, prickling a little with embarrassment for fear he was secretly laughing at me. (I didn't tell him that only a few days before I had telephoned the Communist Party headquarters to ask if they needed any women guerrilla volunteers. "We don't know anything about that here!" a Cockney voice had answered firmly.)

Giles said he would try to help. He told me he had a friend who was a translator of French poetry, and who had contact with pro-Loyalist people in Paris. I begged him to get a letter from his friend to introduce me to them.

"What'll I tell them you want to do in Spain?" he asked.

"I could be a nurse," I said doubtfully, thinking that once there it wouldn't be hard to join the guerrillas after all. Giles agreed, and a few days later he met me again and produced the letter. My spirits sank when I read, *"Mlle. Mitford est une nourrice expériencée."*

"Your friend can't be a very good translator," I said crossly. *"Nourrice* means wet nurse. He should have said *'infirmière.'* How can I go to Spain and pass myself off as an experienced wet nurse?" However, I kept the letter just in case. Giles told me that I should probably have to count on spending at least two weeks in Paris, and even at that there was no assurance of getting to Spain.

Meanwhile, our stay in London was coming to an end and we were to go to Scotland shortly. I was in an agony of indecision as to whether or not to use the *"nourrice"* letter. The main difficulty would be the two weeks in Paris. There was every likelihood that once I left, and the hue and cry was on, I should be dragged back home, a completely unbearable thought.

In the end, I accompanied my parents to Scotland.

Once there, my problems seemed thrown into full focus. It was even duller than Swinbrook, because there was nothing

much to read. My Scotch cousins seemed to me to be unbear-
ably countrified, and they didn't even go in for our sport of
"shocking the Grownups"; in fact, they were thoroughly nice,
well-brought-up girls. Cousins Joe and Bridget Airlie, the
parents of these nice girls, came to visit frequently. Politically the Airlies agreed in general with my parents, or could
perhaps be more accurately described as slightly to the left
of them as they didn't think much of "that feller Hitler."
They disapproved of Boud and the publicity she had brought
on the family by her various fascist junkets.

Cousin Bridget and my mother would spend long hours
conversing, I felt sure, about me and what a problem I was becoming. Perhaps as a result of these discussions, my mother
made arrangements to take Debo and me on a world cruise,
with a girl of my age called Dora Stanley. Even the exciting
planning of the trip was marred by my bad temper. I remember one whole evening was spent bitterly debating whether we
should be allowed to disembark from the ship at Port Said.
My mother maintained that it would be "unsuitable" for us,
but I insisted I wanted to see the White Slavers in their natural habitat (we were all sure that they constituted the major
population of Port Said), and even muttered that being a
White Slave would be a nice change from Scotland — which
effectively broke up the evening.

"You're very silly, little D.," my mother said, and stumped
up to bed.

After one of these rows I would be angry with myself
because I realized dimly that my mother was trying her best
to get me to "snap out" of the gloomy moods I had fallen into.
Actually, the whole world cruise was being planned mostly for
my benefit, as it would be at least two more years before anyone would have to start worrying about Debo, who was only
sixteen. She had given up lessons some time ago because she

said they made her head ache, but she was always gloriously
happy in the country and so far showed no signs of "giving trouble."

Reading and listening to the agonizing news from the Madrid
front, the farce of England's "nonintervention" policy, and
the barbarous cruelty of Nazi and Fascist forces in Spain, made
me feel like a traitor to everything decent in the world. I
despised myself for living in the lap of luxury, supported and
kept by the very people who were making the "nonintervention" policy possible.

Shortly before Christmas the papers carried another long
story about Esmond, this time in the form of a dispatch from
him in the *News Chronicle:*

> 12 DAYS AGO WE'D 120 MEN — NOW 37 [the headline
> read]. WINSTON CHURCHILL'S NEPHEW SENDS GRAPHIC
> WAR MESSAGE.

The story was datelined from Albacete.

> Esmond Romilly, 18-year-old nephew of Mr. Winston
> Churchill, and a member of one of Britain's oldest families,
> is winning laurels for his gallantry under fire while serving
> in the International Brigade, which is fighting for the Span-
> ish Government in defense of Madrid.

The story continued in Esmond's own words:

> We've just returned after twelve days on the Madrid front.
> Experiences to date:
> Air bombing of our positions
> Crossing open-ploughed fields under machine-guns and rifle
>   fire
> Shelling from our own tanks
> Too much death about everywhere ...
> Our company started 12 days ago with 120 men. Present
>   strength 37.

This conversation piece sums up the way the war is being fought:

"Can you give me a light for my hand grenade?"

"Sorry, old man, no matches . . ."

This is the land of *mañana*. Sometimes one goes to the wrong front and back again. Madrid, of course, does not look too bright — with continual air raids and heavy bombardment. Three of our people have been killed by dum-dum bullets.

Yesterday in Madrid we saw a British Parliamentary delegation. They seemed amazingly out of place — Tories and Liberals enquiring about the hot coffee.

The section we're in is German. Some of them are desperately brave. Their idea is to walk in front of the tanks like men with red flags in front of trains in 1840.

Worst experience so far — digging in behind trees in a ploughed field under machine-gun fire.

Then we had the order to duck back into cover. Slipped into a shell hole, and fell — then a shattering roar which nearly blew my eardrums to pieces. It was one of our own tanks firing from five yards behind me.

Most of the people here have now given up the idea that they will ever return to Britain. The figures in our own company tell why.

Naturally, we take prisoners, but everyone on our side would shoot himself rather than be taken prisoner.

When we came here I thought we should be in trenches, but there are none at all in our sector . . .

The militia is officially no more, and I am now, therefore, a member of the Spanish Republican Army.

I am sure we shall win, however . . . But what a victory it will be.

I clipped the story out and kept it in my copy of *Out of Bounds*. A few nights later, the Airlies threw a "servants' ball" as part of the Cortachy Christmas festivities. Various gamekeepers, grooms, footmen, cooks, housemaids and their families assembled at the Castle for the event. The men all wore kilts and the women their best dresses. At the appointed time, we and the Ogilvy family descended to the ball. I fought back tears as I watched my cousin Joe Airlie, as "head of the family," lead off with the housekeeper, and Cousin Bridget with the butler. It all seemed so revoltingly jolly and out of place, so smugly in contrast with the daily news headlines. As the bagpipes squeaked noisily away, I sat in stony boredom and silence.

That night, there was some discussion of the *News Chronicle* story: "Poor Nelly, she must be worried; what thoroughly awful boys those two are, bad eggs, that's what. Pity their father didn't take them in hand more when they were little." As usual, the proposal of a good horsewhipping closed the discussion.

Shortly after this, the newspapers reported that Esmond Romilly had been "invalided out" of the Spanish war and was back in England recovering from illness in a hospital.

Our stay in Scotland was almost over, and the next two months were to be given over to intensive preparations for the world cruise. We should all need new clothes, for all kinds of climates ranging from tropical to bitterest cold. My mother, Debo and I were to return to our house at 26 Rutland Gate to make the necessary preparations to sail in March.

Just before we left, an invitation arrived for me to spend a weekend at Cousin Dorothy Allhusen's at Havering House near Marlborough. When my mother told me about the invitation, a thrilling idea struck me. Perhaps Esmond would be there. Cousin Dorothy was the elderly relation who had volunteered to become his guardian when he was freed from the remand home. I knew he had stayed with her for long periods of time, and had in fact written *Out of Bounds* while living at her house. Therefore, I reasoned, she must be one of the very few Grownups with whom he was still on friendly terms. Should I at long last meet him? I superstitiously tried to banish the thought from my mind, fearful that to dwell on it might invite disappointment.

15

COUSIN DOROTHY's house was deliciously comfortable and pleasant. Unlike most English country houses, the rooms were always glowingly warm. You got the feeling that the fires burned in the fireplace continuously all winter. Being a childless house, it had a quiet, timeless, clean quality often missing in the houses of other aunts and cousins. There were many old-fashioned touches; oranges stuffed with cloves in the chests of drawers, early morning tea in your bedroom, and savory at the end of dinner — hot stuffed mushrooms or chicken livers wrapped in bacon. Cousin Dorothy was fond of company and was specially nice to young people, also in contrast to most of the grown-up relations.

I was the first of the guests to arrive for the weekend, having come down by an early train on Friday afternoon. Over tea in the drawing room, Cousin Dorothy told me who the other guests would be: "A very nice young American couple" (she was known to "go in for Americans" quite a bit) "and your cousin, Esmond Romilly. He's just back from Spain, I expect you saw it in the papers."

For a moment I felt physically faint with anticipation.

Of course, I had been in love with Esmond for years, ever since I first heard of him. Although I had a strong belief that you can make anyone fall in love with you if you really concentrate on it — my older sisters had told me this was so, and I felt it must be true — now that I was about to meet him I was full of doubts and misgivings.

I thought gloomily of all the competition I must face from his unknown women friends; I visualized Elizabeth Bergner-like waifs in the East End, glamorous older women in the left-wing movement, even brave guerrilla fighters behind the lines in Spain. All of them beautifully thin, no doubt.

I spent an unusually long time getting ready for dinner. In the pink glow cast by the pretty lampshades in my bedroom, I thought I really didn't look so bad. I could hear the bustle of the other guests arriving downstairs.

My dress was mauve lamé, street length; it was quite pretty but not very comfortable. I noticed to my annoyance that it had a slightly tinny smell. When I left my warm room for the freezing moment on the landing and stairs, I was tingling with nervousness and sweating slightly.

The other guests were assembled round the fire in the drawing room.

"Decca, this is Mrs. Scott, and Mr. Scott; my young cousin, Miss Mitford; and this is your cousin, my dear, Esmond Romilly. You must be cold, may I give you a glass of sherry?"

The introductions completed, I started chatting with Mr. Scott, a young American schoolteacher, looking at Esmond out of the corner of my eye. He was shorter than I had imagined, very thin, with very bright eyes and amazingly long eyelashes.

At dinner, I sat between Esmond and Mr. Scott. It wasn't until halfway through dinner that I got a chance to talk to him.

"Esmond, are you planning to go back to Spain?" I asked.

"Yes, I think I'll be leaving again in a week or so."

No point beating about the bush — it was now or never. Feeling strangely like a diver about to plunge from a great height into unknown waters, I said in a low voice, "Well — I was wondering if you could possibly take me with you."

"Yes, I could, but don't let's talk about it now," he answered, glancing round to see if anyone was listening. He seemed to have been expecting my question, and already to have made his mind up about the answer. Later I found out that Peter and Giles had told Esmond about my unsuccessful efforts to get to Spain, and that with his usual enthusiasm for fellow runaways he had been thinking over ways to help me.

Cousin Dorothy treated Esmond with the greatest affection, rather as a very fond mother would treat a mischievous little boy. He in turn played right up to this, and there was quite a bit of joking between them about the filthy state of his socks as discovered by the maid who did his unpacking, and whether his state of health would permit the enormous amounts of pudding he was consuming.

After dinner she pressed him to tell about his experiences in the International Brigade; but he was more interested in discussing England's policy toward the civil war, and how it could be changed. He refused to be led on as a "social lion" or to show off in any way about his exploits. The Scotts were obviously enormously impressed with him. I was content to sit back and listen, for it seemed to me that an objective of a lifetime was about to be reached. For some reason I never had a moment's worry that Esmond would change his mind, or that we might be prevented from leaving.

That night I lay in bed absolutely rigid with excitement and anticipation. I woke up long before the seven-thirty arrival of tea and toast, and was the first down to breakfast. Esmond arrived on the scene soon after. "We'll talk about plans later," he said rapidly, between gulps of egg and sausage.

After breakfast there was the usual desultory gathering of guests in the drawing room, rustling of morning papers, lighting up of cigarettes.

Esmond seemed to be looking for an opportunity to detach me from the others, like a spillikin player carefully removing one of the ivory sticks without disturbing the whole collection. He suggested going for a walk; the Scotts looked up hopefully. "We won't be long," said Esmond firmly, and with enough finality to prevent them from coming with us.

We walked out into the freezing, muddy countryside, Esmond talking nervously and rapidly, head down against the wind. He plunged immediately into the plans for our getaway. The *News Chronicle* had already offered him an advance of £10 to return to Spain as their correspondent; I could come along as his secretary. "But I can't type," I said, feeling hopelessly stupid and inadequate. Esmond assured me that wouldn't really matter, as he did all his own typing anyway. I told him about my £50 Running-Away money. His face lit up delightfully. "That's absolutely wonderful," he said with great interest and enthusiasm; it seemed to make up for my lack of typing ability.

The really pressing problem was, how should I carry out my part of the plan? How could I manage to be away from home for any length of time without arousing suspicion? Of course I had been thinking of nothing else all night, and proudly unfolded to Esmond the course of action I had devised. I would confide the whole scheme to my cousin Robin, who was now married and living in the country, and tell my mother that I was going to Robin's for the weekend. Robin, in turn, would be persuaded to cover up for me if anyone should try to reach me at her house.

Esmond immediately vetoed such a plan. He patiently explained that it violated several prime rules for successful running away; not a living soul should be told, it would be too risky; a weekend would be far too short a time for getting to Spain, as we might easily be held up by unforeseen circumstances. I was slightly disappointed, as I was already looking forward to a long chat with Robin and Idden, and savoring their shocked reaction, as soon as I got back to London.

We were approaching a field of stubble.

"D'you think you could run all the way across that field with full equipment?" Esmond asked suddenly.

"Oh — I'm sure I could," but I must have grown slightly pale, because he laughed and said:

"Well, you might not have to. But it wouldn't be a bad idea to spend the next few days practicing that sort of thing, just in case."

I was relieved when he dropped the subject and returned to methods of escape. We should need at least two clear weeks, he insisted. I must think of some adequate excuse for being away from home for that length of time, something that would be sure to meet with my parents' full approval, so that the danger of their finding out would be reduced to the barest minimum.

Suddenly it came to me in a flash. I had just received a letter from the Paget twins, girls who had been debutantes at the same time as I was. They had written to say they were spending several months in Austria; therefore there was no danger that my mother would run across them in London. She barely knew their aunt, with whom they lived, so there was little risk in that direction, either. I could forge a letter from the twins asking me to join them in Austria.

Esmond was immediately enthusiastic. He turned the idea over and over, examining it from every angle, discussing it in his odd rambling way, whittling it down and amending it.

Rather than Austria, he suggested, I should make the invitation come from Dieppe, where the Paget aunt could have taken
a house for a few weeks. In that way, my fare would be paid
as far as Dieppe by my parents, and a few pounds of my Running-Away money would be saved. I was fascinated by his
extraordinarily practical way of looking at things, the realism with which he appraised difficulties in our way, and the
ingenuity with which he devised methods of surmounting
them.

Esmond offered to help me draft the letter from the Paget
twins. I was relieved, because I didn't trust myself to carry
out even the simplest part of the plan alone.

When we got back the drawing room was deserted, and we
set to work with pencil and paper.

"What are you two plotting?" Cousin Dorothy had suddenly come in.

"Oh . . . I was just showing Decca part of an article I'm
writing." I was greatly impressed by the ease with which
Esmond lied, though he was obviously annoyed by the interruption. Taking my cue from Esmond, I hardly spoke to
him when the others were present. Our next opportunity to
discuss plans was on the London train on Monday morning.

Esmond advised me not to tell anyone he had been at Cousin
Dorothy's for the weekend. He was extremely cautious, an-
ticipating every possible leak.

"After all, some people already know you want to get to
Spain," he said. "If they find out we were both there, it
might make them think."

We decided to leave on the following Sunday, giving us a
week to get papers from the Spanish Embassy and other necessary equipment.

"Does your father have an account at any of the department stores? I could do with a good camera, and we don't

want to spend any of your cash till we have to." I was secretly a little shocked at this idea, but readily agreed to go along.

We parted at the station, after agreeing that I was to ring him up at his mother's house in Pimlico Road promptly at ten each morning. If Esmond telephoned me and my mother or father answered, he might be asked to identify himself. However, just in case some unforeseen emergency should arise and make it necessary for him to telephone, we settled that he should announce himself as Robert Brandon, a young man I had met last summer at a dance.

I took a taxi to our house in Rutland Gate, feeling very odd indeed. As children, my sisters and I had often discussed how one would *know* if one were actually in love. Apparently others wondered about the same thing, for the Advice to Lovelorn columns were full of the comforting thought, "Don't worry, dear, you'll know when Mr. Right comes along." ("Or the Duke of Right," Debo used to add hopefully.) Now I could see the truth of this advice. I was completely, deeply committed; I hadn't been able to take my eyes off Esmond all weekend. I had watched the Scotts succumb to his extraordinary charm, like trees slowly falling before the wind. Although Esmond was the youngest person in the party, he had seemed like a star around which everything revolved. A wind, a star, he represented to me all that was bright, attractive and powerful, and I did wonder what he thought of me. There had been one slight indication; one night the party at Cousin Dorothy's had played a primitive sort of parlor game, then popular, in which each guest gave the others marks for various qualities — beauty, sense of humor, intelligence, sex appeal and so forth. The scores were added and announced, and the papers kept anonymous. Terrified of being discovered, I had gone down in my dressing gown after everyone else was asleep to salvage the crumpled sheets from the waste-

basket. I discarded two neatly penned papers as Scott products; another, in a spidery and old-fashioned hand, must be
Cousin Dorothy's; and I recognized my own. That left an un-
tidy penciled scrawl, in which I got straight "10's" — the top
mark. This must be Esmond's paper. Other than that I had no
clue.

It seemed somehow surprising that nothing had changed at
home. My mother was doing household accounts at her desk
in the drawing room.

"Hullo, Little D. Did you have a nice time at Cousin
Dorothy's?"

"Yes, very nice. Delicious food, too."

"Were there many people there?"

"No . . . just some Americans called Mr. and Mrs. Scott."

"Well, now we must start thinking about clothes for the
world cruise. There are some good sales just now, and tomorrow Dora and her mother are coming to lunch. I thought
you and Dora could go shopping, so don't make any other
plans." I was greatly annoyed, having counted on a week free
of any interruptions in which I could concentrate on all
the million things that might have to be done to complete the
Running Away plans.

"Why can't we wait till next week?"

"Well, for one thing, Dora's mother is insisting on her having typhoid injections. Such a lot of nonsense, I always think,
I shouldn't think of letting you children have all that awful
stuff pumped into the Good Body. And Dora wants to get
her shopping over before having to go for the injections."

This was bad news, but making a fuss might arouse suspicion. I hung around nervously all day, unable to settle down
to anything. Cousin Bridget came to tea, and there was the
usual family talk.

"I saw poor Nelly the other day," said Cousin Bridget.

"Of course she's fearfully upset about Esmond. What a fearful little creature he is!"

Later I learned that Cousin Bridget thought I behaved very strangely; that she noticed I had become "deathly pale," and fled from the room.

That night, I was to accomplish Part 1 of the Running Away plan. The last post usually came at about ten-thirty. I had the forged letter from the Paget twins in my dressing-gown pocket, and went down the seven flights of stairs from my room to the front door. Nothing must go wrong; I must act out every detail. I even stooped and pretended to pick up the letter. My heart pounding furiously, I walked back up to my mother's bedroom and knocked on the door.

"Come in . . . That you, little D.?" My mother was sitting up in bed reading, her hair down over her shoulders. Luckily the reading lamp cast a shadow in the place where I was standing, as I could feel my face beet-red.

I cursed my choking voice as I said, "Look, I've just got a letter from the twins. They want me to come to stay with them in Dieppe . . . here . . ."

I handed her the letter, and hoped she wouldn't notice I was trembling all over. Would she recognize my writing? I had done it very carefully, slanting it in the wrong direction, with long thin spidery letters. I had selected "40 Rue Napoléon" as a suitable fictitious Dieppe address, having forgotten to find out from Esmond the name of a real street there. The letter was filled with appropriate "circumstantial" remarks, such as: "Our aunt has rented a lovely little white house down by the sea . . . we'll be quite a party, some boys from Oxford are coming over in a rented motor car so we shall be able to tour round . . . " This last had been suggested by Esmond, so that I should be able to write to my mother from various towns in France as we journeyed south without exciting suspicion.

"Well, it all sounds lovely," my mother said doubtfully, "but the only trouble is, you do have an awful lot to do to get ready for the world cruise. What about your clothes? Really, I think two weeks is too long . . ."

"Yes, I know," I was speaking very rapidly, "But I was thinking I could get some lovely French clothes in Dieppe. I should so love to go, it all sounds so heavenly, couldn't I possibly go?"

"I see they want you next Sunday. Well, I suppose it would be all right. You might not be able to stay the whole two weeks, though." (Success! It seemed unbelievable.)

"Oh, good, I'll write to them right away. Also, I was wondering if I could have an advance on my dress allowance so that I can get my things for the cruise while I'm in Dieppe." (This idea had flashed into my mind as I stood there, and I knew Esmond would be pleased.)

"Yes, that sounds sensible. Well, goodnight, darling, we can talk about it all in the morning."

I fled in relief, excitement mounting in me like a storm. "I'm going to Spain with Esmond Romilly," the magic words repeated themselves over and over in my head all night.

"What in the world are you doing up at this hour?" Nanny demanded to know at seven the next morning.

"Nothing, darling." I swept her off her feet with a hug.

"Stop that foolish nonsense, Jessica. Now come here, I want to sort out your underclothes to see what you need for the cruise."

It seemed like hours till ten o'clock.

"Can't meet you till tomorrow," I told Esmond in a low voice.

"What? Why not?"

"Can't explain. The letter was OK, though."

Hours till lunch; everything that day seemed to be going in slow motion — the arrival of Dora and her mother; the few minutes in the drawing room sipping sherry before lunch; the parlormaid coming to announce "Luncheon is served" — it all took place in a haze of unnatural normalcy. Conversation at lunch revolved, of course, around the cruise; I was finding it difficult to pay attention, and two or three times I had to be jerked back into reality by my mother.

"What's the matter with you, little D.? You seem so absent-minded today."

Lunch over, Dora, her mother and I set forth for the shops. I must say I felt a bit guilty as I watched them select three-guinea tropical topees and other suitable wear for the hot Indian climes to which I knew we should now never go.

"See you tomorrow, then, about one," Dora said when we had finished the shopping.

"WHAT?"

"Yes, Lady Redesdale asked me to lunch again tomorrow, didn't you hear?" I hadn't heard, and was determined to avoid another day like this one. I decided I should have to devise some Esmond-like scheme to get rid of Dora as soon as possible.

By the next day it was imperative that Esmond and I should meet. "Two-thirty at the main entrance of Peter Jones," I told him.

At lunch Dora said, "Lets go to a movie this afternoon."

"Oh no, I can't . . . I've more shopping to do."

"I'll go with you."

"But it's very dull shopping — just things like stockings."

"Well, I'll go. I don't have anything else to do."

Having failed in all efforts to shake her, I firmly took her to Peter Jones. We stood looking at gloves and stockings on the main floor for a little while.

"I just remembered, I've got to pay a bill upstairs," I told her. "Would you wait right here? *Don't move.* I'll be right back. But don't go away or I'll never find you in this crowd."

I ducked round to the front entrance; luckily Esmond was already there, and we left rapidly in the direction of the Spanish Embassy.

A very handsome, very tall Spaniard looked over Esmond's paper and my application.

"And what is your purpose in wanting to travel to Spain, Miss Mitford?" he asked.

Esmond answered for me.

"She's coming as my secretary. You see, I expect to be very busy at the front, and getting the stories, and I'll need someone to do my typing. Miss Mitford generally works with me on assignments, and she'll act as my assistant . . . "

"Yes, yes, I quite understand — I fully sympathize." The Spaniard's face became wreathed in smiles and to my consternation he gave a broad Latin wink.

"However, the request is a little unusual; I'm afraid it will have to be processed by Señor Lopez. He can be reached at our embassy in Paris."

"What'll we do?" I asked Esmond when we left.

"I'm just trying to think. We'll have to go to Paris first, I suppose. Let's go and buy the camera now, and get your Running-Away money out of the bank."

I told him about the advance on my dress allowance, and he was evidently delighted at the promise I was beginning to show as a runner-away.

"Thirty pounds more, that's really excellent," he said.

After buying a very complicated and expensive kind of camera, and charging it to my father's account at the Army and Navy Stores, we selected a good running-away outfit for me. Having pored over pictures of Spanish guerrilla women fighters in the weekly illustrated papers, I knew exactly what I wanted, and found it; a brown corduroy ski suit with a military-looking jacket and plenty of pockets. We also bought name tapes bearing the legend DECCA MITFORD, INGLESA, which Esmond assured me would protect my things from getting appropriated.

When I got home, Debo said, "Dora's been telephoning all afternoon. She's perfectly furious, said you deliberately lost her in Peter Jones. Where were you all this time?"

I dialed Dora's number.

"Really, Dora, I TOLD you to wait for me, you know how long bills and things take." She insisted she had waited for over an hour and a half. "I must have just missed you then. I'm awfully sorry. Good luck with the typhoid injections, I hope it doesn't hurt too much . . ."

The rest of that week Esmond and I managed to meet daily without further trouble. On Saturday we made final arrangements for the next day.

"I'll be down at the far end of the station," Esmond said. "Now for heaven's sake don't look in my direction or anything. Safest not to speak till we're on the boat. Everything all set? See you tomorrow."

Next morning I sat on my bed watching Nanny pack. She gave a little trouble over the running-away suit: "Really, darling, what do you want that awful thing for? Not at all nice to take to Dieppe, I should think."

"Oh, Nanny, it'll be just the thing for motoring in, do let me take it."

My parents took me to the station in a taxi. I caught a glimpse of Esmond in the distance at the end of the station.

"Have a lovely time, darling, and be sure to write. I'll write to you, it's 40 Rue Napoléon, isn't it — let me be sure I've got it written down." My mother was rummaging in her purse for the letter. "Goodbye, then, you're sure you remembered to wire the twins about your arrival time?"

Once settled in the train, I had time to collect my thoughts and assess the situation. I was quite sure I had left my father's house for the last time, as indeed turned out to be the case. And while I didn't regret the decision for one minute, I did have some severe pangs of conscience about not having left any message, even with Robin, about my real plans. My stomach turned over at the thought of the scene at home when they finally found out. But an even worse possibility to contemplate was that they might somehow find out prematurely that I wasn't with the Pagets. Suppose my mother should run into the Paget aunt somewhere in London? It wasn't very likely, but still . . . The twins were safely in Austria for another couple of months, so no risk there . . . Anyway, if some such disaster should befall, I was quite certain Esmond would find a way out.

During the brief week of our acquaintance the opinions I had formed about him through reading *Out of Bounds* had been strongly confirmed. He seemed to have the magic combination of determination, intelligence and courage which would take him wherever he intended to go, and I had already developed an unshakable confidence in him. Also, he seemed now to take it for granted that he was in full charge of carrying out my plans to run away. I worried over how babyish and inexperienced I must seem to him — although I was almost a year older than he. How I regretted not having learned to speak Spanish, or to type, or to be a journalist, in all those wasted years at Swinbrook! During the last week I had risen early every morning and done physical exercises against the dreadful day when I should be required to run across a field of stubble with full equipment; but the exercises had only consisted of trying unsuccessfully to bend down and touch my toes, and I wasn't too sure that this would really help . . .

Once during the train journey to Folkestone, Esmond

walked past my carriage to give an encouraging grin; and soon we were on the boat, past customs and passport inspection, really on our way.

We took rooms in Paris in a small hotel on the left bank. Next morning we presented ourselves at the Spanish Embassy.

"Sorry, Señor Lopez left for London last night."

"But — that can't be! They told us at the Embassy in London we should find him here!"

"Very sorry. He is not expected back for two weeks. But you can reach him in London."

Esmond was fuming. He pleaded and begged to see someone else about my papers; but we were assured that Señor Lopez was the only person who could help us. We wandered off to the Bois de Boulogne. Esmond paced restlessly up and down.

"We must think . . . What's the best thing? We have the alternative of going South and trying to cross the Pyrennees . . . no, I think those borders are closed by now . . . or return to London and try to find Lopez . . ." He was pondering alternatives out loud rather than talking to me, as though he knew he would have to be the one to make all decisions.

That afternoon we caught the first train back to Dieppe; the only thing for it was to return to London and try to find Señor Lopez.

There was a four-hour wait for the next boat to Folkestone. Esmond was suddenly struck with an idea.

"Let's see if there really is a Rue Napoléon," he suggested. "There probably is one in every French town."

We inquired in a café, and found there was indeed a Rue Napoléon, a mile or so from the dock in a residential section. Not only was there a Rue Napoléon, there was a No. 40. We rang the bell. A courteous Old World type of Frenchman in a red brocade lounging robe appeared at the door.

"Is there by any chance a letter for Miss Jessica Mitford?"

I inquired. "I gave my friends the wrong house number by mistake, and hoped perhaps . . ."

"Why, yes, there is," he answered. "As a matter of fact I was just going to give it back to the postman — he'll be here any minute; you are lucky." He handed me the letter with my mother's familiar round handwriting on the envelope.

We retired to a café on the wharf, hardly able to believe our good luck. It seemed a portent for the success of our plans. The letter, written the day I left, was full of the usual home news: "Aunt Weenie came to tea today, and Debo went riding in the Row." We borrowed a piece of writing paper from the *garçon,* and I wrote: "Arrived safely . . . so glad you saw Aunt Weenie, I hope she is well . . . I hope Debo had a nice time riding in the Row . . ." We exultantly posted my letter. It should arrive the next day with a Dieppe postmark; that should keep things quiet at home for a bit.

16

WE STILL HAD almost two hours before the boat would leave. Esmond suddenly became preoccupied and silent. He suggested walking down by the quai. We passed rows of waterfront cafés with their bright, painted fronts and inviting handwritten menus tacked on the doors. We leaned over the railing and watched craft of all sizes and shapes manoeuvering about in the rough, windy Channel.

"There's somehing I've got to talk over with you," he said, very seriously. (Had he decided after all that the search for Señor Lopez was too difficult and time-consuming, and that he must continue to Spain alone?)

Another long silence.

"I'm afraid I've fallen in love with you."

We selected a suitable café in which to celebrate our engagement over *fines à l'eau.*

Some sailors joined the festivities, offering toast after toast to *les fiancés,* and we almost missed the sailing of the channel steamer.

Now there was a new complication to be added to the planning department.

"How on earth can we get married?" I said. "We'll probably both have to get our parents' permission."

"Oh well, don't let's worry about that," answered Esmond, with a sardonic grin. "A lot of people say long engagements are the best thing."

We arrived back in London very late at night, and at Esmond's suggestion took a cab to Peter Nevile's house.

Peter came to the door in his dressing gown, looking rather sleepy and cross. For a moment, he was even crosser when he heard our news. I have since learned that it invariably annoys a person's "best friend" to hear of an engagement which comes as a complete surprise and which he or she has had no hand in promoting.

However, he cheered up when we began discussing the probable reactions of my family.

We decided I should draw up a letter to my mother for Peter to deliver at an appropriate time. Esmond was rather worried over this plan, as it violated a number of his tried and true rules for successful running away, such as "never tell a living soul," and "never put anything in writing." But I pointed out that eventually my parents were bound to notice when I didn't return from Dieppe, and didn't show up for the world cruise. I was very anxious that they should not have additional worries over where I was or with whom.

The letter began dramatically, "Darling Muv: By the time you get this, I shall be married to Esmond Romilly."

Peter was understandably nervous about having to deliver this odd message.

'D'you mean I've got to beard the Nazi baron in his den?" he drawled, in his sardonic semi-American accent.

"Oh, come on, Nevile, you know you'll love it . . . of course, they'll probably horsewhip you," Esmond added reflectively, "but it really isn't much to ask. Tell you what: Decca's frightfully rich, you know, she's got almost eighty pounds, or at least she did before we had to go in for all this ridiculous crossing and recrossing of the Channel. So we'll buy you lunch at the Café Royal, to celebrate."

This was a dangerous risk to take.

The Café Royal was a huge, old-fashioned restaurant in London rather famous in those days as a common meeting ground for writers, artists, journalists, politicians, society people. Among the hundreds of patrons who flocked there at lunchtime there might be many we knew. During the two hours we sat there, consuming red wine and omelet (the cheapest food on the menu — Esmond was still conserving what was left of the eighty pounds), I saw a couple of friends of Nancy's and Esmond also saw some people he knew. We waved hilariously at them, for once abandoning caution. Our luck held, and nothing came of these chance contacts.

The elusive Señor Lopez was nowhere to be found in London, so the same night we returned to Paris.

The next two weeks were consumed in a frustrating series of appointments with various Spanish officials. Time was passing at a frightening rate, and we seemed to be getting nowhere. We traveled to Bayonne, a port in the South of France near the Spanish border, posting letters to my mother in towns on the way. ("Having a lovely time with the twins ... We are now touring France in a car brought by one of the boys from Oxford ... ")

Esmond was getting increasingly restless. The two indispensable practical ingredients of our plan — time and money — were fast being dissipated. It seemed likely that any day now my mother would discover my defection from the family ranks.

In many ways, this was a far from ideal honeymoon. Esmond was tormented by practical worries, and I felt completely inadequate to help solve them. But we got to know each other faster than would have been possible under more normal circumstances. Esmond had an infallible nose for the cheapest possible accommodation, and we stayed in Bayonne in a small hotel, crowded with Basque refugee families from the northern part of Spain. Every day we checked at the Basque consulate for my authorization to travel and for possible news of transportation. We went for long walks in the town, during which Esmond told of his experiences on the Madrid front.

Within a few weeks of the first news of the Fascist rebellion, he had set out for Spain on his own, without telling any of his friends, fearful that he might be rejected and sent back because of lack of military training. For once in his life, he regretted his refusal to join the O.T.C. at Wellington. Knowing nothing of the organization of the International Brigade, he had simply bicycled to Marseilles in hopes of boarding some cargo ship bound for Spain. There he learned that young men from all countries were already flocking to the Spanish front, and he fell in with a miscellaneous group of volunteers — French, Germans, Italians, Yugoslavs, Belgians, Poles — sailed with them to Valencia, and was sent to the training camp at Albacete.

There was as yet no English battalion, so Esmond and fifteen other Englishmen were attached to the German Thaelmann Brigade. He was relieved to learn that most of these were also completely lacking in military training; they came from every conceivable walk of life — car workers, farmers, restaurant owners, university students. The training at Albacete was extremely brief, and within a few days the battalion was sent to the Madrid front. There they were in almost continuous action, living the muddy, bloody, confused life of foot soldiers. A week before Christmas, in a single disastrous battle, all but two of the English group were wiped out. Esmond and the other survivor, ill with dysentery and battle fatigue, were sent back to England, entrusted with the heartbreaking task of visiting the relatives of the dead.

An enormous part of his preoccupation in Spain had been with such small mechanical details as keeping his cartridge belt properly buckled, keeping track of his equipment, and generally learning the most elementary details of normal efficiency.

Esmond seemed to have been born without the slightest sense of dealing with the physical world around him. One had the feeling that he had never even really learned to tie his shoes. The simplest act of opening or closing a perfectly ordinary suitcase was a mystery to him. Once, at a later time, Peter Nevile complained that he was incapable of opening and shutting doors because he had never understood the mechanism by which the doorknob acts as a lever to control the latch. He would get into a fury of frustration with his portable typewriter, the workings of whose ribbon and the shutting of whose case were quite beyond him. Needless to say, the expensive, complicated camera I had so rashly charged to my father's account at the Army and Navy Stores remained unused after one or two unsuccessful tries.

Esmond's encounter with fascism in Spain, and above all the horror of his final action in the battle of Boadilla, had done much to solidify the direction his life had taken since the age of fifteen. He was no longer a dilettante, playing around the edges of the struggle of his generation, nor a mere *enfant terrible,* baiter of the traditions of the rich and powerful. He had become a committed partisan of the fight against fascism.

As for me, I was still only on the threshold. My intentions were serious; running away meant more than just a wild, exciting adventure — but it meant that, too. I was secretly shocked and disturbed at Esmond's assumption that I should never again see my family. Life at home, with all our silly jokes and private languages, huge Christmas gatherings, Nancy's bright clownishness and Boud's immense, strong personality, still meant something to me. I was rather looking forward to introducing Esmond at home, seeing my father glower at him and grind his teeth as he always did to sons-in-law, hearing Esmond demolish Boud and Diana in debate. But Esmond's extraordinary single-mindedness and direct purpose would have rendered all this impossible. He regarded my family as the enemy, and discouraged all discussion of them.

My quality of what he called upperclassishness irritated him. Esmond had a chameleonlike quality in his relations with people around him; he had an ability to become a part of any group he was with. In Bayonne, he quickly assumed the *accent du Midi,* a more guttural French than that spoken in the north, and fell easily into the latest slang. We mingled with sailors and workmen in the cafés, and Esmond was immediately part of them. In contrast, my schoolgirl French, learned at the Sorbonne and from French governesses as a child in England, struck a sour and irritating note.

An outburst of "upperclassishness" on my part led to the first and only quarrel of our lives. We were sitting one evening in a crowded French café, drinking wine with some chance acquaintances we'd struck up there. A rough-looking man wearing the inevitable Basque beret came in with a big dog, muzzled and on a leash. He started beating the dog over the face with a switch; the dog yelped and whined, and people in the café began laughing and cheering the man on. I was frantic.

"Tell him to stop," I shouted to Esmond. "The cruel brute, can't you do something?"

Esmond became furious. "Come on, let's get out of here". He pulled me up and out of the café.

"What right have you got to try to impose your beastly upper class preoccupation with animals on these people? You're behaving like a typical English tourist. That's why English people are so hated abroad. Don't you know how the English people of your class treat PEOPLE, in India and Africa and all over the world? And you have the bloody nerve to come here — to THEIR country, mind you, and start bossing these French people round and telling them how to treat their dogs." Esmond was in a rage. "I can tell you, when we get to Spain you'll see plenty of horrible sights, bombed children dying in the streets. French people and Spaniards don't give a damn about animals, and why should they? They happen to think people are more important. If you're going to make such an unholy fuss about dogs you should have stayed in England, where they feed the dogs steak and let people in the slums die of starvation ... "

I stuck to my guns, and we quarreled all night.

The next day, full of contrition for all the unkind things said, we made up. I was beginning to understand dimly the truth of what Esmond was driving at.

Finally, when we were near despair over the difficulties of leaving for Spain, a mysterious messenger arrived from the Basque consulate. He handed us a paper which read:

Se autoriza a embarcar en el vapor URBI *para ser trasladado a Bilbao por su cuenta y riesgo a la dadora de la presente* DNA JESSICA MITFORD

Bayone 13 *Febrero* 1937

This ship it is in Basens.

The good ship *Urbi* was docked, surprisingly enough, where the paper said it would be — at the harbor of Basens near Bayonne. It was a tiny cargo boat. As far as we could see, the only cargo consisted of about a dozen chickens, already looking rather seasick as they scratched around on the deck.

Led by the Spanish captain who didn't speak a word of English, we descended into a large dining saloon, neatly set up for the evening meal. The crew of about fifteen men assembled, and we sat down to a glorious dinner. Course upon course was passed around; thick Basque vegetable soup, écrevisses, beef stew, chicken, cake, fruit, accompanied by gallons of red wine and full glasses of brandy. I could see that I was going to enjoy the voyage immensely. The captain and crew spoke only Spanish, and Esmond was trying out a few phrases he had learned in Madrid; as the evening wore on, toasts were drunk to everything under the sun, from the "engaged couple" to "Death to the Fascistas!" There was wonderful singing, more eating, more toasts . . .

Toward midnight the party broke up and the crew left for their various tasks. The captain motioned us to follow him, and conveyed through sign language that we were to have his cabin, the only cabin on the ship, as the crew all slept in hammocks on the deck.

The cabin was furnished in the style of a cheap hotel room. There was a large, heavy, old-fashioned chest of drawers, an easy chair, and several smaller chairs.

Shortly after we retired, the sputter of engines and creakings of timber gave sign that the journey was under way and the ship was heading out into the Bay of Biscay.

We were suddenly awakened by a series of grinding sounds and loud thuds. The ship was lurching and rocking violently; all the drawers had fallen out of the chest and were sliding across the floor. Another great rhythmic lurch, and they slid back to the wall, accompanied by the framework of the chest, which was rocking crazily. Joined by the chairs, our suitcases, shoes and every other movable thing in the cabin — which seemed to include just about everything — the chest and the drawers once more advanced to the bunk, and once more slid noisily back to the wall. I managed to crawl out of bed, avoiding furniture as I went, to the basin, where I said a sad farewell to the vegetable soup, écrevisse, stew, chicken, cake, fruit, wine and brandy . . .

The movement of the ship became so violent that Esmond and I had to take it in turns to hold each other in the bunk. Even at that we fell out several times. More trips were made to the basin until there was nothing left to get rid of.

All the next day the crashing and banging of furniture continued. Esmond went up on deck for a little while, and came down to report that the sailors said there was a stiff breeze. I wondered vaguely how the captain managed to keep his stuff from getting ruined; the only ships I'd been on before had neatly battened-down compartments for everything movable in case of storm, even a clamp for the toothbrushes.

That night, an alarm was sounded that a Franco submarine had been sighted not far off. All lights were extinguished. I couldn't help guiltily feeling hopeful that the submarine would find its mark and put us out of our misery. Esmond was worried about me and brought drinks of water, which I immediately threw up, too weak by now to make the effort to reach the basin. I was vividly and gratefully aware, however, of his concern — a side of Esmond not often seen in those days, and certainly not apparent in the long journeyings of the past few weeks about France and England. The organized brutality of Wellington, the viciousness of the Remand Home, the rough and tumble of life alone in London for a boy of his age, had hardly been conducive to fostering the quality of tenderness in Esmond to any marked degree. Like most eighteen-year-olds, his personality was still in a state of flux. To me he seemed part hero, part adventurer, part bad boy — just as I had always imagined him, in fact. Lying in a semi-conscious haze of acute seasickness, I was glad to observe the glimmerings of kindness.

The cabin stank of vomit, the furniture continued to make its sliding, scraping journey back and forth, back and forth across the floor . . . But on the third day, there was suddenly and blissfully a miraculous stillness. The furniture, though topsy-turvy and scattered all over the cabin, stayed where it was. We had arrived in Bilbao.

I struggled up and into my clothes, still shakily weak from three days of violent seasickness.

No need to worry about upperclassishness now. My clothes were filthy and crumpled, my hair smelt of being sick. Two weeks away from Nanny had already taken their toll. Long since vanished were the neat sheets of tissue paper carefully arranged in the folds of my underclothes to prevent them from getting crumpled. Once, while we were in Bayonne, Esmond had been absent-mindedly trying to see if he could make a pair of scissors work, and had practiced on my best suit, which now had large gashes in the skirt.

We threw our stuff into the suitcases and staggered out on deck.

The chickens seemed to be more dispirited than ever, I noticed. They had stopped scratching around for food and were huddled gloomily together near their coop.

We said goodbye to the captain and crew, who surprisingly looked none the worse for the dreadful experiences of the last three days. An immaculately dressed Spaniard dashed up the gangplank to meet us.

"Mr. Romilly and Miss Mitford? I was notified that you would be arriving today. We are always honored and pleased to have the chance to welcome foreign journalists. Allow me to introduce myself. Señor ———, Foreign Minister of the Basque Republic. And now, being English, I'm sure you are anxious to see the boxing? Fortunately a match will be starting in a few minutes. If we hurry we can be there for the beginning." We smiled and thanked him, and reluctantly followed, thinking how much more appropriate a nice hot bath and clean bed would have seemed just at that moment.

A long black limousine took us to the stadium where the boxing was to be held. As the Foreign Minister had predicted, we didn't miss a minute of it. For four hot, stuffy hours we watched the tiny figures deftly dancing around and only occasionally hitting anyone, in the spotlight of the ring below. The Basque crowd was cheering its head off, and we could only hope that the Foreign Minister attributed our stony silence to the well-known English characteristic of stoicism.

17

Life in Bilbao had for me far more the quality of a dream than of a dream come true. It seemed so absolutely extraordinary to be there, with Esmond, to realize that this was actually me living in Spain; and to think that a few hundred miles away over the sea there was Rutland Gate, unchanged, the quiet smooth life of the family flowing on unrippled, marked only by breakfast, lunch, tea, the six o'clock BBC news, dinner, bedtime, all following their normal progression . . . I could visualize aunts coming to tea, casually asking my mother, "Where's Decca?" "She's staying in Dieppe with the Paget twins," Muv would answer placidly. "She seems to be having a very nice time, from her letters."

Reality still seemed to be centered at home, with the family, and to have little to do with the rattling third class French trains, the crowded Bayonne hotel, the swaying, grinding cargo boat of the past ten days; or now with the grim, serious town of Bilbao. It was like living in a protracted vision.

I felt bemused, a convalescent barely out of the anesthetic after a major operation which had severed at one great sweep of the knife all old ties, habits, patterns of living.

Esmond, on the contrary, settled down immediately to the

essentials of living and working in Bilbao. I followed in his wake, briskly trudging to government offices, press headquarters, information centers, lining up arrangements for interviews and news stories. I was trying to get in focus this big blur of a gray seaport town, to understand the heroism of its pale, determined people, who went steadily about their daily business in the shadow of the knowledge that the attack would not be long in coming.

That February the front was still quiet. The opposing armies in the Spanish war were locked in the battle for Madrid. There were few foreign journalists in Bilbao, and those who came were treated royally by the Government. We found to our surprise that free room and board would be provided by the Foreign Press Bureau in one of the large hotels.

Although the fighting was far away, the town was near starvation. Meat, milk, eggs, butter were completely unobtainable. Breakfast, lunch and dinner were indistinguishable, as all consisted of rice and *garbanzos* (chickpeas). In the cafés you could buy thick, sweet black chocolate served in cups, accompanied by slices of grayish bread. Half-starved children crowded round the café patrons, begging for a spoonful of chocolate or a piece of bread.

After a few days in Bilbao we were taken to the front by some people from the press bureau. It was a long day's trip in an Army car over miles and miles of rough mountain roads. Our companions from the Basque press bureau pointed out the encampments along the way.

"That's a Communist battalion over to the right . . . Now further on you can see a company of Anarchists . . . Over to the left there is a battalion of the Basque Catholic Nationalist Party . . ." Apparently the army in that part of Spain was organized along lines of political beliefs.

The front was high on a hill, overlooking a deep ravine.

Across the ravine, about half a mile away, we could see the enemy soldiers and cannon. "Italians," said the man from the press bureau, and spat.

A few cannon and machine guns were spaced at rather distant intervals on our side.

Our companion suggested I might like to shoot a rifle. He showed me how to look through the sight at the tiny figures on the other side of the ravine. I pulled the trigger and it went off with a tremendous bang, knocking me backwards. The bullet had lodged in a nearby tree. My "fire" was returned in much the same desultory fashion by the enemy.

The strange sense of unreality deepened.

On the way back we stopped briefly in a village in "no-man's-land," a stretch of several miles between the two fronts in another sector.

Garbage was piled in the streets, and the village seemed almost completely deserted. A few old women in long black dresses were picking among the garbage. We were told that they had refused to be evacuated along with other refugees, and preferred to stay in their homes, living off what vegetables and poultry they could raise.

Our days in Bilbao began to assume a routine. In the mornings we would check at the Press Bureau for news, or interview government officials for background stories. Afternoons would be spent typing the stories for transmission to the *News Chronicle*. There was very little going on in Bilbao at the time. The town seemed to have settled into a state of anxious anticipation. Cafés were crowded with people listening to the news broadcasts, following each of which the crowds would respectfully stand at silent attention for the playing of not one, but four, anthems, symbolizing the United Front — the Basque National Anthem, the Spanish anthem, the "Internationale," and the Anarchist hymn.

I was consumed with curiosity and anxiety about what must by now be happening at home.

One day, on returning to the hotel, we were told that the Basque proconsul of the British consulate had been round to see us. This was cause for alarm. What could he want? We had carefully avoided all contact with British consulates in our travels.

The next morning the proconsul returned. He was a young, good-looking Basque, and spoke English with a strong accent. We learned from him that a "proconsul" is a national of the country in which the consulate is located, and that his job is to act as a sort of liaison between the consulate and the local authorities.

"I have received a telegram," he said, smiling broadly. "The telegram is in code. It concerns you two, I believe."

"Could we see it?" asked Esmond.

"Yes, certainly. Here it is, and here is the code book. Let us see if together we can decode it." We felt that this must be rather an unorthodox procedure, but readily agreed to help with the decoding.

The telegram said: "Find Jessica Mitford and persuade her to return." It was signed by Anthony Eden.

"And now, I must answer the telegram. What shall I say?" asked the proconsul. We helped him to draft and code the reply: HAVE FOUND JESSICA MITFORD. IMPOSSIBLE TO PERSUADE HER TO RETURN.

"Normally Mr. Stevenson, the British Consul, takes care of all this sort of thing. But unfortunately he is now in Bayonne on consulate business, and he may not be back for some days."

We assured the proconsul that he had handled the affair in the very highest tradition of British diplomacy, that no one could have done better in his place. However, we anticipated the return of Mr. Stevenson with great misgivings;

somehow, we foresaw that he would prove to be a much tougher nut to crack.

Our meeting with the proconsul served to focus our attention once more on the urgency of getting married. We made inquiries of the Basque authorities, and were informed to our surprise that even in the middle of a civil war people under the age of twenty-one could not get married without their parents' consent. Some anarchists we met in a café offered the services of a priest they had taken prisoner ("We could find ways of making him do it," they said), but it would have meant a two-day journey and we weren't sure just how legal such a marriage would prove to be.

A few days later, we were summoned to the British consulate for an audience with Mr. Stevenson.

Mr. Stevenson, a middle-aged, tweedy man with reddish mustache and balding head, was seated at a large desk in this drab little corner of England on foreign soil. He was surrounded by English neatness and orderliness and exuded English lack of charm, in contrast to the delightful proconsul. He did not rise to greet us.

"You two have caused a great deal of trouble," he announced in curt, official tones. "I have instructions to return you to England immediately, Miss Mitford. When can you be ready to leave?"

"But I'm staying here, I don't intend to leave."

"Mr. Stevenson, I suppose you are aware that you have neither the authority nor the power to make Miss Mitford leave against her will," Esmond broke in, assuming his out-consuling-of-consuls manner.

He sounded so authoritative and in control of the situation that I almost caught myself feeling a little sorry for Mr. Stevenson. How could he hope to win against such an adversary? We argued for half an hour, then we left to return to the hotel. The first round with Mr. Stevenson had ended, we felt, in a draw. While he had not succeeded in his objective, our security was badly shattered.

Next day Mr. Stevenson came to see us.

"Miss Mitford, I have just received word that your sister and brother-in-law are coming to Bermeo tomorrow on a British destroyer to see you. Now you must realize that you have given your family a very great deal of anxiety by your actions. I think the least you can do is to go and meet your sister. She has come all the way from England with her husband just to see you, and to be assured that you are well and safe."

"Which sister is it?" I asked.

"Mrs. Peter Rodd. I am going to Bermeo on business tomorrow, I have to meet the captain of the destroyer. I shall pick you up here at six o'clock in the morning."

"We'll let you know what we decide," said Esmond firmly, showing him the door.

We spent long hours discussing whether or not I should go. If I refused, Nancy and Peter would probably come to Bilbao and cause embarrassing scenes. On the other hand, perhaps there was a plan to kidnap me and forcibly take me on board the destroyer.

"Of course, I'm much stronger than Nancy, but Mr. Stevenson looks disgustingly fit. He and Peter could probably drag me on to the destroyer." We finally decided I'd better go; the thought of Nancy and Peter descending on us at the hotel was too awful to contemplate.

The port of Bermeo is only thirty miles from Bilbao, but the drive took almost two hours of slow progress on the stony mountain roads.

As usual, it was pouring. The proconsul had told us that the Spanish tend to blame English children for the eternal rain there because of their jingle, "Rain, rain, go to Spain, and never, never come back again."

Mr. Stevenson led me to a bench on the wharf, and disappeared to do his business.

Hours and hours went by; not a sign of the destroyer. I had nothing to read, no one to talk to, and the wait seemed eternal.

Finally the destroyer appeared and docked, and officers and men came ashore. I was actually very excited at the thought of seeing Nancy, and extremely anxious to hear news from home. Had Peter Nevile delivered the letter all right? Did Muv and Farve understand that there was really nothing much to worry about? Had they been unduly worried? Were they frightfully angry, or only fairly cross? I had a thousand questions to ask Nancy.

I searched the group from the destroyer, but there was no sign of Nancy or Peter. The tall, handsome captain of the destroyer came over to me, looking very English and familiar after these weeks spent among a darker race. He might have been one of the Australian sheep from deb dance days.

"Miss Mitford? Look, I'm awfully sorry, your sister didn't come after all. Bad show. But we do want you to come on board for lunch, you must be starved." Indeed I was; I had had nothing to eat all day, as we had left too early for the hotel breakfast of *garbanzos* and rice.

"I'd love to, but I can't."

"Oh, too bad. We'd really love to have you. Roast chicken, bread sauce, peas, mashed potatoes, chocolate cake, all that sort of thing, you know." He rolled the words slowly, with tantalizing emphasis. "As a matter of fact, our ship's cook really outdid himself in honor of your visit, we were so sure you'd come."

I could practically feel my gastric juices working at the thought of the roast chicken and chocolate cake, but I remained firm. I couldn't leave just now, I had come with Mr. Stevenson, he might think it rude of me to go off for lunch; but the captain had an answer to demolish each objection.

"Well, I'll tell you the real reason I can't come. I have an awful feeling you'd lock me up as soon as we got aboard, and take me back to England."

He was outraged. "What a ghastly idea! What do you take us for, kidnapers? Look here, I give you my word as an Englishman that we'd do no such thing. You would come on board for lunch, then we'd take you right back on shore in plenty of time to go back to Bilbao with Mr. Stevenson."

I looked closely at his boyish, open face. The serious blue eyes gazed back into mine; not a trace of dissemblance there. He certainly did not appear to be a tricky type — he would be incapable of the smallest deceit, I decided quickly, wondering with part of my mind what sort of gravy there'd be with the chicken.

"Well . . . let me see if I can reach Esmond by telephone. I promised him I wouldn't go on the ship under any circumstances."

I reached Esmond at the hotel and told him what the captain had said.

"Don't go," said Esmond. "It's obviously a plot. Make them bring the roast chicken on shore — as a matter of fact, you might bring some of it back here for me."

I told the captain I would have to decline the invitation, and his hurt expression made me so uncomfortable that I couldn't bear to add insult to injury by suggesting that the lunch should be brought on shore.

The long afternoon dragged by. I sat haughtily on the bench until at sundown, stiff with cold and hunger, I joined Mr. Stevenson for the return trip to Bilbao. I was inwardly raging at Esmond for being so super-cautious about the lunch. That nice captain certainly would never have double-crossed me, after giving his word of honor.

I got back to find Esmond pacing up and down in a violent temper. He had just received a telegram from Hastie's, my father's solicitors. It read: MISS JESSICA MITFORD IS A WARD OF COURT STOP IF YOU MARRY HER WITHOUT LEAVE OF JUDGE YOU WILL BE LIABLE TO IMPRISONMENT. I was horrified, and very much disturbed. In all of the many hours I had spent wondering what course of action my parents might take, and what efforts they might make to get me to come home, a threat of prison had certainly never occurred to me. This, then, meant total war. I was beginning to see that Esmond's intransigent attitude to my family, far from being overdramatized and unnecessarily uncompromising, was far more realistic than my own.

Shortly after this we heard again from Mr. Stevenson. This time, he produced an "ace in the hole" against which there was no possible counterstrategy. He pointed out that the Basque government was counting heavily on British facilities to evacuate women and children, refugees from the anticipated offensive. He threatened to refuse further co-operation in the evacuation program unless we agreed voluntarily to leave the Basque territory. Since we were staying in Bilbao as guests of the government press bureau and were relying on them for help in getting stories, he would notify the press bureau that unless they severed all relations with us he in turn would withdraw British assistance from the refugees.

This fantastic piece of bargaining brought home to me the strength and ruthlessness of the forces ranged against us. In a final stormy session with Mr. Stevenson, we capitulated; but not before Esmond had exacted a bargain that we should return, not to England, but to the south of France. We embarked the next day on a destroyer for St.-Jean-de-Luz.

18

NANCY AND PETER RODD were waiting for us at St.-Jean-de-Luz. We saw them at the end of the gangplank; Nancy, tall and beautiful, waving at us with her gloves, and Peter, rather square and stocky, hands in pockets in his usual "tough" attitude. They were completely surrounded by press photographers, and we descended the gangplank in a barrage of popping bulbs.

"Could we have a statement, Mr. Romilly? Are you married? What are your plans?"

We quickly fought our way through the newspaper people and piled into a waiting taxi.

"Decca, really you are a naughty little thing," Nancy began, "worrying us all like that. Poor Muv has been in floods ever since you left, and so has Nanny. Nanny keeps saying you didn't have any suitable clothes to fight in."

"I certainly did," I answered indignantly. "I got a special suit at the Army and Navy. She almost wouldn't let me take it."

Peter turned to Esmond.

"I say, old man, so you want to join the ranks of old Redesdale's sons-in-law. I certainly can't recommend such a course. The Mitford girls are notoriously poor, you know. Virtual church mice. All that glitters is not gold, remember that . . ."

Esmond was not amused, and answered stiffly that we shouldn't dream of accepting an allowance from my father, even in the most unlikely event that one was offered.

"We were all amazed that you didn't come back last week on the other destroyer," Nancy continued. "Everything was all arranged for the captain to lure you on board by promising delicious things to eat, but he said you wouldn't be lured — Peter thought it all up, wasn't it rather clever of him?"

"I saw through *that* stupid trick at once," I retorted, wishing it were true. "Perfidious Albion — that's just what the captain looked like; he had a typically treacherous face. Anyway, I think you're all perfect, utter beasts and so is Hastie's, threatening to put Esmond in prison."

The army of press photographers was waiting for us at the hotel where Nancy had taken rooms for the night, and we once more had to run the gantlet.

From what Nancy told me, and from what I learned later, I was able to piece together what had happened at home since I left.

My mother was surprised and rather worried at getting my letters from Bayonne. She was concerned that the Paget twins' tour was becoming such a lengthy one, as the time for the world cruise was drawing near. Toward the end of the two weeks, she tried to put a telephone call through to 40 Rue Napoléon, Dieppe, only to learn that neither I nor the twins had been heard of there. She then rang up the Paget aunt's house in London, and after a mystifying conversation full of cross purposes learned that the twins were in Austria, and that no arrangements had been made for me to meet them.

I had apparently vanished without leaving a trace. Scotland Yard and the Foreign Office were called in to conduct a search. News of my disappearance began to filter through to family and friends.

"Everyone sent flowers — it was just like a funeral," Nancy said. "Poor Muv in the drawing room, wringing her hands, Nanny crying about what must be the state of your underclothes by now with no one to wash them for you, visitors arriving and flowers every few minutes . . . the place was like a hothouse."

A major London newspaper had soon got wind of the story. They sent a reporter round to offer the newspaper's facilities. Their correspondents stationed in Europe would be alerted to help find me, if my parents would give them all details. They promised there would be no publicity whatsoever. My parents trustingly confided in them. Next day, the newspaper's front page blared forth the story — only, in their haste, they had named Debo as the runaway instead of me. This was to become the subject of a libel suit, which was finally settled in Debo's favor for £1000. (Esmond never quite got over the unfairness of this. "You did all the work, and Debo got £1000 out of it! Let's take it to court, I'm sure any judge would see the absolute injustice and award the money to us!")

Peter Nevile, away in the country, read the story in the paper and hurried back to London. The time had come for him to deliver his message.

He found the family sunk in the deepest gloom. By this time they were quite convinced that I had really become a victim of the Counter-Honnish White Slave traffic.

Peter handed the letter to my father.

Idden told me later that she was downstairs in the Mews, where she was living for a few months, at the moment of Peter's visit. Suddenly she heard a noise that she thought could only be the Amberley blowing up at last; but it turned out to be Farve, reacting to Peter Nevile.

"Worse than I thought!" were his first words. "Married to Esmond Romilly!"

Peter made a hasty exit — just in the nick of time, it turned out. There was talk afterwards of assigning Tuddemy to horse-whip him for his complicity in the affair, but to Peter's relief this never came to anything.

Now family councils began in earnest. Peter Rodd came forward to offer his services. He masterminded the Ward in Chancery operation. If I were made a ward of the court, he reasoned, a judge would have jurisdiction over my move-ments. The judge could bring into play all the law enforce-ment machinery, arrange to have me extradited from a foreign country, issue orders governing my actions, place me in a Home for Wayward Girls if I disobeyed his instructions . . .

Aunts and cousins came forward with their suggestions. I should be allowed to marry at once, a divorce would then be secured, and I should be settled in a flat in London, to live out my days as a social outcast . . . Even Hitler had his say. Boud told him, "My sister Decca has run away to Spain with the Reds."

Hitler sank his head in his hands. *"Armes Kind!"* he sighed.

Debo went around sadly singing new words to a popular song: "Somebody stole my Hon, Somebody stole my Hon; Some-one came and took her away, She didn't even Say that she was leavin' . . ."

Meanwhile the newspapers were having a field day.

"You were the first one in the family to be on posters," Nancy told me. "Boud was frightfully jealous."

The wildest speculation as to our whereabouts was head-lined daily. FIANCE AND PEER'S DAUGHTER TRAPPED IN PEAK HUT? JESSICA MITFORD FEARED LOST IN PYRENEES! MR. ROMILLY AND DECCA BELIEVED IN BARCELONA . . .

Our arrival in St.-Jean-de-Luz was the occasion for more

wild stories. Self-styled "close friends" among London journalists ground out their own fanciful account of our adventures:

"The night before they left we gave them a farewell supper in the West End. They were too excited to eat much. They just had some champagne and foie gras sandwiches. Then they went to the dog races at Clapton. They were lucky. They won about ten pounds."

"I helped them to plan their runaway romance. Three weeks ago I received a telegram from Esmond which ran: DIVINELY HAPPY MORE NEWS LATER."

Esmond was wild with rage at these outpourings. One of the journalists "assigned" to us in St.-Jean-de-Luz was particularly assiduous. He followed us to the dining room, remained with his ear glued to the door of our room. Once Esmond caught him eavesdropping outside a telephone booth where I was making a call.

"You'd better damn well leave us alone or I'll punch you in the nose!" Esmond threatened. Next day, this remark was rather oddly paraphrased: " 'I am with the girl I love,' Romilly told me last evening."

In St.-Jean-de-Luz, Nancy and I had long arguments over whether or not I should return. Her arguments were most ineffectual:

"Poor Dora, she had such a severe reaction from the typhoid injections that she had to go to hospital for days. Now, if you don't go back the cruise will be called off and she'll have gone through all that agony for nothing."

I was getting increasingly bitter and angry at the attitude of my family and their extreme attempts to prevent Esmond and me from marrying. I had of course realized that running away would bring on a family row — a storm that would have to be weathered. But I was amazed at the truly awful lengths my parents had gone to, the devious plotting to force my return, the threats of imprisonment made against Esmond, the way the

Rodds were now uniting with the Grownups against me.

Nancy and Peter left the next day, having failed completely in their mission. Esmond and I went on to Bayonne, a few miles up the coast from St.-Jean-de-Luz.

Gone were the armies of photograpers and reporters; gone were Nancy and Peter. The chase was ended, we were victorious. And now at last we had time to assess our situation.

After engaging a room at the Hôtel des Basques, we walked slowly along the river, discussing the future. It looked very, very bleak. We had exactly nine shillings between us, barely enough for two days' room and board at the hotel. French law forbids foreigners to work without a permit, and permits are virtually impossible to obtain. Should we have to crawl back to England anyway, starved out? We had nowhere near enough money for the fare back. It would be unthinkable to ask my family for help, after the way they had behaved. To return to Spain would mean a repetition of the events of the last few weeks — our time would be spent eluding British Consuls and news reporters. Besides, we felt that all the recent publicity about us had already harmed the cause of the Spanish Republic. The endless stories about our adventures had driven the war news off the front pages, as well as making a farce of our own convictions.

We were miserably wretched as we walked along the dark, windy riverbank. It seemed as though we had come to a dead end. While we had no doubts that we should eventually end up together, it began to look as though I might be forced to consider wiring friends for funds to return, at least temporarily.

"Let's go back to the hotel," Esmond finally suggested. "Perhaps by tomorrow morning we'll have thought of something."

This was the sort of situation in which Esmond was at his best. One could almost see the intricate cogs and wheels of his brain turning, as he pondered a solution to the seemingly impossible. Now the full extent of his resourcefulness came into play.

The next morning, he presented himself at the local offices of Reuter's news agency. Within the hour, he had persuaded them to retain his services as interpreter for dispatches from the Basque front, which could only be heard on the Bayonne radio. He pointed out that, although the front was quiet at the moment, action might start any time, and offered to translate the nightly broadcasts from both sides.

Reuters agreed to pay two pounds a week — which by a fortunate coincidence happened to be the exact price of weekly room and board at the Hôtel des Basques for the two of us. Esmond was to listen to the six o'clock evening broadcasts, type up a translation, and deliver it daily to Reuters. Fortunately, they did not realize that neither of us could speak Spanish.

Esmond returned to the hotel and explained to M. Erramuzpe, the Basque proprietor, that in order to pay our weekly bill we should have to have his help in translating the Spanish broadcasts into French. We would then write up the English translation. M. Erramuzpe saw the point at once. Every evening the three of us huddled round the radio. The Loyalist broadcast came first, followed by dispatches from the Franco side. News was skimpy, as little action was taking place. M. Erramuzpe would listen, then report:

"Intermittent firing on the Oviedo front . . . occasional skirmishes . . . four prisoners taken with their mules . . . "

When the Loyalist broadcast was over, M. Erramuzpe would shut off the radio.

"But we're supposed to report the dispatches from both sides. That was part of our agreement with the newspaper people."

"Nada, nada," said M. Erramuzpe with finality. "From the Fascist side, nothing but lies. Why should I waste my time?"

In the end we had to make up the Franco dispatches as best we could, drawing from the Loyalist news: "Occasional firing on the Oviedo front . . . intermittent skirmishes . . . four of our men taken prisoner with their mules . . ."

Our life once more settled into a routine. Esmond had started writing *Boadilla,* a book about the Spanish war. He worked every morning, cursing the unknowable workings of his portable typewriter. At noon came an enormous Basque meal; hors d'oeuvre, the inevitable cabbage soup; meat swimming in spicy, greasy sauce, and unlimited red wine. In the afternoon we sometimes went to the beach at Biarritz or St.-Jean-de-Luz with a journalist whose acquaintance we had made. In the evening, our nightly tussle with the radio broadcasts; then another huge meal, eaten very late, in the company of refugees from Bilbao or Guernica who crowded the hotel. Most of these were older women, dressed in long, dark dresses as though in mourning. Pale, thin children would join them to struggle through the rich meal, often carried out halfway through, slightly tipsy from the red wine.

I often reflected, then and later, on the strange beginnings of our life together. Most honeymoons, after all, are preceded by at least some period of acquaintance, family introductions, an engagement. Here we were, strangers only a few weeks ago, now suddenly alone together against the world — or at least against our families! It was a little like being castaways meeting for the first time on a desert island, or explorers coming face to face in a lonely jungle.

I used to watch Esmond as he worked furiously on *Boadilla,* brown head bent over the typewriter, papers scattered all over the floor, wondering how much he minded being separated from the struggle in Spain.

He seldom spoke of his decision not to return to Spain, though he referred to it once in *Boadilla:*

> The first British battalion was being trained at Albacete. It was part of the section of a thousand Englishmen who, in February, were to hold the most vital positions near the Valencia road under twelve days of the biggest artillery bombardment of the war, then counterattack and make Madrid's road safe for months — perhaps for good. I might have gone back and joined those men, who are the real heroes of the Spanish struggle. But I did not go. I got married and lived happily instead . . .

It was plain from his occasional deep moodiness that the decision had been a hard one to make. An old contradiction had been partially revived: "living materially in one world and spiritually in the other." The news from the Madrid front, where the battle of Teruel was raging, filled him with gloom.

One night, sitting with the black-garbed refugees in the hotel dining room, we heard over the radio that Guernica, capital of the Basque Republic, had been totally destroyed by Nazi bombers. An old Basque woman arose, her face distorted by rage and despair:

"Allemanes! Criminales! Animales! Bestiales!" she cried, her voice rising with every word.

The misery of the refugees was in odd contrast to the bright, brassy world of English and American journalists, into which we made occasional excursions.

One of the more successful of these was the night of the celebration of King George VI's coronation. We had learned that free champagne would be dispensed at a party to be given by the British Consul — and that all English people were automatically invited. This seemed to call for temporary suspension of our consul-shunning rule. There were seven in our party, including our journalist friend with the car, without whom we seldom moved if we were going far.

Between us, we consumed fourteen bottles of the free champagne. Soon we were singing Spanish revolutionary songs, giving clenched fist salutes to all who came near our table, drinking toasts: "Freedom for Africa!" "Down with imperialism!" The latter slogan gave Esmond an idea. He demanded paper and envelope, and in an almost illegible penciled scrawl addressed a letter to Winston Churchill.

Churchill was at that time an extremely high-priced journalist for the *Evening Standard*. His articles on Spain were strongly pro-Franco. The Duke of Alba, Franco envoy in England and an old family friend of Churchill's, was a constant visitor at Chartwell. At the same time, Churchill's strongly anti-German opinions had brought him into disfavor with the dominant wing of the Conservative Party, led by Chamberlain and Lady Astor's "Cliveden Set."

Esmond now sought to focus his uncle's attentions on the contradictions in his position. He pointed out that if Franco should win in Spain, Germany and Italy would be left in full command of the fate of Gibraltar, "Britain's gateway to the Mediterranean." He went on to develop the argument that the foremost defenders of the British Empire were today the Spanish Loyalists.

We never received an answer to this letter. But three months later Churchill reversed his position completely, and from then on his articles thundered lavish praise of the gallant Loyalist defenders of democracy in Spain.

Esmond's letter undoubtedly had nothing whatsoever to do with this change of heart. Perhaps it never even reached Churchill, and, even if it did, deciphering it would have been a problem for a code expert. But it was evidence of Esmond's instinctive understanding of the subtleties of politics.

Soon after we arrived at the Hôtel des Basques, I wrote a letter to the Chancery judge who had become my unknown guardian. I argued that he would not be able to extradite me, as I had committed no crime, and that I knew from reading detective stories that it takes at least a year to extradite even a known murderer. I suggested that if I were forced to wait until I was twenty-one to marry, I might already have a family, and that therefore, in the interests of propriety, the marriage should take place rather soon.

It was Esmond, in his best "outjudging judges" form, who actually drafted the letter.

The judge sent his permission by return of post, and I had won the final round with my family.

To our surprise, both our mothers came to Bayonne for the wedding. We were married by the British Consul, who intoned a special service: "By warrant of the Secretary of State for Foreign Affairs I hereby make known that according to the law of England you are man and wife." The mothers sat looking, as Esmond said, "more like chief mourners at a funeral than wedding guests." But they cheered up after the ceremony, and took us and a party of our friends from the Basque consulate to a delicious wedding lunch.

19

AFTER THE WEDDING we were once more, by Esmond's standards, rich. Wedding presents and an advance from the publisher of *Boadilla* had brought our funds up to undreamed-of
heights — over fifty pounds.

I was all for buying some new clothes and having blowouts
at good restaurants, but Esmond had other ideas.

"I've been thinking a great deal about boule lately," he
announced. Boule is a sort of junior gambling game played
in French casinos, mostly patronized by those who, like ourselves, were under twenty-one and therefore banned from the
roulette rooms.

When he spoke about boule, Esmond's face assumed the faraway expression of one seeing a vision of happiness; the look
of a child on his way to his first circus, or a mother shown
her newborn infant for the first time. It was a soft, radiant
look, full of excitement and promise for the future, and one
that I was to come to know well over the next few years.

On this occasion, Esmond had devised an absolutely water-
tight system for winning. As he told me of it, hammering restlessly away at the boundless possibilities, I too became
convinced. It was so extraordinarily simple, yet so absolutely

sound! There is a choice of seven numbers in boule. We
would pick a number, say 4, and put a very small amount on
it — one franc to start with. Every time the 4 failed to come
up, we would multiply our investment by 7 — to 49, to 343
to 3401 and so on. Acutally our potential fortune would
increase in direct proportion to the failure of 4 to win; for
eventually it would be bound to come up, and by that time we
should have thousands and thousands of francs on it. It seemed
amazing no one had thought of it before.

We settled on Dieppe as the ideal spot in which to make
our fortune at the boule table. Several hundred miles north
of Bayonne, it would be a handy taking-off place from which
to return to England in grand style. We decided that after
the first big win we should be in a position to start again
with an investment this time of 2 francs, to be increased to
14 and then 98, and so on with each losing bet.

Our journalist friend had left for Bilbao, and he had asked
us to keep an eye on his ancient car, which he had left in a
Bayonne garage.

"Don't know if you can really trust these French garage
people," he had said. "So give an eye to it once in a while,
will you?"

Esmond pointed out to me that we shouldn't be able to
keep our promise to him if we left without the car, and that
we had better take it along with us to Dieppe.

We bought various pieces of equipment for our trip: a small
tent, two large cotton sacks for mattresses, to be stuffed with
straw along the way, two frying pans, two forks, a portable
petrol stove.

"By the way, can you cook?" Esmond asked.

"Well, I had a lesson once at the Cordon Bleu in Paris,
but they only taught how to separate egg whites from the
yolks. That won't be any good for a camping expedition.

Besides, I've forgotten what you're supposed to do with them after separating them. I'll go and get Mme. Erramuzpe to teach me."

Since we were to leave the following day, Mme. Erramuzpe said she would only have time to teach fried eggs and steak. So fried eggs and steak it was, for the two weeks it took us to travel up the coast to Dieppe.

The camping trip was idyllic. Every night we set up our tent near a river for washing purposes. We bought milk and eggs from farmhouses along the way, and steak and bread when we passed through towns. We used one frying pan for the steak and the other for the eggs. ("That way," Esmond pointed out, "we shan't ever have to bother washing them.")

We were madly conserving money for the big day in Dieppe. Esmond noticed a sign at one farmhouse for "homemade oil." He inquired from the farmer whether the oil would be suitable for use in the car, which was needing to be re-oiled at every stop. The farmer answered that it would serve excellently as a motor oil, so since it was extraordinarily cheap we loaded up with it. After that, the car began going slower and slower. First we were passed by all the other motor traffic; then by cyclists; finally, as we approached Dieppe, little girls rolling their hoops whizzed by us.

On the outskirts of Dieppe we parked our car by a river as usual, unloaded the suitcases, and set up the tent. Then we chugged slowly into town. We sat drinking brandy in a café, waiting for the casino to open at dusk. We had already selected the expensive restaurant in which to celebrate our winnings over dinner.

Finally the casino opened, and we headed for the *boule* table. First the number 4 kept coming up. This annoyed Esmond, as in order to keep his system he couldn't double until it lost. He won about 6 francs in succession.

"This isn't working. I think I'll switch to 3; it hasn't come up at all yet. At this rate it's going to take us all night really to cash in."

He was right about No. 3. It hadn't come up yet, and it never did — not all that night. Something had gone frantically wrong. We realized afterwards that it had something to do with multiplying by 7. If you keep doing this, you soon reach an astronomical number — even a larger number of francs than we had received in exchange for our fifty pounds.

It didn't take long to clean us out. About two agonizing hours, and we were through. Gloomily, in driving rain, we got into the car. It took over an hour to drive the ten miles back to the tent. We arrived to find that the river had risen with the evening tide, and tent, mattresses, suitcases were floating in a foot of water. We salvaged what we could and drove back to Dieppe to wait for the morning.

"We'll have to discuss what to do next," Esmond said.

It seemed the acme of understatement.

We wandered into an all-night café. The proprietor came up to ask what we wanted to drink, but we didn't even have the price of a glass of wine. After having witnessed by now so many examples of Esmond's amazing ability to get out of the tightest places, I couldn't get too upset about this new crisis.

Esmond was just mentioning the possibility of exchanging the car for a fishing boat when we heard a shout of greeting. A friend of his, a former correspondent of *Out of Bounds,* suddenly appeared in the doorway of the café, silhouetted against the pouring rain outside. Esmond introduced us. His name was Roger Roughton, and he was just on his way home from a holiday in France.

Roger bought us a drink, and we sat and talked at length about the evils of gambling and the pitfalls of systems.

Roger was of the view that in order to make any money at

gambling one would have to run one's own game, and be the "house." Esmond was inclined to agree, and proposed a weekly Vingt-et-Un game, in which no expensive equipment would be needed. We had got as far as drawing up a list of "Possible Suckers," such as Giles, Robin and Idden, the Paget twins, Philip Toynbee, the Peter Rodds, Tuddemy, and various other friends and relations, when Roger let slip the information that he had just acquired a huge furnished house in Rotherhithe, looking right out on the river — an ideal spot for a gambling den.

Esmond was immediately on the alert. "I didn't know you had a house! How many rooms has it got?" he asked, flashing me one of his conspiratorial looks under his thick eyelashes. The house had four stories and seven rooms, completely furnished with grand piano, beds, stoves, for a total rent of only £2 a month.

We regretfully decided to leave the car parked on a Dieppe street. It really wasn't working any more. "These journalists certainly don't know how to take proper care of their things," Esmond said.

Living with Esmond was like going for a walk in a fairy story, I decided. You never knew whether some sinister troll disguised as a British consul or a croupier might be lying in wait round the next corner, or when the thorny briar forest would magically part to admit you into the enchanted palace. A day later, having borrowed the boat fare from Roger, we moved into 41 Rotherhithe Street.

20

THE BUS RIDE to Rotherhithe from more familiar parts of London (Kensington, Hyde Park, Oxford Street) takes well over an hour. It winds past miles and miles of workers' flats with such incongruous-sounding names as Devon Mansions, Cornwall Homes. Nine or ten stories high, these gloomy red brick structures house a shorter and paler race of people than the inhabitants of London's West End. In appearance, dress and speech they differ so radically as to give the impression of a different ethnic group.

Our house in Rotherhithe Street was wedged between warehouses, across the street from one of these teeming flats. The drawing room took up one entire floor, and looked directly out over the river. On the next floors were various bedrooms where Roger (and frequently others) slept. Esmond and I settled into the fourth floor, where there were a couple of rooms and a kitchen.

I had a vague ambition to prove myself as an efficient working class wife, keeping everything bright and clean and attractive; but Idden's predictions that I wouldn't be much good at that sort of thing were borne out after a few abortive efforts. With great fanfare I seized a broom and spent hours sweeping the stairs, only to be discovered by Roger, who critically pointed out, "You're supposed to start at the top and sweep down." He patiently explained that my method of washing up after meals, soaping, rinsing and drying each piece, lacked rationality, and urged the assembly line method, first soaping everything, then rinsing, then drying, all in one batch. Since I couldn't seem to get the hang of it, and since Esmond never noticed the state of the house, I soon gave up and abandoned the field to Roger.

Cooking presented few problems, as we seldom ate at home. Someone had given me a book of recipes by Boulestin, but as most of the recipes called for a pound of butter, a quart of cream, a wineglass of brandy, breast of chicken, lobster, and similar items, we could only afford to eat at home on rare occasions, and generally ended up with fish and chips at the nearest Lyons teashop.

Esmond got a job as copywriter for a small advertising agency in the Strand. We kept our actual living expenses well within his five-pounds-a-week salary, mostly by the simple expedient of never buying anything. Esmond was always trying to pile up enough capital to start a night club, or buy a milk bar, or get a car, and to this end we would take whatever was left of his weekly income and go to the greyhound races every Friday night. But these expeditions usually ended in disaster. Esmond, making his boule face, would display the almost touching faith of the inveterate gambler in the dog of his choice, but nearly always, as the race drew to a close, incredulous despair would replace his enthusiastic optimism, and we would frequently end up having to walk home, without the price of a bus ticket.

We even tried the gambling den idea a couple of times. Roger contributed part of the £10 capital, and we invited twenty or thirty people, and set up a game of Vingt-et-Un. But somehow even being "the house" didn't work for us, and by the end of the second session we had lost most of the capital. The following day we noticed a small, perfectly round hole in the drawing room window facing the river. Esmond insisted that the river police must have found out about our illicit gambling operation, and had been shooting at us from their boat. I pointed out that a more normal way for them to proceed would have been to come round to the front door to register a complaint. Whether Esmond really believed his fantastic theory I never knew, but in any event we discontinued the gambling sessions after that.

I now began to meet some of Esmond's friends for the first time. Social life consisted mainly of "bottle parties." The hosts provided food, which could be just potato chips or might go as far as ham sandwiches, depending on the state of finances, and the guests brought their own drinks, ranging from beer to whiskey. A prime objective of the host would be to end up ahead, with a certain amount of liquor left over to last through the coming week.

The parties were frequented by a motley crowd of journalists, writers, night club singers, students. Of the many who drifted across the scene, like bit players in a movie, only a few now stand out in my memory; Peter Nevile, Roger Roughton, Philip Toynbee, Esmond's brother Giles . . .

Philip, who was, I learned, the "T.P., Rugby" of the Mosley meeting article in *Out of Bounds,* was a constant visitor at Rotherhithe Street, and he would frequently stay for days at a time. His rather romantically cadaverous face seemed out of tune with his personality, which was that of a warmly exuberant, overgrown puppy. He had an enormous capacity for getting outrageously drunk. On these occasions he would wander round the room saying hopefully: "God, I want to sleep with somebody!" If there was a party going on, he would approach all the unattached girls to that effect, or he would grab the telephone and call around town. I was continually amazed at how often this unorthodox and indiscriminate approach was rewarded with success, and how often there would be "one more for breakfast" when Philip was staying at Rotherhithe Street.

Esmond and Philip had first met when Philip, then sixteen, had run away from Rugby. Esmond, only fifteen, was at that time living in London in a furnished room, supporting himself by various odd jobs of journalism and selling advertising space. He had become a sort of unofficial center for boys who had run away, and Philip had stayed with him briefly before finally deciding to return to complete his education.

Philip was our only link, if rather a disreputable one, with the now-estranged world of London society. Although a member of the Communist Party, he still found time to take in a good number of debutante dances during the London season, and he would regale us with accounts of these.

"Couldn't you take along a little paper bag and bring us back some of the delicious food?" we urged. But the most he brought back were bits of juicy gossip about my family and former friends, and stories of what was being said about us.

On one occasion Philip was asked by the Communist Party to participate in an election campaign in a mining town in the north of England. It so happened that he had been invited to a houseparty at Castle Howard, not far from the mining town, for the weekend following the election. Not wanting to return all the way to London, he had packed a suitcase with clothes suitable for both occasions. He made a very funny story of his desperate efforts to conceal the full evening regalia, white tie and tails, which lay guiltily hidden at the bottom of his suitcase during his stay in a coal miner's cottage.

While Esmond laughed uproariously at the story, it underlined one of his main objections to joining the Communist Party. He felt that it was overloaded with young upper class intellectuals, and therefore was operating on an unrealistic basis. Most of our friends were Communists at that time, and we heard from them a great deal of the inner-Party gossip. Much of this seemed to consist of expulsions for trivial reasons, people getting "fed up" and resigning, long drawn out and rather pointless feuds, petulant quarrels over real or imagined slights. The ex-Communists, those who had resigned or been expelled, were generally the worst of all, as they would turn bitterly against their former comrades and frequently ended up as all-out enemies of everything they had ever stood for. Yet we knew that there was another side to the Communist Party. Internationally, and to some extent within England, it had proved itself to be a driving force in the fight against fascism and for collective security against the Axis powers. The Communists had done a tremendous job of focusing the nation's attention on the plight of the unemployed, organizing thousands from all parts of the country for hunger marches and other forms of direct action. In all the great battles for progress of the thirties, Communists had proved outstanding for their courage and singleness of purpose.

Esmond's opinion of Communists he had met in Spain was summed up in *Boadilla* in a description of Hans Beimler, political commandant of the Thaelmann Battalion:

"I put him immediately in my mind into the category of Real Communists. This was a purely personal definition I applied instinctively; to fit it you had to be a serious person, a rigid disciplinarian, a member of the Communist Party, interested in all the technical aspects of warfare, and lacking in any such selfish motive as fear or reckless courage."

Our friends who tried unsuccessfully to recruit us into the Party would generally oversimplify the reasons for Esmond's refusal to join: "He's incapable of submitting to discipline," or "He's too much of an individualist." Esmond's real reasons were considerably more complex. True, his nature was one that resisted discipline, yet he had proved himself quite capable of submitting to discipline when it was obviously necessary to the objective, as in Spain. But he saw no need for the kind of discipline for discipline's sake that seemed to be practiced in the English party, and he was determined to stay clear of the petty inner-party squabbles, the pigeonholing of people as "deviationists," "petty-bourgeois disrupters," etc., of which we heard so much from our Communist friends. Though the Party's goals were generally the same as his own, there were rather too many false theatricals attached to membership to suit the more sober mood in which he had returned from Spain.

The Bermondsey Labor Party was much more to our liking. At the monthly meetings, held in a shabby hall not far from Rotherhithe Street, vigorous discussions would take place on the important political events of the day. Tired, white-faced dockers and their wives would join in singing "The Red Flag," still the Labor Party's anthem in that part of London. Fundraising campaigns for milk for Spanish orphans or for aid to Hitler's Jewish victims were planned and carried out, often in defiance of the wishes of Transport House. If they lacked the glamor and the special, high-flown language of some of our Communist friends, these members of the local Labor Party branch seemed to display a seriousness of purpose and a down-to-earth understanding of issues that quickly won our respect. The Labor Party in that section of London was considerably more militant than the Party's official spokesmen. It was said that the schoolchildren lined up to boo Princess Mary, symbol of hated charity, when she made her infrequent expeditions to the local orphanage.

On May Day the entire community turned out, men, women and children, homemade banners proclaiming slogans of the "United Front against Fascism" waving alongside the official ones. The long march to Hyde Park started early in the morning, contingents of the Labor Party, the Co-ops, the Communist Party, the Independent Labor Party marching through the long day to join other thousands from all parts of London in the traditional May Day labor festival.

Everyone took lunch in a paper bag, and there was much good-natured jostling and shouting of orders, and last-minute rounding up of children who had darted away in the crowd. Philip and Roger taught us some new songs to sing on the way — parodies on Communist songs: "Class conscious we are, and class conscious we'll be, And we'll TREAD ON THE NECK of the bourgeoisie!" — "Oh, 'tis my delight of a dirty night to bomb the bourgeoisie!" — and a sarcastic version of the "Red Flag": "The People's flag is palest pink, It's not as red as you might think."

We had been warned that the Blackshirts might try to disrupt the parade, and sure enough there were groups of them lying in wait at several points along the way. Armed with rubber truncheons and knuckle dusters, they leaped out from behind buildings; there were several brief battles in which the Blackshirts were overwhelmed by the sheer numbers of the Bermondsey men. Once I caught sight of two familiar tall blond figures: Boud and Diana, waving Swastika flags. I shook my fist at them in the Red Front salute, and was barely dissuaded by Esmond and Philip, who reminded me of my now pregnant condition, from joining the fray.

The blissful contrast between life with Esmond at Rotherhithe Street and my former drab existence was a source of constant delight and I was joyfully looking forward to the birth of the baby. Sometimes I would dream I was back at home, the governess breathing down my neck at a drawing lesson, saying, "Very nice perspective, dear"; or dancing with a blank-faced young man; or fighting with Boud about Spain; or coming home in the drenching rain from a walk at Swinbrook. The leaden, trapped feeling would only vanish when I was fully awake.

We did not see much of my family or people from the old life, though we resumed relations after an uneasy fashion with some of them. I got the impression from my mother that, although she was too loyal to Farve to criticize any of his decisions, she really regretted the severity of the measures he had taken. Sometimes Esmond and I would meet her for dinner at a restaurant, but these would tend to be frosty occasions, made awkward by unspoken bitterness on both sides. We were barely "on speakers" with the Rodds because of their underhanded co-operation with the Revereds. Debo was not allowed to come to Rotherhithe Street, nor did she particularly want to; she was now in the middle of her first season, and her mind was on more important matters. I kept in touch with her through long telephone conversations. Tuddemy, the only member of the family whom Esmond really liked, came to see us quite often, dining with us when I had managed to save up enough money to eat at home, and even joining in the "bottle parties."

During these months at Rotherhithe Street I landed my first job, doing market research for Esmond's advertising agency. The work was occasional and on call, and for the most part out of town.

Market research was considered slightly above selling or office work; the pay was higher and it was the kind of employment that might "lead to something better." It attracted a mixed assortment; my co-workers, all women roughly between twenty-five and forty-five, were ex-chorus girls, wives of businessmen, friends of copy writers, aspirant newspaper reporters.

We traveled by train in teams of six or eight, herded by the supervisors, to manufacturing towns in the Midlands or the north of England. Since we received, in addition to our salaries, a flat amount for living expenses, our strategy was to find the cheapest possible rooming house, where we often piled into a single room to sleep two or three to a bed, thereby saving a considerable portion of the expense allowance.

The work itself was based on a very new idea recently imported from America. We were told that its originator was a Dr. George Gallup, a person with the unusual but descriptive title of Pollster. The objective was to compile information for the use of the advertising agency about public reaction to various products, and to this end we were provided with elaborate forms to be filled out in the course of door-to-door interviews. The questions, of course, varied widely according to the product. Interviewing for a breakfast food or household cleanser was fairly plain sailing, while the form dealing with a deodorant was likely to contain the question: "How often do you find it necessary to wash under the armpits?" — with the attendant risk that the market researcher might face swift ejection by the housewife thus approached. The supervisor cautioned us that the Dr. Gallup method included a built-in safeguard against cheating on the part of interviewers, and inferred that somehow *he* would know if we should be so dishonest as to fill in the questionnaires over a nice cup of tea in the nearest Lyons.

At night we straggled in one by one to report the day's work to the supervisor, and later to cope with the acute discomfort of the sleeping arrangements. In the feminine squalor of the overcrowded room, the topic of conversation was always the same: Sex and Men, discussed without a trace of warmth or humor. Men, whether husbands or lovers, existed only to be milked or tricked out of every penny they were good for, and sex was the weapon so graciously supplied by nature for this purpose. One member of our team won the respectful admiration of the others for a particularly clever trick she had worked out to get her husband to give her extra money. Shortly after her marriage, several years before, he had approached her with great embarrassment and haltingly explained that he knew there was a "certain time of the month" when women had unusual expenses, and that she shouldn't hesitate to ask him for three or four extra pounds when that time arrived.

"The silly oaf!" her flat, rather brutal voice continued. "I've been getting three pounds ten every month off him for the past ten years. He don't even know enough to know how much a package of sanitary napkins costs."

Listening to her story, and to the approving comments of the others, I felt I had arrived at a rock bottom of degradation I didn't know existed before. The market researchers opened up a whole new side of life; I was repelled yet fascinated, at the same time rather hoping these were not the workers of the world destined to lead the revolution. There didn't seem to be much danger, as none of them were remotely interested in politics; their newspaper reading seemed confined to crime news and the ever popular antics of dear little Princesses Lilibet and Margaret Rose.

My co-workers were kind enough to me; they treated me rather as an odd little mascot, and called me "The Baby." I loved the adventurous trips to parts of England I had never seen before, and the glowing feeling of actually earning money, but was always glad when the end of an assignment came and I could return to the relative innocence and purity of Rotherhithe Street. The intrigues begun at drunken bottle parties, the unbounded license of Philip and other friends, were at least carried on in a spirit of exuberant romance, and had nothing in common with the horrifying, calculated frigidity of the Market Researchers.

The baby was born a few months after our return to England. She became the center of my existence. Esmond gleefully watched her grow, learn to smile, learn to wave her feet and catch them with an unsteady hand. We planned her future, growing up among the rough children of Rotherhithe Street, born to freedom and May Day parades, without the irksome restraints of nanny, governess, daily walks and dull dances; or perhaps we'd take her to Paris to live, a little gamine trudging to a lycée with books in satchel . . .

The Labor Party had established free health clinics throughout the East End, and to one of these I took her weekly for weighing and free cod liver oil. An epidemic of measles broke out in the neighborhood, but the health clinic nurses assured me there was nothing to fear — a breast-fed child was immune to such illnesses. Perhaps they did not know that immunization can only be conferred by a mother who has had the disease; or perhaps, in that teeming part of London, it never occurred to them that a person might reach maturity without having had all the usual childhood illnesses at some time or other. In any case, they were tragically wrong. When she was four months old the baby came down with a terrifying, flaming case of measles, and within a few days I had caught it from her. Esmond frantically engaged nurses to look after us day and night; my temperature rose alarmingly, until I became lightheaded and delirious. I recovered to find that the baby was dying of pneumonia.

She lived on for a few horrible days, gasping for each breath under an oxygen tent. Nurses came and went, their standardized cheeriness concealing horror like a smile in a bad dream; then it was all over.

Esmond and I fled like people battered into semi-consciousness in a vicious street fight. He took charge of all our plans, drew out our savings, made the necessary travel arrangements, and the day after the baby was buried we left for Corsica. There we lived for three months in the welcome unreality of a foreign town, shielded by distance from the sympathy of friends, returning only when the nightmare had begun to fade.

21

WE RETURNED to Rotherhithe Street late in the summer of 1938. Although mass meetings and fund-raising parties for the Loyalists cause attracted as much support as ever, the atmosphere had changed. The victorious feeling of the early days of the war had seeped away forever. Even the magnificent Ebro offensive of that July, into which the Loyalists threw all their resources, did not basically change the desperate situation. Franco remained in control of three-fourths of the country.

As the offensive simmered down into a series of indecisive battles it was clear that slowly, day by day, the war was being lost, and that slowly, one by one, Loyalist supporters in England were beginning to give up hope.

In the drafty meeting halls from Bermondsey to Hampstead Heath where they gathered to raise money for Spanish relief, the mood of the huge, grave audiences seemed out of step with the ever more strained optimism of platform speakers.

At the same time, the Spanish war was driven off the front pages by events in central Europe, where lines were being drawn for the last, bitter battle for collective security against

the Axis. A million Germans were massed along the Czech-
oslovak frontier. Newspapers quoted Goering as saying he
had definite information that if the German army marched into
Czechoslovakia the British would not lift a finger.

It was hard to tell what the British and French policy
makers were really up to. The discreet, impervious men of the
Cliveden Set, with their furled umbrellas so symbolic of furled
minds, came and went on their missions to the embattled area
and said little. Lord Runciman went to Prague with forty
pieces of luggage and enraged the Czechs by hobnobbing
with Nazi leaders. What else he was doing in Prague did not
emerge very clearly from news reports.

Throughout September the shadow deepened. At Rotherhithe Street there was much uneasy talk about what the outcome might be, whether this last clear chance to stop Hitler
and avert war would be taken. None of us thought very
seriously that this time there would be an outright capitulation to Hitler. Sheer numbers would prevent it. If ever the
determination of millions seemed a tangible force, it was then.
I thought back to the great parades we had seen in Bayonne
— anti-fascist youth, socialist youth, communist youth, marching under the banners of the Front Populaire in never-ending
thousands. Fragments of their stirring marching songs came
to my mind — we could never quite get all the words:
*"Prenez garde! Prenez garde! C'est la lutte finale qui com-
mence!"* and *"Ça ira, ça ira, ça ira, ça ira, tous les fascistes on
les pendra!"* They'd never let their government knuckle under
to Hitler. Russia would never let it happen. The English
workers would never let it happen; even the frequently insular
Trades Union Congress issued thunderous declarations against
throwing the Czechs to the wolves, and warned that this
might be Europe's last chance to prevent another world war.

Feelers put out by the Chamberlain clique to test reaction

to a sell-out of Czechoslovakia were meeting everywhere with rebuff: When the *Times* blandly suggested that the Sudeten German territory of Czechoslovakia should be permitted to secede and merge with Germany, this proposal ran into loud opposition, not only throughout Europe but from most of the English press.

I was in Southampton on a market research job when the news came through that Chamberlain and Daladier had sealed the fate of the collective security policy to which their governments were supposedly committed. In the early dusk groups of people were gathered at street corner newsstands — an unusual sight for England, more reminiscent of emotional Paris, where a fall of government, a financial scandal, or even a particularly interesting murder case often causes such spontaneous interest in the evening headlines. "PEACE IN OUR TIME!" The huge black type quoted the Prime Minister's first words to the press at the airport on his return from Munich. The incredible had happened: complete capitulation to Hitler's terms; a free hand for the Nazis in Czechoslovakia . . . could Chamberlain possibly hope to get away with such betrayal? Only the week before we had attended a huge, jammed meeting called by the Left Book Club in an East End London hall, one of scores held at that time to protest appeasement of the Nazis. The big, orderly crowd seemed so determined, the speakers so eloquently convincing — surely the meeting was proof that this new move by Chamberlain would never be accepted.

I showed the paper to a fellow market researcher. "Chamberlain? Oh — Chamberlain," she said vaguely. "But the paper says he's for peace. That's good, isn't it?"

Later I wandered out into the streets of Southampton, half expecting to find signs of a spontaneous uprising; but to my surprise people were placidly going about their business as usual, with no hint in the air of the disaster which lay just a few hundred miles away. Already news programs were describing the confusion and despair of the inevitable multitudes of refugees — a phenomenon with which Europe had become all too familiar with each successive move of Hitler's since 1933.

A day or so later the local papers carried an announcement of a protest meeting to be held by the Southampton branch of the Communist Party. I went, hoping for the best; but the meeting was a sad little affair with more people on the platform than in the audience. My co-worker's comment, "He's for peace, that's good, isn't it?" apparently summed up a good part of popular reaction to what had happened.

I was more than usually anxious to get back to London, to find out what Esmond thought of the new situation. I found him in a serious, unhappy mood. He was on the whole out of sympathy with our Communist friends, who continued to go through the motions of political activity as though from long-ingrained habit — busily they rushed from meeting to meeting, cranked out thousands of mimeographed leaflets, exhorted to action — but now it all seemed like useless gesturing. The time when these activities could have any meaning in terms of influencing events had passed. The anticipated storm of indignation simply didn't materialize.

Indeed, an enormous wave of blind relief swept England, relief that for the moment at least the plunge would not be taken. But it was relief without hope, like news that a dreaded operation has been postponed for the doctor's convenience; despite the reprieve the cancer would grow and flourish, and one day the inevitable moment would come. By that time, it might even be too late. The specter of a completely Nazified Europe a few years hence seemed not impossible.

All sorts of emergency measures were being taken by the

Government to prepare the people for war. Thousands lined up patiently to be measured for gas masks, only to find out that because of the haste with which the masks were manufactured the parts which were supposed to intercept gas had been inadvertently left out. Trenches were dug in Hyde Park, causing mass discontent on the part of nannies, who complained that their little charges were always falling in. Apart from the bitter jokes caused by these inept arrangements, the atmosphere was on the whole one of dreary calm, of apathetic bowing to the inevitable.

Conversation now dwelt, not on "what we'll do *if* war breaks out," but rather on "what we'll do *when* war breaks out." There was already question about which side England might find herself on. Philip, who still managed to move at least part of the time in exalted circles where it was possible to garner interesting political gossip from the Other Side, was convinced there was a real possibility that the Chamberlain Government might go full circle, that England and Germany might team up against Russia.

How long this drab limbo, neither war nor peace, might last was anybody's guess. It could be a matter of months, or several years. Conscription was a foregone conclusion, and it would not be long before England was transformed into a great, gray, semi-military camp. "One vast O.T.C.," as Esmond put it with shuddering disgust, "with overtones of an eternal Boy Scout jamboree. You wait and see; in no time there'll be a wave of Stiff Upper Lipism, followed by a nauseating epidemic of Gray-Haired Motherism (bravely choking back the tears, you understand), and the small matter of who we go to war with, and why, will be entirely lost sight of."

I had never seen Esmond so depressed and restless. Ahead of him lay the prospect of the kind of discipline, centered around the inconsequential, that he had hated and resisted all his life — the well-shined shoe, correctly angled cap, smart salute — those hallmarks of modern armies, which had been so pleasantly lacking in the International Brigade. Yet the end use to which this discipline would be put remained obscure, and the decision was now firmly and irrevocably in the hands of the appeasement crowd.

If Esmond reflected at that moment the despair of a generation that has lost control of its own destiny, he was not one to remain in despair for very long. Turning over and discarding possible alternative plans of action and modes of existence, the idea suddenly flashed upon him: we'd go and live in America until the war began.

22

POLITICS ASIDE, two other elements had entered our lives which effectively tipped the scale in favor of emigration: the Process Server and my hundred pounds.

The Process Server was a pale, sad-looking youth in the employ of the London Electric Company. Fortunately for us, he was not particularly good at his line of work; the most transparent disguises — Esmond's false mustache, top hat or worker's cap, my dark glasses — would effectively muddle him for the few moments needed to escape. He would stare sorrowfully after us, his brow wrinkled with puzzlement, as we quickly dashed round a corner or disappeared from his view down the Underground.

I felt guilty about the Process Server, because in a way I had been unfairly trapped into responsibility for his haunting presence. No one had ever explained to me that you had to pay for electricity; and lights, electric heaters, stoves blazed away night and day at Rotherhithe Street. When the enormous bill first arrived we thought briefly of contesting it in court on the grounds that electricity is an Act of God — an element, like fire, earth and air; but legal friends assured us this would get us nowhere. It was unthinkable that we should pay, so we moved out of the Rotherhithe Street house to a furnished room near the Marble Arch.

Somehow, the Process Server found out where we were staying. Every morning before going to work we peered cautiously out of the window to see if he was coming down the street or lurking at a corner. We regretfully abandoned the disguises because he had seen them all so many times. If he was in sight, we would go back to bed, as Esmond had a theory that it was illegal and in some way a violation of Magna Carta to serve process on people in bed. Sometimes we stayed in bed for as long as two days, fearing that our tormentor was still in the neighborhood. Though enjoyable to us, these lost days were becoming a source of irritation to Esmond's boss.

Obviously, life in England had become untenable, in more ways than one. Besides, on my twenty-first birthday I came into a great windfall, a trust fund of one hundred pounds, and we were casting around for a suitable way to use it.

My mother had established savings accounts for all of us. With the birth of each child, she had started making weekly deposits of sixpence into these accounts, which, together with interest, would reach the sum of a hundred pounds by the time we were twenty-one. Only by luck was my hundred pounds intact, for many years before my older sisters had inadvertently lost a good portion of their savings when they sank some money in one of my father's many "damn sound investments." Debo and I had escaped, being considered too young to sign up for the venture.

An American by the romantic and Western-sounding name of "Mr. Reno" approached my father in the early twenties about this particular project. Mr. Reno had invented a sort of tank, for which he produced plans and blueprints; when built, the Reno tank would be able to descend into the depths of the ocean and bring to the surface the golden treasures of the days of piracy and the Spanish Armada. "Think of it — great chests of gold bullion!" my father would say, rubbing his hands. He made an enormous investment of his own, and raised additional money from uncles and friends who were anxious to share in the pirate gold.

The five oldest Mitford children were allowed to put up twenty pounds each of the savings my mother was keeping for them. I remember shedding hot tears of rage as they described the enormous fortunes they would soon own — not to speak of fabulous jewelry, heavy gold chains, priceless gems that would doubtless be dredged up in Mr. Reno's tank. But my mother was adamant; Debo and I were under seven, and too young to make our own financial decisions.

Debo and I had our day of rejoicing soon afterwards, when it was learned that Mr. Reno had taken off for America without leaving a trace. "Really *very* dishonest of him — I can't imagine what he must have been thinking of," Muv said. The other sisters put up a halfhearted argument that Debo and I should be forced to share in the loss, since we would readily have invested our money too if we had been allowed to. But for once justice prevailed, and our savings were kept intact.

The sum of a hundred pounds seemed just the right amount for the purpose of emigration. It was neither large enough to start a business or invest for income, nor small enough to spend on a few parties and good meals out. Yet a third of it would purchase two one-way steerage tickets to America, leaving a nice round sum, over $300 at the prevailing rate of exchange, to live on for a while until we found work.

To our disappointment, the American Consul to whom we now applied for the necessary papers did not look at matters this way at all. Indeed he expressed great surprise that we should consider starting a new life with so small a capital, mentioned there was danger we might become a public charge, and told us that we should have to show a guarantee of financial support amounting to at least fifteen dollars a week before he would consider giving us immigration visas.

We canvassed various friends — Philip Toynbee, Peter Nevile, Giles — and suggested they should underwrite a guarantee of financial support in case we should become penniless, but we were met on all sides with firm and indignant refusals. "He'll give you the papers, all right; just say the Magic Words," Peter advised. The Magic Words, it seemed, were Land of Opportunity, Rugged Individualism, Free Enterprise. With Peter's help, Esmond concocted and memorized a brief appeal in which the ritual words were repeated a number of times, and we presented ourselves once more to the Consul. No sooner were we in his office than Esmond became transformed into his idea of red-blooded Americanism. "Sir," he began, "my wife and I hold dear a most heartfelt, deep and sincere faith in the ability of your grea-a-a-t country, the Land of Opportunity, the United States of America, to provide, through its Free Enterprise system, a modest but adequate living for those young people who, like ourselves, are imbued with the spirit of Rugged Individualism." He went on this way for some time, Sincerity and Forthrightness actually shining in his eyes.

If Esmond had suddenly assumed the appearance of a cross between Mr. Oover in *Zuleika Dobson* and Spencer Tracy, the Consul didn't seem to notice. As Peter had predicted, the words had an enormous, almost mesmeric, effect on him. With a faraway look in his eyes — which were no doubt seeing the windswept main street of some midwestern town, swarming with rugged individualists — he uttered the words of consent: "Well, I guess I'll take a chance on you kids."

Now that the trip was becoming a reality, Esmond hit upon an idea which would enable us to travel all over America and get paid for it. We would get some of our friends to come, too, and offer a lecture tour covering various phases of English life. Our idea of America, like that of most English people, was limited and not a little distorted. We pictured it as a vast nation of Babbitts whose eyes were uniformly riveted on English royalty, Mothers and Dads, and Sex.

"Women's clubs are the very thing!" Esmond explained. "They have them all over America, and this'll be just the sort of thing they love. They'll simply *eat* up Philip Toynbee." I remarked that this was a most unappetizing thought, but Esmond assured me he was merely repeating an American turn of phrase he had just picked up from Peter.

In short order, we lined up three co-lecturers. Sheila Legge, one of the ex-chorus-girl-market-researchers, agreed readily, and Esmond promptly assigned a subject for her lecture: "Men, from the Ritz to the Fish and Chips Stand." The young male secretary of a well-known poet, who had just parted from his employer in one of those petulant flare-ups which often mar such relationships, was easily persuaded to prepare to be eaten up by the women's clubs; his rather suggestive topic was to be "From Guardsman to Poet's Secretary." Philip was to speak on "Sex Life at Oxford University," and in addition to offer a special Father's Day talk titled, "Arnold Toynbee — Historian, but First and Foremost 'Dad.'" I was to describe "The Inner Life of an English Debutante" (Esmond thought they would like to hear about the delicious dinners and suppers we used to have during the season). Esmond himself would be manager of the expedition, occasionally helping out with lectures on such surefire subjects as "Is Princess Elizabeth Really the Monster of Glamis?" "The Truth about Winston Churchill," "How to Meet the King," "Sedition Spreading at Eton."

In the atmosphere of almost electric excitement which Esmond always managed to create when developing a new plan,
the five of us met to draw up a prospectus suitable for mailing
out to lecture agencies. It began in typical Esmond style:
"Dear Sirs: King George and Queen Elizabeth are not the
only people leaving these shores for America this year. We
are also coming."

We even got as far as having a special series of photographs
made for enclosure with the lecture outlines. There was a
leering Philip to accompany "Sex Life At Oxford University,"
and a filial Philip for the Dad's Day lecture. Sheila, showing a large expanse of the limb from which, we assumed, she
had got her surname, was pictured in a sultry pose near the
main entrance of the Ritz, with the poet's ex-secretary lounging
langourously nearby, symbolically clutching a slim volume and
a guardsman's cap. But no sooner had we assembled all this
promising material than our fellow lecturers began to drop out
one by one. A sudden turn in Philip's love life required
his presence in England; the poet's secretary made up with
the poet, and resumed his post; Sheila was unable to raise the
money for her ticket. Our frantic efforts to shore up the
situation were to no avail. We regretfully decided that our
plans would have to be revised and the lecture tour junked.

Now we concentrated on getting letters of introduction
from anyone and everyone we knew who had ever been to
America or who knew any Americans. They were addressed
to as wide and varied an assortment of people as those from
whom we had secured them: artists in Greenwich Village;
tycoons on Wall Street; movie people, poets, kind old ladies,
journalists, advertising people.

My own impressions of Americans had been culled from
various sources, ranging from books read in childhood, such
as *Little Women* and *What Katy Did,* to Hemingway and
the movies. I knew that they lived on strange and rather

unappetizing-sounding foods called squash, grits, hot dogs, and corn pudding. On the other hand, cookies sounded rather delicious. I visualized them as little cakes made in the shape of cooks with sugar-icing aprons and hats. From seeing *The Petrified Forest,* I gathered that Americans often made love under tables while gangster bullets whizzed through the air.

Peter Nevile was the only person we knew who had actually been to America; and Esmond, with his usual thoroughness in such matters, enlisted Peter's help in briefing us on the language, manners and customs we should encounter in the Land of Opportunity. We spent an evening at his house being initiated.

"Never say, 'I say!' Say, 'Say,'" Peter explained patiently. "Things on the whole move much faster in America; people don't *stand for election,* they *run for office.* If a person says he's *sick,* it doesn't mean regurgitating; it means *ill. Mad* means angry, not *insane.* Don't ask for the left-luggage place, it's called a checkroom. A nice joint means a good pub, not roast meat . . ." He listed a variety of Christian names we should encounter, some taken from English titles such as Earl and Duke, some from American states such as Washington, Georgia, Florida. "On the other hand," he went on, lapsing into his American accent as he warmed to his theme, "you'll hardly find anyone christened Viscount or New York. There's really no special logic to it." He instructed us in the use of "gotten" and "you betcha" (under no circumstances to be pronounced, "you bet you"), and filled us up with a certain amount of misinformation to the effect that "pediatrician" was a fancy name for a corn specialist, and "mortician," a musician with necrophilic bent who plays only at funerals.

"'Twenty' is pronounced 'Twenny,'" Peter continued, "and be sure to leave out the first 'T' in Interesting, too. Then, you'll have to know a few stock rejoinders. For example, you'll find people generally say 'I'll be seeing you' instead of 'goodbye.' Then that leaves the field wide open for you to answer, 'Not if I see you first,' which will show you are on your toes, alert and amusing. Alternatively, you may be able to raise a laugh by saying, 'Abyssinia.' Another thing, if someone pays you a compliment — you're looking well, what a pretty dress, and so forth — you are supposed to say 'Thank you,' instead of just mumbling inaudibly. You have to be on the lookout for what is considered a compliment, too; for instance, an American may say, 'That dress is the cat's pajamas.' Don't take this as a criticism, it's meant as just the opposite."

When I suggested, in what I imagined was best American idiom, that I guessed it was time for us to scram home, Peter's parting advice was: "You'll need a crooked lawyer in New York; can't get on without one. Why don't you wire the British Consul there and tell him to have one meet you at the boat?"

23

We sailed for New York on February 18, 1939, on the Canadian ship SS *Aurania*.

Tom, Philip, and Nanny — an oddly assorted, yet appropriate three — came to see us off in London at the boat train. Nanny, looking so much smaller now I was grown up, was grumbling mildly at the idea of our leaving England — "What do you want to go to America for, darling, those horrid earthquakes, and those tea bags, oh they sound nasty, my cousin says you can't even get a proper cup of tea there" — and she was still audibly worrying over my underclothes.

Tom, at this moment my only link with the family, dimpling and blithering in the background, added: "Yes, Little D., and don't forget to wash them every night. I *happen to know* American girls always do." "Oh Tuddemy, you've been committing it again, you *are* awful, what's to be done about you?" (this in Boudledidge, so that Nanny wouldn't understand).

Philip was all exaggerated, exuberant sorrow that we were leaving without him, and only giggled halfheartedly when Esmond noisily reminded him, "Keep a stiff upper lip, Toynbee! And keep the Home Fires burning. We owe it to the Mothers of England."

We got our last smell of London — a lovely, exciting railway smell, tiny bits of soot floating in the nipping cold, stagnant air — and the train was off. It was almost like running away all over again; no regrets, no premonition of changes that might have taken place if I should ever come back. If "the future lay ahead," as an American politician once so beautifully and simply expressed it, I didn't give it a thought. We were off to America, the future a great blank canvas on which anything might appear. It was an enormous relief to put three thousand miles between the family and myself at that particular time. Relations with them had deteriorated badly; I hardly ever saw any of them, yet there they were — and there was the niggling discomfort in the background of the impending war in which Boud and I would be on opposite sides.

Esmond passed the train trip spinning an improbable fantasy about the possibilities that might show up in the course of the sea voyage. We might meet some great industrialist who, impressed with our new-found Ruggedness and Individualism, would ensure our future then and there, or possibly a movie talent scout, traveling incognito, would sign us on the spot and offer to pay our fare to Hollywood.

One evening at sea was enough to convince him that such did not abound in the steerage class. Our fellow passengers were Canadian tourists, and Polish refugees who had managed to get on the immigration quota. Since there was little to liven up the voyage, we devoted our attention to taking sides in the continuous battle that raged between these two groups.

Some of the Canadians had taken it upon themselves to preserve the Anglo-Saxon purity of the steerage class bar from the "foreigners." The bar was small, generally crowded, and stuffy. A group of Canadians generally managed to monopolize it early in the evening. "This place stinks of polecats," they said loudly when some of the immigrants tried to come in. Esmond, assuming his most super-English-upper-class-public-school manner, escorted a group of Poles through the Canadian phalanx. "I really must apologize for these ghastly Colonials. They're virtually uncivilized. Too bad we couldn't have sailed on an English ship." For once he was enjoying outsnobbing the snobs.

At last the long, dull journey came to an end. It turned out that once more there was a Lord on Board, but since he had been traveling first class we only met him at the last moment, in the long queue of aliens waiting to be processed through immigration formalities. He was directly in front of me, and I watched him filling out the long form required of tourists. The burly, sour-faced immigration officer read it through, pointing with his finger in the style of one unaccustomed to reading. Coming to "Occupation — Peer of the Realm," the officer crossed out this answer and wrote in "Nil." It seemed a symbolic and fitting incident to mark our arrival in the New World.

Soon we were in a cab, in the wide, bright streets of New York, on our way to the Shelton hotel, where Peter Nevile had reserved a room for us. We had been rather appalled at the rates — $3.50 a night without food — but he assured us that the main thing in America was to "put on a good front." The Shelton turned out to exceed our wildest dreams of American mass-produced luxury. The magnificent lobby and bellboys, the immense size of the place, the thickly carpeted corridors, had nothing in common with any English hotel. The dark gloom of the London Ritz with its elderly, grave staff, the genteel, organized discomfort of English middle class hotels, seemed much more than a mere three thousand miles away; we seemed to have stepped onto another planet. Fascinating signs in the elevator announced available services in this Brave New World: ROOM SERVICE, COMPLETE VALET SERVICE, SWIMMING POOL ON PENTHOUSE, HOUSE DOCTOR ("I wonder what on earth a house doctor is," Esmond said); it seemed like a city in itself. We put our things down in the aseptically clean bedroom, got out our letters of introduction, and descended to the bar.

The Shelton Bar was our first vivid impression of America. We sat in a dim, plushly upholstered corner ordering dry martinis, absorbing the amazing unEnglishness of it all. We watched the incredibly beautiful and ageless-seeming women, in their faultlessly lovely tight black clothes and gleaming shiny shoes; the raucous and often aging businessmen shoving up around the bar. An orchestra played unfamiliar popular songs that would eventually reach England, months or a year later.

We agonized over the letters of introduction. Armed with immense sheets of Shelton writing paper and grandly inscribed Shelton envelopes, we set about writing notes to enclose with the letters — "Dear Mr. So and so, my friend Peter Nevile . . ."

"No, why don't you put 'my *great* friend Peter Nevile'?"

"Well, how's this, 'my *very good friend* Peter Nevile' — it sounds more businesslike, don't you think?"

"Or how about 'my *dear* friend Peter Nevile' — no . . . too sugary."

" 'Peter Nevile, a very good friend of ours, gave us the enclosed note to you' . . ."

"Or 'our *mutual* friend Peter Nevile' . . . mutual sounds very American to me . . ."

"Or how about the informal touch? I understand Americans like that sometimes, such as 'I expect you remember old Peter Nevile, he met you when he was in New York' . . ."

"Oh no, that's hopeless, because it sounds as though they

might *not* remember him. That's not putting on a good front . . ."

We argued interminably over the phrasing of each one; for these letters were to be the open sesame to the world beyond the Shelton Bar. At last they were done, and we scuttled out into the freezing night air to mail them.

Next day, we hardly dared leave the hotel for fear of missing a telephone call. Restlessly we paced the room or went down to check at the desk for messages. In this state of anxiety, we discovered something that cast a deep shadow over our next twenty-four hours in New York. We had not had a single response to the letters; yet they should have had plenty of time to arrive. Suddenly a truly awful thought occurred to me. "Esmond, have you noticed that the dustbins and the pillar boxes here are exactly alike? They're both dark green, and both have slots for putting things in. *You don't suppose* . . ."

We rushed outside the hotel. There was a dark green mailbox, right next to a dark green garbage can. At night, in the dark, accustomed as we were to bright red English pillar boxes, it would have been so easy to make the fatal mistake.

The next day was one of horrid suspense. We made innumerable trips from the room to the desk, to see if there were any letters or messages. To pass the time away, Esmond sent for the house doctor, partly to find out if he really existed and partly because of a slight sore throat. The house doctor not only existed, he came up to the room, prescribed aspirin, and charged us five dollars — much to Esmond's fury, as he had assumed this service was included in the price of our room.

At long last, the telephone rang. A pleasant American voice said, "Mrs. Romilly? I got your letter. I'll be more than happy to meet a friend of Peter Nevile's and hear some news of him." We breathed again. The letter problem solved, we set about exploring New York.

24

THOSE FIRST DAYS in New York were filled with opportunities to check our prior conceptions of America against reality. The Times Square–Broadway–42nd Street area lived up to all expectations, with its bright, movielike quality and the added musical comedy touch provided by pickets forever circling in front of the Brass Rail restaurant, delivering in unison their eternal message: "Brass Rail on Strike. Please Pass By."

Of course we were told that New York is "not typical" of America — how untypical we were not then in a position to judge — but we did get the impression there was a distinct New York personality. The unique feature of this personality seemed the bright spark of momentary interest lit in New Yorkers by the most casual of contacts.

A stranger asked for directions would, for the brief second spent talking on the street, throw himself vigorously into one's problem, questioning the very wisdom of one's plan, often suggesting a completely different course of action:

"Could you direct me to the Museum of Modern Art?"

"It's two blocks over, but the Picasso show closed last Wednesday. If you wait till next week, there'll be a Van Gogh exhibit. How long are you folks planning on staying in town? Tell you what, why don't you take in the Museum of Natural History today?"

A lady shopper, stopped in full flight for directions to Macy's, might elaborate her answer: ". . . but, honey, their sale don't start till Friday. Try Bloomingdale's, it's closer anyway." Often they would add, "You're from England, aren't you? How long are you staying? How do you like it here?"

Roaming the streets of New York, we encountered many examples of this delightful quality of New Yorkers, forever on their toes, violently, restlessly involving themselves in the slightest situation brought to their attention, always posing alternatives, always ready with an answer or an argument.

The letters of introduction brought a flood of invitations to the greatest variety of social functions we'd ever known, and for a while we basked and wallowed in the fabled American hospitality.

Having lost the carefully compiled descriptive list of the people to whom we had written, we had no way of knowing whether the person we were about to meet was a dear old friend of Cousin Dorothy's, a business acquaintance of Esmond's boss in the London advertising agency, or a dashing young friend of Peter Nevile's. In some ways this made it more exciting: "Like hunters not knowing if they're stalking a deer or a rabbit," Esmond said.

In contrast to the predicament we should have been in had a similar situation arisen in England, our ignorance about the "contacts," as Esmond now insisted on calling them, hardly mattered at all. Even the old and rich treated us with surprising warmth and informality; they were devoid of the familiar quality of "disapproving auntism," really a form of automatic rudeness to the young, so ready to pop out bleakly at one from their English counterparts.

The lack of bleakness we noted in the natives of this fascinating terrain extended to their dwellings, uniformly as cozy and sheltering as greenhouses. The lovely blasts of heat which greeted one on entering seemed to go with the quick friendliness of the occupants, a welcome change from England, where it was a too-common experience to find the midwinter temperature in someone's drawing room the same, degree for degree, as that outside.

We felt like explorers in a territory that encompassed apartments and offices throughout Manhattan, with occasional excursions on the terrifying parkways to outlying suburbs.

The "contacts" fell into roughly three groups, into which Esmond, with his incongruous mania for classification, began to list them. There were the Grant's Tombers, those inclined to take us to see monuments of interest rather than suggesting cocktails or dinner; Possible Job Getters; and — since we had not been in America long enough to discover how few of its inhabitants really spoke in the accents of Peter's enthusiastic rendition — the Genoowinely Innaresting People.

The one thing common to contacts of all three categories was the inevitable question, "Do you like America?" This always stumped us a bit at first.

"It would never occur to us to ask a foreigner if he liked England," Esmond pointed out, "because, if he did, so what? And if he didn't there would be nothing one could do about it."

We often wondered what the contact would say if one answered, "Loathe it." However, this was fortunately far from the case, and we were able to answer truthfully, "Oh, very good — wonderful . . ."

Esmond wrote to Peter: "There's one little fly I notice. People here — I mean even the intelligent ones — are so damned nationalistic. They keep bringing up points of history and the American War of Independence — whereas you must admit one's own mind is completely blank on that subject." Esmond's schooling, though considerably more thorough than mine, had left him also vaguely under the impression that America had had to be kicked out of the British Empire for misbehavior, but we were quickly disabused of this theory by the Grant's Tombers.

By the end of the first few weeks in New York we felt we knew almost as many people as we did in London. Our acquaintance, while it hardly constituted a cross section — for it was heavily weighted with publishers, advertising people, editors — was kaleidoscopic in its variety. It ranged from radical to conservative, from Park Avenue millionaires to young wage earners, with a sprinkling of dancers, artists and writers thrown in.

Among the dozens of new places, faces and experiences, a few still stand out sharply in memory: the lavatory at Random House, fixed up like a miniature library, lined from floor to ceiling with such appropriate titles as *Gone with the Wind, Mein Kampf, King John;* the fascinating Graham and Meyer families; the Time-Lifers; the English tailoring fanciers; the Park Avenue snobs.

We met Kay Graham at a party, and immediately put her down as a Genoowinely Innaresting one. She was about our age, very pretty and clever, and an ardent New Dealer. Before the evening was over, she invited us to stay at her family's country house for the weekend. "But won't your parents be *furious?*" I asked doubtfully, visualizing the scene that would have ensued if I had proceeded without permission to ask two foreign strangers to stay at Swinbrook. She seemed surprised at the idea; after I met her parents I could see why.

Their house in Westchester County, which we had been told was a sort of millionaire's suburb of New York, was the most luxurious place I had ever seen — like an English country house in size and surroundings, only twice as comfortable. There were none of those unexpected inconveniences — cold bath water, electric lights that don't work, inedible food — so often suffered in similar settings in England.

Kay's parents, Eugene and Agnes Meyer, were so unlike my own — or any English parents, for that matter — that they hardly seemed like parents at all. They behaved like kindly Fairy Godparents, even to their own children. Although the senior Meyers were leading Republicans and their children inclined to be radicals, and in spite of political arguments that raged all weekend, they all seemed amazingly fond of each other. Mr. Meyer even seemed to like the men his daughters had married. I couldn't help thinking back to Farve's designation of his sons-in-law, to whom he referred with dark displeasure as "the Man Mosley, the Boy Romilly, and the Bore Rodd."

Kay and her husband, Phil, took delight in verbally pummeling Mr. Meyer into a corner, trapping him in the contradictions of his point of view. One evening at dinner, after they had him on the ropes, I was emboldened by this unfamiliar relationship between old and young to ask, "But surely, Mr. Meyer, you're not in *favor* of capitalism, are you?" He looked at me across the laden table for a long, twinkling moment while his children and Esmond roared, before giving the reply that best summed up his entire point of view on the subject: "Yes."

Later, Kay told us a funny story about the previous election. She and her parents had worked furiously in the campaign — on opposite sides. On election night, Kay was at a friend's house, sitting up late to hear the returns. In the wee hours her father telephoned her from his Westchester County mansion to report jubilantly: "The rural areas are going heavily

Republican! We just got the results from Westchester County!"

Having learned that Eugene Meyer was the owner and publisher of the *Washington Post,* we immediately assigned him to the top of the list of Possible Job Getters, in case we should one day find ourselves in that city.

Although the Meyers were "in favor of capitalism," and perhaps because they were strong anti-fascists, their company never gave us the uncomfortable feeling of "fraternizing with the enemy" which occasionally marked our excursions into other strongholds of the American rich.

After a long and unsuccessful day with the Possible Job Getters, it was soothing and pleasant to relax among satin cushions in somebody's Park Avenue penthouse. Unfortunately, too many of the owners of these havens of good food and unlimited whiskey proved to be humorless, fascist-minded types — the forerunners of McCarthyism — and sometimes we felt we had plumbed a depth of snobbery and racism the like of which even I had never experienced before.

Too often we ended up quarreling with our hosts. One of these undertook to enlighten us about her fellow countrymen. Esmond was making a check list on a piece of paper as she explained the various classifications. He wrote down as she talked: "Negroes — potential criminals. Poor whites, Italians, etc. — worse than Negroes. Jews — poisonous. People on the WPA — scavengers who won't work. Democratic Party — trash. President Roosevelt — a criminal lunatic who couldn't get a job."

"That must add up to just over seventy per cent of the people here," he said. "What a horrible country we've come to! How can you stand living here? We'd certainly never have left England if we'd known all this beforehand. Come on, Decca, let's dash over to the hotel and see if we can get quick reservations for the next ship sailing for home . . ."

And dash we did, leaving our hostess open-mouthed with astonishment, and our dessert untouched. "It did look good, too," Esmond said regretfully, "but one has to draw the line somewhere."

One invitation from a Possible Job Getter bore the ominous words, "Black Tie."

"That's good, I happen to have a black tie," Esmond said. I quickly disabused him.

"I think it means a dinner jacket, only they call it a tuxedo here," I said. "If we're going, you'll have to get hold of one somehow." It would have been a violation of all our rules to turn down an invitation. Esmond consulted the headwaiter at the Shelton Hotel, and returned with a gloomy report.

"He says a tuxedo would cost at least forty dollars at the only places he knows of. He says you can rent them, but even that costs about fifteen dollars. So that's out . . . I think I'll go and see what I can find in a cheaper part of New York."

He arrived back very late, but victorious.

"Look!" he exulted. "Only six dollars, waistcoat and all. I got it at a little place on a street called Third Avenue. It's a wonderful place for shopping. The salesman let me have it extra cheap, because the last person who had it had been shot in it, and that's supposed to bring bad luck, so no one else would buy it."

The tuxedo fitted all right. I looked carefully for the bullet hole but couldn't find it. The worst part about the suit was the satin lapels, which gleamed and shone like mirrors. I rubbed face powder in them, dimming the luster somewhat. We debated whether or not to take out the enormous pads in the shoulders, which gave Esmond the appearance of a prizefighter, but decided against it, for fear it might bring about a total collapse of the coat.

"After all, they'll probably never see you again, so they'll go on thinking those are your normal shoulders," I said.

Thanks to the power of suggestion, Esmond's tuxedo was a great success. I carefully avoided catching his eye when our host was heard to say: "There's nothing like English tailoring. Say, that tux is a beauty; where did you get it, Savile Row?"

There had been a small flurry of publicity shortly after we arrived, when the New York papers briefly revived the story of our running away to Spain. We were pleased to find the news accounts on the whole sympathetic, and more accurate than we had been accustomed to in our experiences with the English press. *Time* Magazine quoted Esmond as saying, "We came here to get away from a terrible, deathlike atmosphere of depression and hopelessness. England is one of the saddest places in the world."

As a result of all this, we met two people about our age who worked for *Life* Magazine: Liz Kelly, a *Life* researcher, and Dave Scherman, a cub photographer, who had been assigned to interview us. We were fascinated by them, for they seemed so typically American — Liz, fresh from Nebraska, Small-Town-Girl-Makes-Good-in-Big-City written all over her; Dave, with his quicksilver repartee — and soon we were great friends. Dave came out quite naturally with expressions we'd only heard in the movies: "That guy's a low-down, good-for-nothing heel," or "Can you beat it?" They often came to see us, and we regaled them with accounts of the Grant's Tombers and our excursions into Park Avenue life.

We inadvertently got poor Dave into serious trouble with his superiors at *Life*. Esmond casually remarked to a *Daily Mirror* reporter, "The most hard-boiled American I've met so far is a photographer on *Life*." The next day, the *Mirror* carried the quote in one of its columns. Dave came rushing over.

"Listen, you crazy people, don't go around telling other newspaper guys I'm hard-boiled. My boss didn't like that crack *one bit*. He bawled me out but good about your quote in the *Mirror*. He said *Life* men don't talk tough. We're not *supposed* to be hard-boiled in our racket. Get it?"

We apologized profusely, but couldn't help roaring slightly because Dave's speech of protest was one we could just imagine being delivered by Humphrey Bogart himself, cigarette butt casually hanging from one corner of his mouth.

The possible Job Getters were taking up most of our days. Esmond had a sheaf of introductions to various advertising people, and this list was frequently added to by suggestions from the Genoowinely Innaresting People or even by the Grant's Tombers.

Our cash reserve was getting depressingly low. Life at the Shelton was making fierce ravages on what was left of the hundred pounds. "The trouble is," Esmond told me disconsolately, "I seem to make a great hit with the secretaries and people in the outside office. But then when I get down to the interview they tell me that my English advertising experience won't help much, as England is twenty years behind America in advertising. I suppose they mean this sort of thing." He showed me an ad in an old copy of the London *Evening Standard*. "Seller's Bouillon Cubes . . . As Good as Beef Tea." "In America they never just say something's *as good as* something else. Specially if it's only as good as something so depressing-sounding as beef tea . . ."

One firm suggested that he should submit a sample of "soap opera." "I wonder what on earth that is," Esmond said. "I told him I'm not a bit musical, but he said that didn't matter."

We made some discreet inquiries, and found out that a soap opera is a dramatized serial story, usually about a small town druggist and his family. Esmond worked on one, but his druggist sounded more like a mixture of a British Army Officer and a north of England character actor, with a few "I guesses," "swells" and "lousys" thrown in. When he submitted it, the cruel suggestion was made that he should seek a job as an office boy somewhere where he could "start at the bottom and work up."

In the end, I was the first one to land a job. Having shamelessly invented a long background in the fashion industry in London and Paris, I was hired as a salesgirl at Jane Engel's Dress Shop on Madison Avenue, at twenty dollars a week.

"You should have seen me, starting at the bottoms and working up," I told Esmond after my first day. "Getting the customers' clothes on and off, I mean. Really, it's frightfully difficult, I had no idea. Either the dress gets caught halfway, and the poor thing stands there struggling and protesting with muffled screams, or else *everything* comes off and she's all bare and shivering. I suppose I'll get on to it after a while."

Most of the other salesgirls were young, uniformly pretty, friendly and uncomplicated. They had none of the aura of warped and embittered selfishness which had been such a distressing feature of some of the market researchers. Free and easy and aboveboard, they were full of curiosity about me.

"What does your old man do?"

"*Do?* Well he listens to the wireless most of the time. There's a mag called the *Radio Times* which is his favorite thing. It only comes out once a week, but he's an awfully slow reader so he's generally still poring over it when the next issue comes."

"No, but I mean what does he do, like my old man's a shoe salesman?"

"Goodness, what a terrifying thought! No, I shouldn't think anyone would want him selling their shoes, I'm afraid he's rather a subhuman."

I could see I was rapidly being classified as an odd one, and sought to make recovery.

"Actually he has done a lot of things in his time. He has a dear little gold mine in Canada, staked a claim to it when he was very young, with a person called Harry Oakes who staked the next door one. There isn't actually any gold in my father's, but he and my mother often used to go there for months at a time to dig about hopefully. Then he's frightfully interested in new inventions." I told them about Reno's tank, and about one of the few investments Farve had passed up. Early in the century an inventor approached him with a machine that could make little squares of ice in the home. "Never heard such damned foolishness in my life," Farve had roared. "Feller must be loony. Little squares of ice, indeed!"

The girls were full of sympathy, and assured me that in America who a person's folks are doesn't matter a bit, here I would be judged strictly on my own merits without regard for unfortunate heredity.

Another problem was solved about this time; we managed to find a rented furnished apartment. "Charming one-room walk-up (this is American for a flat without a lift) in picturesque old-world Greenwich Village — quaint unhaunted quarter full of the breath of old New York," Esmond wrote to Peter in best Grant's Tomber's style.

The apartment was a dear little place, more like a bedsitter really, but efficient and comfortable in spite of its tiny size. It was furnished *en écossais* with cheerful plaid covers and curtains. Everything in it was geared for space conservation; the Murphy bed (and, Esmond claimed, even a Murphy kitchen and Murphy bath, both were so tiny and self-effacing), the neat dining nook into which chairs fitted as in a doll's house.

It would do nicely until we found the gold that lay just beneath the pavement in New York. Esmond felt that all we need do now in that regard was to sit back and exploit our Old Worldishness for all it was worth. But shortly after we acquired the apartment, we found to our distress that two could play at that game.

25

ONE DAY I was called to the telephone at Jane Engel's. A deep voice with a strong North of England accent inquired, "Is this Mrs. Romilly?" The caller explained that he always liked to meet newly arrived English people in New York, that he'd seen our name on the passenger list, called the Shelton, and been referred to my place of work. I wished I hadn't given them my number at the Shelton. This sounded like an awful bore. "I can't talk now, I'm working," I told him shortly. He was quite persistent, so finally I gave him our home number, just to get rid of him. I had forgotten the whole incident by the time I arrived home.

Esmond was pacing up and down in the flat in a high state of excitement.

"That man who telephoned — he's absolutely fascinating! I must tell you the whole thing, quickly, because he's coming back here soon. I really think we've hit on something good."

The man told Esmond that he was Mr. Donahue, brother of Steve Donahue, the world-famous racing jockey. He had come round to our flat that afternoon, and Esmond had learned his whole life story.

Mr. Donahue first came to America many years before, as a youth. In a short time he lost over $80,000 at the races. It nearly broke his heart. He returned to Lancashire and his uncle told him: "Go back and beat them at their own dirty game!" He had taken this advice. He now gambled only in the small races, in which he paid the journeyman jockeys $100 apiece to throw the race to the horse he was betting on. In this way he had amassed a huge fortune, and had traveled all over the U.S. He knew people in Florida and Hollywood. He could guarantee to get us the autographed photo of any film star we'd like to name.

"But the really wonderful thing is, he's willing to let us in on the betting," Esmond said. "Of course that's very risky from his point of view, because if too many people get in on it the odds will go down sharply, and the whole thing could be ruined."

"He sounds to me like rather a crook. I don't think we ought to have anything to do with it," I said doubtfully.

"Of course he's a crook! That's the whole point. That's what makes it such a sure thing. He told me that after he lost the eighty thousand he decided he'd 'take a nickel off a dead man's eye.' That's just the way he talks. Here's the way I've got it figured. He probably thinks we've got a lot of money and he's planning to get it away from us. So he'll let us have a couple of small wins, just to get our confidence. Then, when he's got us in the palm of his hand, so to speak, he'll really move in on us."

"Yes, but if we do make a couple of small wins, he really *will* gain our confidence. What then?"

"No, he won't." Esmond was getting impatient. "Don't you see, he's planning to take us for a LONG ride. He's much too important a crook to be interested in some piddling amount. Then when we've won say around $500, we'll simply stop there. The SHORT ride versus the LONG ride, that's what our policy should be."

"Another thing, about the autographed pictures of Hollywood stars. Anyone can get them, just by writing. I know, because Robin and Idden used to send for them all the time."

"Yes, but that's just part of his trying to win our confidence. I wasn't in the least bit taken in by it, naturally. Look here, in a few hours we shall have won over $150."

I suddenly got very suspicious.

"WHAT? You don't mean to say you've given him any of our money?"

"Well, not really. I only gave him a check, and if he turns out to be trying to cheat us I'll stop it at the bank."

"How much did you put on?"

"Forty dollars. We've still got twenty-seven left in case of emergency, if you should get fired or something. If he doesn't show up tonight, I promise I'll stop the check. Look, here are our horses. We've got twenty on Braving Danger in the fourth race, and twenty on Starlight in the sixth." Esmond was rustling the green sheet as he spoke.

"I wonder why he suddenly decided to let us in on it," I said. "After all, he hardly knows us."

"He explained that. It seems he's one of the sort of Englishman abroad that is always on the lookout to help his fellow countrymen. Also, he's very fond of young people, he told me. He hasn't got any children of his own, and he's always regretted it, so he tries to help struggling young couples. Of course, I didn't believe a word of all that; if you ask me he's just out to make a lot of money. That's why I think we should definitely stop after making about $500."

The doorbell rang. "See? There he is now," Esmond said triumphantly.

Steve Donahue's brother was a short, stocky man with a

weatherbeaten face and sad, kind eyes. Esmond introduced us and made some drinks.

Mr. Donahue sat heavily down on one of the kitchen chairs, shaking his head gloomily.

"I don't know what happened in that last race, that I don't," he said, in his soft Lancashire brogue.

"Oh — we didn't win, then?" Esmond and I asked together.

"You won $70. Braving Danger came in. But it seems we were doublecrossed in the sixth race. If I ever catch up with that jockey, I'll wring his neck, that I will."

"Seventy dollars! That's really wonderful. When do we get it?" Esmond asked.

"Pay-off's tomorrow. I'll meet you at Jack Dempsey's bar, around noon. Jack's a very dear friend of mine, a very close acquaintance, that he is. Let's see; I only made $4500 today. Should have been over $10,000. That dirty, doublecrossing jockey . . ."

Mr. Donahue stayed for a long time. He told us about his sad love life, many years ago. He had loved a lass who worked in a mill in Wigan. He had never married her, but he'd had a daughter off her, and both mother and daughter had died shortly after. He told us all about his racing life in America. He owned several stables of race horses in various parts of the U.S.

"In England, racing is the sport of kings; it's a king's sport, that it is," he told us. "In this dirty country, it's as crooked as a nine-dollar bill. It fair breaks your heart to think of it."

"You talk just like someone out of one of Damon Runyon's books," said Esmond. "I've read a lot of his stuff."

"Damon Runyon! He's a very dear friend of mine. Would you like to meet him?" asked Mr. Donahue. He also offered to introduce us to an English woman artist who was doing a portrait of Brenda Frazier. "She's six feet two, but she's a magnificent artist.

"I've taken a real fancy to you kids, that I have," he said. "You don't mind if I call you 'kids,' do you?"

Before he left, he invited us to go with him to the opening of the New York race track and to run down to Florida for a weekend with him later on.

We sat and roared with laughter after he went. What a fantastic stroke of luck, to be let in on this honest-to-God underworld racket, after only a few weeks in New York!

We telephoned Dave Scherman to tell him we had some exciting news. He came round right away. Esmond quickly outlined the events of the day.

"Why, you poor God-forsaken suckers," was Dave's first comment. "That guy's probably a first class con man. He'll take your shirt . . ."

"Of course, we realize he's a con man. That's why we are in such an excellent position to make some money out of this thing." Esmond explained the theory of the long and short rides so convincingly that Dave was soon anxiously suggesting that he should join in with us as a partner.

"I'm sure Mr. Donahue would love to have you in," I said. "He is awfully fond of young people. Perhaps you could get a few days off from *Life* and come down to Florida when he takes us."

It was agreed that Dave would call us the following evening to make joint plans for future bets.

I extracted a promise from Esmond to bet only our winnings of $70 on tomorrow's race, and to recover our initial investment of $40.

I couldn't wait to tell the other girls at Jane Engel's about our wonderful good fortune. They crowded round, begging to be let in on it.

"But we promised not to tell anyone the names of the horses," I explained. "It has to be kept a terrific secret, otherwise the odds would get ruined."

They pressed money on me. "We'll trust you. Put on $5 for me . . ." "I'll have $2 on, you don't have to tell the names . . ."

I phoned Esmond that afternoon to hear all about the meeting at Dempsey's bar.

"He really does know Jack Dempsey," Esmond told me. "He introduced me to him as Lord Redesdale's nephew!"

"What did Jack Dempsey say?"

"He said 'How do you do,' of course," Esmond answered impatiently. "And he hoped we liked America."

"I don't see how that proves Donahue knows him. What else could Dempsey have said? Anyway, what about the money?"

"Well, Mr. Donahue didn't actually have it with him. There was a little misunderstanding; he thought we wanted to re-invest the whole amount in today's race, so he didn't bother to bring it. I explained we'd decided only to bet the $70 winnings, and he's going to come around at three to return the $40."

I arrived back at the flat rather late, having spent some time looking in shop windows to decide what new clothes to buy with our winnings.

Esmond didn't answer the doorbell, so I let myself in with a key. There was a sound of running water. Esmond was standing in the shower. He looked as though he had been there for hours. Water was dribbling down his face, contorting his expression. "Don't come near me," he said. "Don't touch me." He spoke with concentrated misery.

I knew at once.

"Mr. Donahue" had never shown up. It had been a very short ride, indeed.

26

THAT SPRING the news from Europe was unrelievedly bad. In March, Germany invaded Czechoslovakia, Franco gained final victory with the fall of Madrid, and English war preparations began in earnest. From what we could gather from the newspapers and letters from friends, the preparations were marked by inefficiency, lack of enthusiasm, and uncertainty as to who the enemy would be.

"The National Government, far from having abandoned 'appeasement,' are working to extend it to open collaboration with Nazi Germany," a friend wrote. "Hitler would only be prepared to fight against the Soviet Union if France and England openly joined him; and this I think they are ready to do."

This depressing analysis of the situation was backed up by news stories. The Soviet Union urgently renewed its pleas for reopening discussions with England and France on collective security against Nazi aggression. The Chamberlain Government replied by sending to Moscow an envoy described in the press as a "foreign office clerk," with no power to negotiate anything.

Conscription was introduced in England. Some of the most unlikely people were turning up in the Army. Letters from home gave occasional news of these.

Philip Toynbee wrote us about a mutual acquaintance of ours who was a well-known London homosexual. As a young officer of "the new type," he had been required to write an official report on the visit of a captain to his regiment. "Captain —— is an utter charmer," the report began.

Esmond was jubilant at having escaped the "call-up." He wrote sardonically to Philip:

"Well, sir, I have this message to you and the young men like you in England today. It is this: Do your duty. Don't be a shirker. Every able-bodied man can find some way of serving his country at this critical time, be it in the Territorial Army, Navy Reserve or Air Guard. Less talk of isms and politics — more of the shoulder-to-the-wheel and no-questions-asked attitude ..."

About this time Esmond sold an article to *The Commentator* entitled "Escape from England." He described the "atmosphere of grim depression and resignation" of England in the spring of 1939:

People in England aren't excited or hysterical any more at the idea of the coming war. People are adjusting themselves to a kind of half-life — a life where it's no good making plans, no good thinking at all of the future ... People don't talk about politics very much, either. What's the use? No one can feel any more that they have the remotest control over what is happening. Their only role now is to do what they're told ...

He traced the machinations of the Cliveden Set from their support of Franco, "a gentleman fighting to regain some of the lost wealth and privileges of his class," and their encouragement of Mussolini's invasion of Abyssinia, to the betrayal of Czechoslovakia at Munich. He quoted typical dinner-table talk at gatherings of rich conservatives: "We could learn a great deal from Hitler in this country . . . we need someone like Hitler over here." Contrasting this with Rotherhithe Street meetings for Spanish and Czech relief, he told of the long, losing fight put up by millions of English people for an anti-fascist foreign policy.

In conclusion he wrote: "After escaping from England, what shall I do now if war breaks out? The answer is that I shall go back . . . to fight for the grey of British Imperialism allied to Polish and Rumanian fascism against the black of German-Italian fascism."

We were bent on cramming in as much as possible of life, new people, new scenes, before the inevitable day should roll around.

Early in April, a man we'd met once or twice at parties rang up Esmond to say that he knew of a possible job in a new advertising agency, Channing and Floyd.

"He asked me how much salary I'd require, and I told him $50 a week."

"Oh, Esmond, how could you. Now you'll never get the job. You should have said $25." Until now, $25 had been Esmond's top figure when offering his services for sale.

But the incredible thing was that the man had insisted that no one could possibly live on $50, and Esmond should go for an interview and ask for $125. However, when the time came, Esmond swallowed hard and said that $100 to start would be just fine. To our incredulous amazement, the vice-president of the company agreed readily.

We learned much later that the advertising agency had been set up by the tax accountants of a young playboy millionaire. The express purpose of the company was to lose as much money as possible, thereby reducing the millionaire's income below a certain tax bracket. By an amazing stroke of luck,

we became the unwitting beneficiaries of this noble endeavor.
Esmond wrote to Philip:

> After a great deal of picking, stumbling and scraping, I've
> at last hit on the hidden treasure we came all this way to find.
> As a matter of fact, the story of this is such fairy-book pauper-
> prince immigrant stuff that you may even snort derisively. But
> in actual fact, we had $27 of our money left when I got a job
> at one hundred dollars a week salary. In other words we are
> rich. Isn't that amazing? I'm sure it has a moral somewhere,
> though it looks like a piece of pure farce.
>
> Ah, Philip (all this in Toynbee quotation marks, you under-
> stand), Ah, Philip, I've known the bitterness and the worm-
> wood and the gall, I've known those hard cruel pavements,
> I've known those closed doors, that "Nothing today, Nothing
> today," over and over again till the words seemed to be part of
> the hot sun staring up at me cruelly, mocking me, shouting at
> me from the pavement, screaming the words in my ears till I
> wanted to scream them back. . . .
>
> I.e., I tried to get a job in lots of places and failed. Now I'm
> getting $100 a week, and that's the end of the story.

Since the agency had hardly any accounts, Esmond put in
very little time at the office. The vice-president had a pleasant
habit of leaving for the weekend on Friday mornings or even
on Thursday afternoons, and returning after a late lunch on
Monday. Esmond explained to me that it would be inappro-
priate for him to work harder than the vice-president, whose
responsibilities were so much greater.

In the evenings he would show me the slim results of his
few hours spent at work. "Look, what do you think of this
slogan: 'It's great to sin on Gilbey's Gin.' Pretty snappy,
isn't it? A far cry from 'As good as beef tea'!"

We conscientiously banked Esmond's salary each week and
continued to live on my $20. Our goal now was to build a

big reserve so that in a few months we could start on our Grand Tour of the United States.

There is an apartment building in New York overlooking the river called "1 Beekman Place." Towering above a brawling slum, it is said to have been the inspiration for the movie *Dead End*. The inhabitants of 1 Beekman Place apparently get a delightful thrill from picking their way through garbage-strewn streets, past noisy gangs of street urchins, to arrive in the refined silence of the discreetly ornate lobby of their dwelling. Respectful doormen and uniformed elevator boys bow the way to the fantastically plush apartments.

Shortly after Esmond got his $100 a week job, I was summoned to one of these apartments. Its occupant, a domineering, fortyish blonde called Miss Warren, described herself as a "bachelor girl," the prototype of American career woman on the make.

Miss Warren was in charge of one of the concessions at the New York World's Fair of 1939, and she now proposed to hire me as a sales girl. She lost no time in "placing" herself for my benefit as a thoroughly upper-drawer type of purest English ancestry, and did her best to draw me out about my own connections.

"Have you ever been to Glamis Castle?" she asked with a searching look, in the first five minutes of our conversation.

"Yes, we went there once in the winter, when the family was away and you could see all over the place for a shilling," I answered innocently.

"Oh, I meant when *dear* Lady Strathmore was there . . ."

After cautioning me about being careful to "get acquainted with the Right People in New York," and explaining that once I got used to American accents I should easily be able to distinguish the Right People by the way they talk ("just like in England"), she offered me the job. I readily accepted.

Miss Warren's concession at the fair was a Scottish tweed shoppe, part of Ye Merrie England Village. Ye Merrie England Village was situated in a grubby corner of that flashy, dusty vista of stage-set buildings which made up the World's Fair. The Tudor style booths, cottages and hot dog stands looked no more and no less like Tudor England than the main street of Stratford-on-Avon. A barker dressed as a London beef-eater droned endlessly into a megaphone: "Authennic, folks! Authennic! Better than Billy Rose's Aquacade! Authennic corner of li'l old England!" Twice daily, a group of bagpipers would wend their squeaky way down our part of the fairway, emitting fearful (but "authennic") sounds of disharmony.

Our sales staff consisted of Miss Warren, a couple of phony Scottish lassies with rather incongruous accents, and myself. At Miss Warren's request we all wore plaid cotton dresses bought in Ohrbach's basement. Miss Warren gave daily pep talks, mostly addressed to the not inconsiderable problem of sifting out the Best People ("people who appreciate the Finer Things") from among the surging crowds.

"One good way to tell is by their shoes," she would patiently explain. "Don't be taken in by their hairdos. Shoes and handbags are the most telling." She also noted that women wearing white shoes and gloves are apt to be richer than others because white things are so expensive to keep clean.

Esmond would make occasional forays into the Merrie England Village. On these occasions, much to the annoyance of Miss Warren, he would get down on his hands and knees and pretend to be scouting out the "Best People's" shoes for my benefit.

As the hot, dusty summer wore on, things began to fall apart rather badly at Ye Merrie England Village. People went around accusing each other of "acting un-English" and thereby ruining the authentic atmosphere. Ye Olde Shelle

Shoppe, down the street from us, was said to be on the verge of bankruptcy. The barker's voice took on a shrill note of despair as the thinning fair crowds resolutely thronged in the opposite direction, toward Billy Rose's Aquacade.

Miss Warren got engaged to a Bachelor Boy of uncertain age called Honey Bunny. Honey Bunny often came to Ye Merrie England Village, and he and Miss Warren would talk baby talk and read passages to each other out of Christopher Robin.

The smell of cotton candy and hot dogs and the sound and sight of Miss Warren and Honey Bunny were getting to be rather too much for me. I was relieved when Esmond announced that he had been fired. It seemed that the millionaire backer of the agency had succeeded, with Esmond's help, in losing his quota for that year, and the company was being disbanded.

Now that Esmond had lost his job, there was nothing to keep us in New York. We had several hundred dollars saved up, I said goodbye to Miss Warren and the Scotch lassies, and we began to plan in earnest for the Grand Tour of the U.S.

27

WE PLANNED the Grand Tour only in roughest outline, to include the obvious essentials. There had to be enough flexibility to allow for any fascinating contingency, for any chance opportunity that might turn up along the way. We might stay in any given place a week, six months, or a year, depending on what sort of jobs we found and on what sort of people we met there. Our tour would begin with a few weeks' vacation in New England.

Esmond listed a few of the obvious goals, tracing our probable route with the help of a map: "Washington D.C., get jobs in the New Deal. New Orleans or Miami, something in restaurant business. Texas: Cowhands. Hollywood: Be movie stars, or at least extras. San Francisco: Longshoremen. Chicago: Underworld."

From friends in New York we got another batch of letters of introduction, this time to people in all parts of the States. One of these was to a movie magnate in Hollywood. Esmond spent hours concocting an improbable background with a French theatrical touring company, and sent this in to the movie magnate, together with a snapshot of himself in which

I also happened to be. To his extreme annoyance a curt note
came back: "We do not think that your experience in theater
would warrant consideration of you for a job with our company. However, your wife appears to be quite photogenic.
If she is in Hollywood, we will be happy to have her come
in for a test."

A letter to the Jay Six Cattle Company of Benson, Arizona,
produced better results. We got a return reply from Mr.
Speiden, the president: "If you two young folks come West
in your adventurings, stop in here. We can possibly give you
jobs punching cows, mixing drinks for me."

This last gave Esmond an idea. "You know, I've always
secretly rather longed to be a bartender," he said. Riding the
bus to work he had noticed a small sign on a Broadway building advertising a bartenders' school. He investigated, and
found that a "quickie" course lasting one week was offered
for $30. The course was guaranteed to teach trainees to make
"over one hundred different drinks."

Esmond enrolled immediately, and set about with his usual
single-minded determination to become an expert bartender.
The "professor" gave him many useful tips: after the third
martini the customer won't know the difference if you make
it mostly with water — but be sure to do this *under* the bar
so that he won't see; if you want to save enough liquor to have
a drink for yourself without the boss knowing, save it on the
frappés, which can be mostly ice; avoid putting your thumb
on the edge of the glass in case the customer is particular.

Esmond insisted on bringing his newly learned techniques
into the home, with the result that our friends were treated
to a succession of disgusting concoctions known as Pink
Ladies, Horse's Necks, Clover Clubs, Cherry Smashes. The
most nauseating of these, and the one of which Esmond was
proudest, was known as a *pousse café*. It was made in a pony

glass, and required knowledge of the specific gravity of seven different kinds of liqueurs. The finished product, with grenadine at the bottom and brandy on the top, had a rainbow-like appearance and tasted like cheap candy.

We bought an ancient Ford for $40. Its owner assured us that it was accustomed to long trips, having crossed the country many times, and that we should have no fear of a breakdown. The only thing wrong with it was that it needed to have the water replenished about every ten miles. Esmond bought a handsome chrome-topped cocktail shaker for this purpose. Sometimes, if we forgot about the water too long, smoke would start to belch out of the motor, indicating that a merry blaze had started under the hood, and on these occasions our emergency water supply would have to be used to douse the fire. But on the whole it was a very serviceable car, and we felt that its oddly blotched, green and brown appearance would blend nicely with the quaint New England byways on which our attention was now focused.

We had consulted friends on appropriate articles to take on the New England vacation. They told us that life in those parts in summertime was extremely informal, we shouldn't need much, just gray flannels and cottons. Esmond translated this advice with great literalness. He left his only suit in New York and packed nothing but underwear, a change of shirts, bathing trunks and the tuxedo, which was brought along in anticipation of a rich, relaxed weekend at the country mansion of Mrs. Curry Appleton.

We had met Mrs. Appleton in New York during the summer. She was an elderly, rather intellectual lady of enormous wealth, derived from the production of certain indispensable bathroom fixtures. We had been told that Mrs. Appleton had quite a penchant for young authors, artists, and poets, and that she had even been known to pay a fee on occasion to foreign

visitors in these fields of endeavor for an evening lecture to
her guests. We had visited her one evening in her immense
Park Avenue apartment. To our great annoyance, as we were
arriving we met W. H. Auden and Christopher Isherwood on
their way out. Esmond had known them quite well in London, but as though by common consent both they and we confined our greetings to a distant bow as we passed in Mrs.
Appleton's foyer. "Trying to muscle in on our racket! They've
got a hell of a nerve," Esmond muttered. Judging by their
expressions, the thought was fully reciprocated.

Mrs. Appleton's butler was an enormously tall and large
Englishman by the name of Horton. "He's quite a character,"
Mrs. Appleton confided. "He used to work for the Duke of
Norfolk before he came here."

Horton fixed us with a look strangely similar to the one
we had noted on the faces of Auden and Isherwood. His eyes
roved appraisingly over Esmond's tuxedo. Did they contain
just the hint of a threat: "If you try to queer my pitch, young
feller-me-lad, you'll be sorry. English tailoring, my eye!"

A very happy outcome of the evening had been the invitation to spend a weekend at the end of July at Mrs. Appleton's
Woods Hole estate. This invitation quickly assumed the proportions of the focal point of our New England trip, the pot
of gold at the end of the rainbow.

We left New York at the end of June. Our itinerary had
been carefully planned to include as many stopovers at people's
houses as could humanly (and geographically) be arranged.

During the next few weeks, we stayed with a university
professor in Boston, young commuters in Hartford, a magazine
editor in Providence.

For the first time since our arrival, something of the American national character began to emerge for us. Much later,
Esmond wrote to me from England: "After the wonderful sim-

ple nice naïveté of Americans it was rather fascinating to get
back to the subtleties and nastiness and undercurrents of a lot
of the sort of English people we know, where every remark
doesn't mean what it seems to but is a sort of a rapier thrust
of some kind." Actually, the "wonderful simple nice naïveté"
charmed and delighted us. It had been present in the newspaper people and intellectuals we'd met, in my co-workers at
Jane Engel's, in the hitchhikers we picked up, even in a distorted way in the Park Avenue snobs.

The illusion, created by a common language, that Americans
are somehow "the same" as English, or even close cousins, was
being dissipated. We began to pick up on the very real pride
of country and talk of "democracy" and "freedom" that we
encountered everywhere. No longer did the anxious question,
"Do you like America?" strike us as a little outlandish and
odd. We began to realize that people asked it because they
really wanted to know.

If some of our new friends seemed a trifle overearnest and
even humorless about their country, at the same time they displayed a kind of enthusiasm and alertness to which we responded wholeheartedly. We were impressed by their unbounded kindness and hospitality, by the streamlined efficiency
of their houses, by their rather wild, uninhibited children.

We tried to visualize the fate of an American couple who
might set out to see England in the way we were seeing
America. "In the first place, it's inconceivable that anyone
would ask them to stay unless they'd known them for ages,"
Esmond said, "and probably not even then if they didn't know
their parents." The freezing houses and often horrid food
to which our mythical American couple would have been subjected, in the unlikely event that they were asked to stay,
was a gloomy thought to dwell on.

The month of July dragged pleasantly on. We saw miles

and miles of the pretty New England countryside, and managed to avoid some of the more Grant's Tombing experiences such as King's Chapel Burying Ground in Boston and the Radcliffe campus.

Finally, on the appointed day, we arrived at Woods Hole.

In the long shadows cast by the late afternoon sun, it looked like an English seaside village. Mrs. Appleton had given no further address or directions, but the first passer-by pointed out the way to the Appleton estate.

We easily found the driveway, and were about to enter through the big swinging gates when a large uniformed cop loomed to block our passage.

"You can't come in here. This is a private residence. Can't you read the sign?" He pointed to a Gothic lettered legend: "Trespassers and picnickers keep out."

"But we've come to spend the weekend with Mrs. Appleton."

"Go on! Tell me another."

We finally persuaded the cop to telephone from the lodge to the house to confirm the fact that we were expected.

Horton, tall, proud, and splendid, admitted us, treated us to one of his quizzical stares, and showed us into the drawing room. "Mr. and Mrs. Romilly!" he announced in a tone overlaid with sarcasm.

Mrs. Appleton, well corseted in a beautiful gray linen suit, greeted us kindly. Four or five other guests in equally faultless country attire were having cocktails. We apologized for being a bit dirty, and explained we had been traveling for several weeks. Soon Mrs. Appleton arose and announced that dinner would be in an hour.

We escaped thankfully to our room, and I quickly unpacked. The tuxedo, now brought out for the first time since we had left New York, had deteriorated badly. It was a mass of tiny wrinkles, a mere wreck of its former self. "I'm afraid its basic six-dollarishness is beginning to show up," said Esmond.

We rang for Horton.

He appeared, breathing heavily, his whole demeanor seeming to say, "I've got your number."

"I wonder if you'd mind pressing this for us," I asked him. "I'm afraid it got a little crumpled in the suitcase."

For the first time, looking at the tuxedo, Horton relaxed and began to twinkle a little.

"It looks like a very pressing job," he said, and bore it off.

Esmond was happily scrubbing up in the shower when Mrs. Appleton appeared at our bedroom door.

"I just wanted to tell Esmond not to bother to dress for dinner. Tell him to wear a dark suit or a pair of white flannels."

"Oh — but Mrs. Appleton — could you wait a minute?"

I relayed the message to Esmond, and heard him spluttering with frustration in the shower.

"Mrs. Appleton," I was back at the door, speaking very carefully and loudly, "he hasn't *got* a dark suit, or a pair of white flannels."

"Oh, that's all right. Tell him anything will do. Just a dark suit or a pair of white flannels . . ." she repeated, and was gone.

Horton had done surprisingly well with the very pressing job, but Esmond was thoroughly trapped. This was one of those few occasions when he seemed genuinely embarassed and ill at ease. I overheard a guest in dazzling white flannels comment to another, "That's the English for you. They always dress for dinner, even in the darkest outposts of empire."

The next morning, when Horton appeared in our room with breakfast, he unbent all the way.

"I know the likes of you don't belong with the likes of 'er," he nodded in the direction of Mrs. Appleton's room.

He sat on our bed and we chatted. He confessed that he had originally been a wrestler in Birmingham, and that a cousin in America had written suggesting that he should get in on the English butler racket. His position with Mrs. Appleton had been his first job.

28

MARTHA'S VINEYARD is a short boat ride across the sea from Woods Hole. Shady forest paths, half hidden by underbrush, lead to innumerable little cabins and cottages, built with studied rusticity but sumptuously equipped for rental to summer guests. What the New Yorkers call "real country." To one of these cabins Esmond and I now repaired.

We were met by Seldon Rodman and his wife, with whom we had arranged to spend some time on Martha's Vineyard. Seldon was at that time co-editor of *Common Sense,* one of the many small, leftish liberal magazines that flourished in America in those days. Its program was described on the inside cover: "a monthly magazine of positive social action devoted to the elimination of war and poverty through democratic planning for abundance."

Seldon was a wiry, slender man with unusually dark and intense eyes. He was a few years older than Esmond, and about as different from him in all ways as anyone could be.

We sat around on conveniently placed tree stumps near the cabin, drinking wine and burying our bare toes in the leafy dust. "And you should have *seen* this butler. About as big as Joe Louis. But he turned out to be really terribly nice. When we left, I offered him a dollar, as a tip, you know. He gave a terrific wink, and said, 'Keep it, young feller! You need it more than I do.'" Esmond was regaling the Rodmans with an account of our weekend adventures, his eyes gleefully sparkling, flashing a knowing look at me from time to time as he added a bit of embellishment to make the story even better. Seldon listened intently, asking a question here and there, and occasionally laughing the creaking-door, almost painful laugh of one who does not laugh often. He was plainly falling under the peculiar spell of Esmond's charm, good humor and ability as a raconteur.

Later on it was Seldon's turn, and in the gathering dusk he produced and read the manuscripts of several poems he had just finished. We were back in more familiar territory, the land of thinkers and writers, the American Rotherhithe Streeters. Merrie England Village, the advertising agency, the Curry Appletons had reverted to mere backdrops, slightly unreal situations that could have been scenes from a particularly vivid movie or novel.

We found that Martha's Vineyard was a summer retreat frequented by people of a great variety of opinions on the left. There were Communists, Trotskyites, independent socialists of all kinds, and even one or two rather moth-eaten anarchists. Arguments raged on all kinds of topics, from art forms to politics, from theories of psychoanalysis to someone's latest novel.

The Rodmans' cabin, where we were staying, was divided into two furnished bed-sitting rooms, bath and kitchen. After a couple of days, Esmond decided that it would be cheaper if we officially checked out of the cabin, thereby saving on room rent. As the main office was some distance away, we were able to continue actually sleeping in the cabin without attracting attention. Each morning we stole quietly out of the cabin, carrying empty suitcases down the wooded paths, and came back by the office as jauntily and ostentatiously as possible, hoping that we looked as though we had been camping somewhere and had just come to spend the day. The Rodmans were delighted but a little shocked by this arrangement. It seemed to confirm their opinion of Esmond, and to lend credibility to his fantastic stories of past exploits.

The days dragged on most pleasantly, punctuated by the casual housekeeping at the cabin, hikes through the woods, hours spent lying on the soft white beach. But in the background there was always the radio, thundering out news of the approaching war . . .

It was rather like being at a really wonderful party when you have a very bad earache. All your friends are there, the conversation is fascinating. But all of a sudden that horrible twinge of pain surges over you again. You have another drink, are getting pleasantly high; but in the background your ear is hurting like mad. Perhaps you shouldn't have come in the first place . . .

Lying in the sand, in the blazing sun, we heard the astounding news over the Rodmans' portable radio: "Nonaggression pact concluded by Soviet and Nazi governments . . . Ribbentrop in Moscow . . . *Daily Worker* silent . . ."

Political arguments raged louder than ever. It was reported that shortly after the news broke, a leading Communist had run into a well-known Trotskyite who had just come to Martha's Vineyard from New York. "What would you say if Hitler and Stalin were to sign a pact of friendship and nonaggression?" asked the Trotskyite. "Impossible. It simply couldn't happen," answered the Communist, whereupon the Trotskyite triumphantly produced the latest *New York Times* with banner headlines proclaiming the pact. The Communists on the island seemed stunned by the news. Esmond took on all comers to defend the realism of the Soviet position.

"For years and years they've pressed for genuine collective security. All this summer they were trying to conclude a pact with England, aimed at stopping Hitler. But the grand strategy of Chamberlain and Daladier has been to engineer an attack by Hitler against the Soviet Union. So, if Hitler carries out his threats and marches against Poland, what do you think the English and French will do then? Sit tight, and hope he keeps going east, of course."

Esmond was equally impatient with those who cried "betrayal" and with the orthodox Communists who, once recovered from the shock, began to interpret the news as meaning that the days of anti-fascism were over and to urge what they called "peace" with Hitler. We heard that Harry Pollitt had been removed from his position as secretary of the English Communist Party for putting out a leaflet, considered ill-timed by his colleagues, calling for aid to Poland against Hitler. Esmond fumed at what he considered the Communists' poverty of political understanding. He was convinced the greatest danger now was that British and French imperialism would fail to prosecute the war fully, that it might still be turned into a fascist crusade against Communism with the Western democracies either sitting on the sidelines or actively coming in on Hitler's side. When the anti-climactic announcement finally came that England and France had declared war, nothing happened to dispel this view. The blitzkrieg against Poland was proceeding in full fury. England and France made not a move.

Letters from home gave us a picture of gloom, low morale, confused outlook. The left had become badly split and disorganized following the Nazi-Soviet pact. The long-awaited war against fascism had finally come in a situation where unity of the anti-fascists no longer existed, and to an England ruled by the pro-fascist Chamberlain Government. Someone in London sent us a copy of *The Week*, Claud Cockburn's very informative "inside" political news sheet. We read:

> There are those in "high places" in London who regard it as axiomatic that the war must not be conducted in such a manner as to lead to a total breakdown of the German regime and the emergence of some kind of "radical" government in Germany. These circles are certainly in indirect touch with certain German military circles — and the intermediary is the American Embassy in London . . .

Esmond's analysis was that so long as Chamberlain remained in power there would be no real war effort, and that in fact some further doublecross might easily be in the making. The story in *The Week* was supported by other rumors of continued negotiations between the Cliveden Set and their counterparts in German industrialist circles. After long discussion, we decided not to go back home until the fighting really started and we knew what side we were going to be on. We would continue our tour of the U.S., keep an eye on the news, and make our decisions as the situation developed.

Shortly after the outbreak of war, Winston Churchill became a member of the Chamberlain cabinet. While we were still at Martha's Vineyard Esmond wrote an article about his uncle for *Common Sense*, prophetically titled, "England's Next Prime Minister." He pointed out that Churchill, "in the political wilderness" between the two world wars as leader of a small minority group of extreme right wing conservatives, was likely to make a sensational comeback — "he is waiting confidently for full power to fall into his hands." While the American press were puzzling over the "enigma" of a Churchill recently allied with the Left on all foreign policy issues,

Esmond explained the origins of this alliance. He portrayed Churchill as a thoroughly consistent champion of British imperialist interests:

Churchill's rise in prestige can be exactly traced to the growth of the issue of British Imperialism versus German and Italian expansion. This issue has, of course, nothing whatever to do with the thing called "Collective Security" or the issue of "Democracy" versus "Fascism." . . . Today, with Churchill's star in the ascendant again, let no one imagine he will lead a popular front government. He may get the support of Labor, to be sure — what else can Labor do but support the man who is going to fight Hitler? — but it will be on his terms and his alone.

29

WE HAD TWO major objectives in mind for our stay in Washington. The first was to try to unravel some of the mysteries of American politics, about which we understood almost nothing. When Roosevelt had first been elected in 1932 there were those political analysts who predicted that he would lead America to fascism, and that the New Deal would prove to be nothing but a fascist labor front. In the intervening years it had become clear how wrong they were, that the New Deal was not only a tremendous force for progress but that it had in all probability saved America from a fate similar to Germany's. Yet we were puzzled about the lack of a labor party in America, and the fact that except for the Communists there was no political party with a program of socialism. As for the Democrats and Republicans, we found them confusing in the extreme. John L. Lewis was labeled "Red" by most of the newspapers — yet he was a Republican; Roosevelt was a Democrat, yet a large number of Democrats in Congress seemed to regard him as the devil incarnate. We hoped for enlightenment on all these confusing questions in the nation's capital, where we had a number of people to look up.

Our second objective was to find some way of replenishing our dwindling cash supply. Somehow, in spite of such economy measures as getting out of paying rent on Martha's Vineyard, we had managed to spend an awful lot during the summer.

We found a cheap furnished room, and devoted our attention to the Help Wanted columns of a Washington daily. As usual, they were depressingly full of "experienced mechanic wanted," "tool and die maker," "carpenters," "house painters," "statistician — college grad.," but Esmond soon came across one which he felt was a perfect description of himself: "Young man, must be intelligent, alert, ambitious, personable. $50 to $60 a week. Ample opportunity for advancement. NO SKILLS OR EXPERIENCE NEEDED." The last words seemed particularly apt and encouraging. We wondered what the job could possibly be. Perhaps some sort of confidential work for one of the Congressional committees? Or researcher on the staff of someone like Drew Pearson? Or working on the campaign committee of some influential politician?

Esmond took immense pains with his appearance, at the same time hurrying frantically for fear that others with no skills or experience would be chosen ahead of him. I was quickly gathering together copies of his articles and job references in case he should need them.

He was gone for most of the day, and finally returned carrying a large cardboard briefcase, with a sheepish-but-pleased expression on his face. "Well, I got the job," he announced. "Wonderful! But what is it? When do you start? Is it going to be $50 or $60?" "Well — wait a minute. I can't exactly explain right off what it is. Let me tell everything just the way it happened, otherwise you won't understand. It isn't *exactly* the kind of thing we thought . . ."

Esmond had arrived at the address given in the ad, and

to his surprise was the only applicant to show up. A receptionist showed him to a small waiting room. There were no clues of any kind to the sort of business transacted there, but on the walls there were several pictures of beautiful ladies, with particular attention focused upon that portion of them between thigh and ankle. He had just about concluded that the job was that of talent scout for a burlesque theater when the manager called him in.

"First off, he didn't say what the job was," Esmond explained. "He kept talking about how it's a nationally advertised product. Every time I tried to get him to explain the job, he sort of slid off the subject, and kept talking about the money one could make and the advancement possibilities. It began to sound quite mysterious and fascinating. He didn't ask to see the job references, so I offered them to him, and he looked them over carefully and said he thought I should be just fine for the job he had in mind. Then he said, would I like to see some of the national advertising? He showed me some copies of *Life* and the *Saturday Evening Post,* and it turns out that the product is Silkform stockings. Also, I don't know yet whether it will be $50 or $60 because they don't actually pay any wages, just commissions on the sales one makes."

While selling silk stockings door to door was a bit of a comedown from the glamorous possibilities that had occurred to us when we first read the ad, it would still provide some sort of income for the duration of our stay in Washington. After his interview with the manager, Esmond had spent several hours with one of the crack salesmen, who had been enlisted to show him the ropes.

Esmond was fascinated by the subtle refinements and advanced techniques used by Silkform. Years before, when he was about sixteen, he had been a door-to-door stocking salesman in England. But the ad through which he had got that job had simply stated: "Door-to-door salesman needed. No salary. Commission only." Instruction in selling techniques had been limited to the one injunction, "Get your foot in the door and keep it there. Don't be talked out of a sale. . . ."

"In this grea-a-a-a-t country we have the know-how. Little Old England sure has a long ways to catch up," Esmond exulted in his American politician's voice. "Come with me tomorrow and I'll show you how it's done. You'll be simply fascinated by it. Wait till you hear all the new expressions I've learned. Perhaps, after you've learned the routine, they'll give you a job, too."

The selling territory assigned to Esmond was in a middle class residential district of Washington not far from where we were living. Esmond opened up the cardboard briefcase and explained the workings of the elaborate kit — for the use of which he had been induced to leave a $5 deposit with the Silkform Company. "The first day, we don't do any actual selling at all. We do a thing called softening up the territory," he explained. "That's done with the magnificent free gifts. Actually, each salesman has to pay for his supply of free gifts, and they cost only one-half cent each, so I'm afraid they are not really terribly magnificent." I came across some penciled sheets in the kit, notes in Esmond's peculiar and almost il-legible handwriting: "All made different by creator," "fasten support," "big toe sightseeing — hard time," "careful house-keeper," "woven exclusively, discriminating American woman," "economy size package . . ."

"What's all this?" I asked.

"Oh, you'll see. Part of the tried and true Silkform method; I copied them down from the salesman's patter. Listen care-fully tomorrow, it'll all come clear to you then."

Before setting out to soften up the territory, we agreed that

I should be introduced as Esmond's assistant, Miss Freeman, rather than as his wife, on the theory that this would sound more businesslike. I was to keep the record of sales interviews on the special form provided by Silkform.

Esmond was careful never to vary from the strategy outlined for him by the Silkform supersalesman. "After all, they've worked it out very carefully over years and years, in the ha-a-a-rd school of Amurrican experience."

We approached our first door, and rang the bell. A woman opened the door, and immediately Esmond was suffused with false charm and obsequiousness.

"Good *morning*," he said, grinning from ear to ear and almost bowing. "We have been given your name by the vice-president of our company, who wishes you to receive one of our magnificent free gifts. This card will entitle you to the gift, Absolutely Free of Charge. No obligation whatsoever. Please put it in a *very safe place,* we wouldn't want you to mislay it, would we? Oh . . ." (as though filled with confusion at the oversight). We forgot to introduce ourselves. I am Mr. Romilly, and this is my assistant, Miss Freeman. And your name?"

"Mrs. Robinson . . . What is this? Are you selling something?"

Esmond was at once overcome with surprise and chuckles at the very thought.

"Why, *certainly not,* Mrs. Robinson. Well, thanks very much. We'll be back tomorrow about this time with your free gift. Goodbye! Put the card in a safe place!" and we backed quickly down the stairs. "Did you get the name? Mrs. Robinson. Be sure to keep track so we can call them all by their right names tomorrow."

We kept at it for several hours, and gradually the interview record filled up. Never once did anyone challenge the fact that their name was supposed to have been given to us by the vice-president of something, and yet we had to ask them what it was. Never once did Esmond give them time to ask what vice-president of what company. In fact, several times he simply said, "We've been given your name by the vice-president," thus leaving the vague impression that John Nance Garner had suggested we call. "We're not supposed to mention Silkform until the very end of the second interview; that would be fatal, it would give away the whole show at once," he explained. If a man answered the door, we'd simply excuse ourselves and say we had come to the wrong place.

The next day's work was more complicated. By now we were armed with a list of names and addresses of the people with whom we had left cards.

"Good *morning*, Mrs. Robinson! And how are *we* today?" Esmond was almost falling over himself with the sort of controlled joy-of-living attitude that he imagined best suited to this work. He didn't give Mrs. Robinson time to answer, or to shut the door, but continued, rather sternly, "Yesterday we left you a card, entitling you to one of our magnificent, free gifts. GET THAT CARD —" his bearing suddenly became authoritative, almost military. He pointed over her shoulder into the dark recesses of the house. Without a word, she turned and walked through her hall, Esmond pace for pace behind her. "See?" he whispered quickly to me. "It works every time." Apparently Silkform scorned the crude, old-fashioned, foot-in-door method. Years of trial and error, fortified, they claimed, by extensive psychological research, had proved to them that the words "GET THAT CARD," accompanied by the commanding pointing gesture, would produce results almost every time. The victim, already half mesmerized, would obey, and the salesman would have achieved his first objective — entrance into the house.

Once inside, it was important to start talking fast — and, once started, not to stop ("Never lose the initiative"). The strategy employed at this stage bore no little resemblance to the famous "Third Degree" of which we had read so much both before and after coming to America. In essence, it consisted of a deft combination of mental torture and physical manipulation designed to reduce the subject to a state of helpless passivity, bereft of independent will, and ready to sign anything as a condition of freedom from torment.

"Got the card? Ah . . . good. I see you're a very careful housekeeper, Mrs. Robinson. Now, if you would be so good as to have a seat . . ." (he was bustling around her living room, rearranging chairs, easing her into one where the glaring sunlight would fall on her face). "There we are! Now, I must explain the uses of the magnificent free gift. It wouldn't be much good to you if you didn't even know what it was for, would it?"

"Well, I don't know . . . I'm awfully busy this morning . . ." Mrs. Robinson was looking helplessly around.

"Ha, ha, ha, aren't we all? But luckily this will only take a minute." Esmond opened his kit and rapidly fished out a grubby little object that looked exactly like a folder of safety matches. "No-o-ow, here we are." He opened the little folder to display some small cardboard sticks with glue on the ends, a few strands of darning thread, and a needle. "When you get one of those nasty old runs in your stocking, here's all you need to do. Just lick one of these Hand-Ee Run Arresters, and apply the end to the run. Then, when you're all safely and snugly back in your home, you can mend it at your leisure with some of this marvelous darning thread." He thrust it into her hand, at the same time flipping from the kit a large bound morocco book, which he dexterously opened to Part I of the Third Degree session.

"Mrs. Robinson, have you ever felt a bit of REAL FRESH SILK?" He produced a long, tangled skein resembling horsehair, and wound one end tightly round her wrist. "Now, PULL!" A brief tug of war ensued. "THAT would certainly have a hard time breaking, wouldn't it? Now, let me show you something." Seizing her unresisting hand, guiding it: "Take this pin . . . that's right . . . now, see if you can make a hole in this little sample of WOVEN real fresh silk, woven exclusively for the use of the more discriminating woman. Almost impossible, isn't it?" (but he withdrew it quickly, because it had been known to happen). "Your big toe would have a hard time trying to go sightseeing through that, wouldn't it? Now, many women don't realize that most brands of silk stocking give you very, very little choice of sizes. You are limited to getting, for instance, a size 9, or 9½, or 10, or 10½. The average stocking manufacturer simply *refuses* to make allowances for legs of different *shapes*. And yet, we're all made differently by the Creator, aren't we? For instance, take your legs and Miss Freeman's here . . ." (but he quickly dropped that line of approach as a possibly dangerous deviant from the supersalesman's injunctions). "Now, just for example, let me measure your ankle with this Hand-ee Ever Ready measuring tape . . ."

"Look here, are you selling stockings?" Mrs. Robinson was suddenly beginning to wake from her lethargy.

"SELLING STOCKINGS? Oh no, you are quite mistaken, Mrs. Robinson. Look here, I want you to go all through this kit, and tell me if you see any stockings for sale there. See? Not a single stocking. I couldn't sell you any if I WANTED to, could I?" He thrust the whole kit at her and was down on the floor with the Hand-ee Ever Ready measuring tape. "Miss Freeman, will you be so kind as to take down these measurements? Ankle . . . 48 inches . . ."

"But it *can't* be," I protested.

"Oh no . . . sorry . . . I got hold of the wrong end. Ankle, 10 inches. Calf, 17. Thigh, 24. Where do you fasten your support, Mrs. Robinson? Oh yes, I see. Length of leg from ankle to upper thigh, 25 inches. Got them all, Miss Freeman? That's right. Now, Mrs. Robinson, as to shades. Let me see. I think we'll make you up a nice economy size package of a dozen pairs. Four of Mist, that goes well with navy, four of Shell, that's for evening wear and social events of all kinds, four of Rust, for more informal wear . . . got that, Miss Freeman?"

Mrs. Robinson was sitting in a kind of daze, thoroughly disheveled, staring vacantly into space.

"Now, here's where we keep the family treasury, ha, ha, ha, am I right?" Esmond had spotted her purse, and now handed it to her. "Just a little deposit, say $10, $5, whatever you have handy . . . thanks. Now if you would be so kind as to sign here." Her limp hand moved across the paper. "Well, it certainly has been very pleasant meeting you, Mrs. Robinson. And now, we don't want to detain you any longer. Good day!"

"Esmond, that *poor* woman. Do you realize she's bought eighteen dollars' worth of stockings?" I said when we got outside.

"I know, it is rather awful. But at least she's got enough to last some time. And you'll be glad to hear that we don't have to make the deliveries. They have a special squad of trained strong-arm men for that, in case the husband is at home when they come."

Not all the victims were lulled with the same ease. One woman even roused herself long enough to ask me, "How did a nice girl like you ever get mixed up with a fellow like this?"

Esmond was disturbingly successful as a Silkform salesman.

In short order he was winning prizes for exceeding the quota
assigned to him, and proudly presented me with a Snugfit
Supersoft Shortie Housecoat and a Brushrite brush and comb
set. He attended the Salesmen's Pep Rally, and came home
singing snatches from some of the rousing anthems he had
learned there, designed to inspire team spirit in all who heard
them:

> (to the tune of *Tipperary*)
> It's a great gang that's selling Silkform
> It's a great gang to know,
> We are all full of pep and ginger
> And our watchword is, LET's GO! Hey! Hey!

> (to the tune of *There's a Long, Long Trail*)
> There's a Silkform trail a-winding
> Into the land of my dreams . . .

Even if the dream of fifty or sixty dollars a week was one
to which the Silkform trail failed to lead, we did end up making enough money to pay for most of our expenses in Washington.

30

OUR EXPEDITIONS into the Silkform territory were pleasantly interspersed with visits to people working in various New Deal agencies, and opportunities to make a fair sampling of the dinners, cocktail parties and lunches that comprised a large part of Washington government life.

Wandering through the different government bureaus, we talked to men and women who had flocked from all parts of the country to work in the National Youth Administration, the Department of Agriculture, the Works Projects Administration, and many more agencies whose myriad names and initials we couldn't even keep straight.

We were immensely impressed by the people we met, some of whom seemed to be hardly any older than we. They lived and worked with a crusading enthusiasm for what they were doing. Everywhere we went, they pressed upon us pamphlets, surveys, press releases, describing the many activities of the New Deal. We were urged to tour the countryside, to visit work camps, the Tennessee Valley Authority, drainage and resettlement projects, to look into schemes for financial aid to farmers — to see for ourselves the dramatic changes wrought by the Roosevelt Administration. How different, we thought, from English government offices, where the very words "civil servant" seem synonymous with dry-as-dust dullness and red tape.

We were told that Washington, like New York, is very untypical of American cities. Yet we couldn't help feeling that much of what was best in America was concentrated here in the capital and was represented by this bright, sincere group of liberals. They had little of the automatic cynicism, the inevitable wisecrack come-back of the New Yorkers; at the same time, they were far from being the dreamy-eyed, muddleheaded idealists portrayed by almost all the press. They were doers of deeds, planners of projects, and above all translators of their country's principles and ideals into real life.

We soon became fast friends with the editor of the *New Republic*, Michael Straight. He was an extraordinarily handsome youth, a couple of years older than Esmond. His wife Binny was just eighteen, and had been considered by her family too young to leave home without her nanny, so we often had dinner with the three of them. Michael had been educated in England, at Dartington Hall. Both Esmond and I knew quite a lot about Dartington, as it had been a storm center of public controversy for years and the target of innumerable angry letters in *The Times*. Mike's stories about the immoral goings on there would doubtless have confirmed the letter writers in their darkest thoughts on the subject.

The Straights insisted on hearing every detail of our Silkform adventures. They howled and roared with laughter, and we would all sit round singing, "It's a great gang that's selling Silkform." Our standard greeting to them was, "Good *morning,* Mrs. Straight, and how are *we* today?" At Esmond's insistence, they furnished us with letters of reference for use in case we should become really stranded in our travels. The letters described me as a highly trained lady's maid who had worked for years in Mrs. Straight's service, and Esmond as an accomplished valet, whose expertise and adroitness in the fulfillment of his duties had become almost indispensable to Mr. Straight.

One day when Esmond was off in the territory, Mike took me to a breakfast gathering of New Dealers in one of the large hotels. I sat next to a tall Southern woman in a huge white hat. She introduced herself to me as Virginia Durr. She spoke in a sort of soft scream, happily devoid of the slight whine I had come to associate with Southern voices. Her approach to conversation was that of the frontal attack. As soon as she learned I was English, she fired question after question at me:

"Well, what in the world do you think of Mr. Chamberlain? I think he's just puh-fectly *awful* . . . Whereabouts did you live in England? I've always been so fascinated by English country life. What in the world did you *do* all day long? How much do you-all pay your servants in England? What does steak and kidney pie taste like? I just adore Jane Austen, and *Cranford,* and I would so love to go to England one day . . ."

I had a hard time trying to catch up and answer all the questions, at the same time trying to explain that things in England had changed somewhat since the days of Jane Austen and *Cranford.*

Actually I was a little ruffled by the insistent barrage. Mrs. Durr made me feel outnumbered, as though I were being cornered by a roomful of reporters.

She soon got bored with my brief answers, and focused her gaze and attention on a red-haired youth across the table. "Why, Red! They tell me you're just about the smartest man on Capitol Hill. Now, tell me, what do they say the President is going to do about . . ."

The person thus addressed squirmed and blushed prettily, but he gave her a detailed answer to her question, and they were soon off discussing the intricacies of New Deal politics.

As soon as Mrs. Durr had had enough of a given topic of conversation, she would close it off gently but firmly. It was as though she had finished a chapter in a book, shut the volume, and put it down to pick up another. This proved a little disconcerting to the one with whom she had been talking, who was frequently left high and dry in the middle of a sentence. She applied her direct-question method to all without discrimination, no matter how delicate the subject: "Jack, I hear you-all had a falling out with John L. the other night. Whatever happened? I thought you all were just about as thick as thieves."

Toward the end of the breakfast, she once more turned her overpowering charm and attention on me: "Why don't you-all come out to dinner with us one day this week? I'd love to meet your husband, they tell me he's a really remarkable young man."

"Oh . . . do they? That's awfully nice of them. Of course, *I* think so . . ."

I was stumbling badly, caught off guard by the unfamiliar directness of the compliment. We arranged that Esmond and I should meet Mr. Durr at his office the following night and drive out to their house on Seminary Hill.

Clifford Durr was a tall, rather stoop-shouldered man of about forty. His appearance was casual yet scholarly, reminiscent of a softened edition of Abe Lincoln. He greeted us with that extra degree of kindness and hospitality which I had noticed in so many Americans; it always gave me the uncomfortable feeling that, no matter how long I lived among them, I should never quite be able to rise to their level of genuine cordiality with strangers.

The Durrs lived in a big, sprawling white farmhouse in a country community about seven miles from Washington. We entered the hall, which was piled high with back copies of the *National Geographic* Magazine, to find Mrs. Durr screaming softly into the telephone. She hung up as soon as we came in — apparently in mid-sentence; I wondered a little about the poor person at the other end — and rose to greet us. "Why, I'm so absolutely delighted that you-all could come! Cliff, honey, go get them a drink. Come on in, and meet Lucy and Baby Sister." She led us into the drawing room, one end of which was filled with a tangled mass of small children. Mrs. Durr strode among them, sorting them out, and produced Lucy, a beautiful little blond child of two. Baby Sister, a newborn infant, was kicking placidly in a pram in another corner of the room.

Lucy was rapidly held up for introductions, and to kiss her father good evening, and as rapidly set down among her cronies, with instructions to "keep quiet, you-all, so Mother can talk to her company."

Mrs. Durr settled down for some more inexorable questioning, completely oblivious of the bedlam which filled the room. Occasionally an extra-loud wail would produce some reaction: "My Lord! Children, won't you-all *please* keep quiet and play nicely . . ." Eventually, without any particular prompting, the children gradually dispersed and Lucy stumped off to bed. In the unnatural quiet that followed it was noticed that Baby Sister had been crying for some time. ("My lands! We forgot to feed Baby Sister!") She was quickly pacified with a bottle, and the grown-up conversation proceeded without further interruption.

Esmond now became the center of Mrs. Durr's attention.

She questioned him at length and in great detail about his views on the war, about what sort of person Winston Churchill was, about his experiences in Spain.

Listening to them talk, I already began to form a different view of Mrs. Durr. She was a real spellbinder, I decided, whose peculiar charm lay in her enormous curiosity about people, her driving passion to find out things, to know about details and motivations, to trace big events to their small human beginnings. No wonder she loved Jane Austen!

She and Esmond were hitting it off famously. By the end of the evening we were on the friendliest of terms. We felt as though we had known the Durrs for years. How long, I wondered, would it have taken in England to develop such a feeling of close friendship? How many hours and hours, spread over how many months, spent in each other's company? First there would have been the preliminary skirmishes, as when two strange dogs approach each other suspiciously for the first time, sniffing but on guard, eying each other closely while walking carefully round. Conversation would of course vary depending on the particular milieu. It might be of the monosyllabic "Oh I say, good show" variety, if it were taking place at a hunting-and-fishing sort of weekend. Or then again it might consist of the carefully turned literary phrase, the judicious (but rather consciously offhand) dropping of well-known literary names, for there are many different ways in which people establish contact with one another. Certain it is that the direct, easy exchange of views and experiences that came so naturally to the Durrs would have not been achieved in a first meeting.

We renewed acquaintance with the Meyer family, who were staying in Washington at the time. Visits to their lovely huge Washington house provided the "contrastiness" which to Esmond was always so much the essence of enjoyable living. Back from the Silkform territory to our squalid rented room, a quick scrub-up, into the ever-present tuxedo, and off to a fabulous dinner party where anyone might show up — from a Hiss to a Pegler, for such was the range of the Meyers' acquaintance.

Ignorance of Washington personalities led to some embarrassing moments. At one such dinner I sat next to a portly young lawyer, a Mr. Pritchard from Kentucky, reminiscent in face and form of Tom's "fat fairs."

"A friend of mine says you're just a 'Dean Acheson Liberal.' What is that exactly?" I asked.

A swift kick under the table from Esmond warned me to drop this line of inquiry; he explained later that Mrs. Dean Acheson was sitting directly opposite me.

Esmond wasn't so lucky that evening either. After dinner Mr. Meyer expounded his views on the Lend-Lease bill which was then being debated in Congress. The guests listened enthralled, attentive not only because politeness would have required it when their host was speaking. Mr. Meyer was a fascinating talker, one with the ability to pinpoint and transmit to an audience the gleanings of a lifetime of varied political experience.

"There are those who claim the British are trying to put one over on us," he was saying, and added with great emphasis, "I say the British are incapable of stealing from us!"

As though drawn by sympathy to the representative in their midst of that gallant little island, all eyes turned to Esmond, who had quietly slipped away from the circle by the fireplace and was busily and methodically stuffing his pockets with some excellent Meyer cigars.

Far from being annoyed with us, Mr. Meyer treated the whole thing as a huge joke. He proved worthy of the designation "Possible Job Getter" a few days later, when he commissioned us to do a series of articles on our adventures in America.

Philip Toynbee has cruelly, but accurately, described these articles as "coy and shameless, a cosy picture of a gallant little English couple fighting against heavy odds to keep their heads above the deep and alien waters of America."

If Mr. Meyer wanted revenge on Esmond for the theft of the cigars, he got it when the articles eventually appeared under the singularly repulsive title, "Baby Blue-Bloods in Hobohemia."

31

THE TWO WEEKS in Washington seemed to last an age, for travel makes time stand still, like a dream which takes one through a long series of adventures while actually lasting only a few moments.

Once more we said goodbye to our new friends, some of whom already showed possibilities of becoming lifetime friends, as we had said goodbye in London, New York, Martha's Vineyard. This was the shape — if shape it can be called — our life had taken long ago; to swoop down on a situation, a circle of people, become part of them for a brief time, glean what there was of interest and be off again. It gave us a satisfactory feeling of having peered quickly but deeply into a particular corner of the world, of having begun relationships which could be resumed as easily months or years later. Even in England, our attitude had been a little like that of explorers, investigating, and then in the privacy of our own house analyzing and cataloguing the natives. In America, cut off as we were by intangible barriers of nationality, this attitude to people around us became more pronounced. Even our best friends, the ones we loved fondly and looked on as our nearest and dearest — Giles, Philip, Peter, the *Life-Timers*, the Rodmans, the Durrs, dotted around the world like flags on a map — had for us an almost two-dimensional quality, for more and more we only really minded about each other.

Perhaps most young lovers share in common to some degree this feeling of oneness, of having "eyes only for each other"; certainly literature of all countries and ages is full of such references. In our case, we had more reason than most to feel bound to one another in a way that excluded people around us. Estrangement from our families, the circumstances of our marriage, our constant wanderings about, the death of the baby, all had conspired to weld us into a self-sufficient unit, a conspiracy of two against the world.

The only area of my life which I could not share with Esmond was my attachment to Boud. Perversely, and although I hated everything she stood for, she was easily my favorite sister, which was something I could never have admitted in those days, above all to Esmond. I had tried, most of the time successfully, to banish her from my mind after the war broke out. There had been little news about her in letters from the family; no one knew exactly where she was or what had become of her. A cousin wrote to say that she had returned to Germany in August taking a pistol with her, with which she planned to commit suicide when the war started. While we were in Washington the papers carried occasional rumors about Boud — that she had entered a convent, that she was dangerously ill. The thought of her, alone and ill — perhaps *dying* (dreadful word! too awful to hold in one's mind for more than a moment) — filled me with terrible distress. I could only take comfort in the thought that Boud herself, to whom loyalty was the supreme virtue, would be the first to understand that the war had parted us forever.

It was easy enough, anyway, to abandon oneself to the day-to-day excitements of the Grand Tour of America.

Esmond was living violently in the present. This he was

extraordinarily good at. His attitude at that time was not so much "eat, drink and be merry, for tomorrow we die" — death was the last thing he expected or anticipated — but rather, "tomorrow our life's work begins, and a long, all-absorbing job it will be." Somewhere, some time in the next months or years, the war against fascism would actually start, and at that point the outlines of real life for us would emerge. Since the Munich Pact, and despite the official declaration of war, the fight had come to a standstill. Esmond was not one to wait around for things to happen; they would happen soon enough, and meanwhile there was an endless variety of places to see, people to savor, situations to be explored.

We started south from Washington, bound for New Orleans, where Esmond was hoping to get a chance to practice his newly acquired bartending skill. But one night, while Esmond was driving and I was supposedly keeping track of our route on the map, we suddenly realized we had taken the wrong road hours ago, and were headed toward Miami. In the dim glow cast by our headlights we already saw orange plantations on either side of the road. It seemed too much trouble to go all the way back; besides, when we stopped to refuel the gas station attendant told us there were hundreds of bartending jobs in Miami. He assured us that any training remotely connected with the dispensing of liquor would come in most handy there, and that Esmond's services would be much in demand.

The Playground of America proved to be the most unattractive town I had ever seen, from the stunted, ratty-looking palm trees to our motel room, from behind the spanking-new white walls of which cockroaches came out by the thousands every night. Here was not the cozy, settled filth of London bedsitters, nor the warm, smelly and somehow human dirt of the Hôtel des Basques, but rather a crawling, mean sordidness. The human population matched their surroundings. The town was getting ready for the winter season; it was a good time for job-hunting, and to this we both applied ourselves. Going the rounds of job interviews, and later working behind the "junk jewelry" department of a large drugstore in which I soon found employment, I had plenty of opportunity to observe the Miamians. They struck me as a humorless, suspicious, narrow-minded lot. It was our first experience of a southern American town. The Negroes lived like a band of ghosts in miserable shacks on the outskirts, their very existence ignored for the most part by the whites. The verbal fire of my co-workers in the drugstore was reserved for use against the Jewish tourists, on whose money the town grew fat, and whose patronage paid their salaries. Many of those with whom we came in contact exhibited a sort of smarmy bonhomie, reminiscent of sugary German *gemütlichkeit,* a front behind which lurked the foulest racism.

The gas station attendant's information proved most inaccurate. Esmond made the rounds of employment agencies and hotels only to learn that the bartending profession was completely closed to outsiders, that bars were run either as family businesses or by long-term, trusted employees. Even an ad in the Miami *Herald,* in which Esmond described himself as "thirty years old, steady, dependable, many years' experience in Paris and London Ritz," failed to draw a single response. Once more I was the family breadwinner, drawing down a wage of $14 for a 48-hour-week.

As usual, Esmond's bad luck was only temporary. He answered an advertisement for "experienced waiters, must have own tux, high class Italian restaurant, opening shortly," convinced the employer that he had worked for years at this trade in the Savoy Grill, and was hired on the spot.

Out came the tuxedo, dealt with this time by me — I did wish Horton had been there — and Esmond went off to re-

port to the Roma Restaurant for the opening night, looking
very spruce indeed, though hardly fitting the part of a seasoned old Savoy Grill waiter. He came back hours later,
crestfallen and thoroughly shaken. The evening had started
most propitiously, with a first-rate Italian meal served to the
help in the lovely huge kitchen. Before the waiters had finished their dessert the first customers arrived, and a team of
two sprang up to serve them. To Esmond's horror, they de-
parted from the kitchen with dishes, sauceboats, water jugs
"sticking out," as he described it, "from every conceivable
finger, several things to each hand, and all up the arm."

Esmond, known for his inability to carry a teaspoon from
one room to the next without dropping it, was too disturbed
by this sight to eat the rest of his dinner. Inexorably, his
turn came. The rest of the evening was a nightmare, as one
angry customer after another, many of them dripping with
tomato sauce or soaked to the skin with wine, called the boss's
attention to the odd behavior of their waiter. The climax
came when Esmond, who was by now desperately trying to
save the situation by sheer energy, rushed through the wrong
door, collided head-on with a laden co-worker, and brought
them both crashing to the floor in an unseemly shambles of
chicken *cacciatore* and broken dishes. The boss, with tears
in his eyes, begged Esmond to consider his employment at an
end. "I decided I'd better leave without making a fuss," Esmond said. "He'll probably be in a better mood tomorrow, I'll
go round and have a talk with him."

Esmond had noticed a delightful little bar in one corner of
the Roma Restaurant, on which he now set his sights. The
next day he presented himself to the proprietor, apologized for
the sad debacle of the previous night, admitted that he hadn't
actually worked at the Savoy ("he seemed to have already
rather gathered that"), and applied for a job as bartender.
The proprietor assured him that no bartender was needed,

the bar was only a sideline which could easily be handled by his own family; but such was Esmond's persistence that with great reluctance the boss agreed to take him on in the capacity of busboy and general handyman, for a wage of $5 a week and meals. "An unhandier man I can scarcely imagine," I told Esmond, "but I bet you'll probably end up having something to do with the bar."

Sure enough, after a week or so of swabbing out lavatories and scouring the huge kitchen pots and pans, Esmond graduated to a position of trust with the Chizzolas, the family who owned the Roma, and was permitted to don the tuxedo of an evening and stand proudly behind the bar. He grew very fond of the brothers Chizzola. There were three of them, John, the "front man" who greeted the customers, took care of hiring and firing, and brain-trusted the business; Paul, the maître d'hôtel, a rather mad young man who lived in a dream world of his own except while plying his trade; and Tony, the excellent cook. They in turn were pleased with their strange new busboy, who made up with enormous enthusiasm for his total ignorance of his duties.

One day Esmond arrived for work to find the Chizzolas in deepest gloom. The Miami police had just informed them that the bar was being operated illegally; they must either buy a license or stop selling drinks. A temporary license, good only for the six months of the Miami season, would cost the fantastic sum of one thousand dollars.

Esmond immediately had a bright idea. He offered then and there to put up the $1000 for the license if the Chizzolas would agree to enter into full partnership with him. Preoccupied with the disaster, and not unnaturally completely skeptical of Esmond's proposal, they curtly brushed him off as one might dismiss an annoying child who offers to bring a gift of the moon and stars.

I was equally incredulous when Esmond told me his idea.

As usual, our bank account was in awful shape, with less than $200 in it. The *Washington Post* articles, which were to bring us $20 each, not only hadn't yet been written but were barely outlined. Esmond, as usual, had eyes only for the rainbow with the pot of gold at the end; he was congenitally incapable of dwelling on the pitfalls and difficulties in a situation. Here was merely one more Gordian knot, ripe for the cutting. His plan was to take the plane to Washington that night, using what was left in the bank for the fare, and borrow the $1000 from Eugene Meyer.

"Likely story!" I said. "Obviously he won't lend it to you. Why should he? Rich people never do lend money without security, that's probably how they stay rich. You'll just be wasting all the savings on the airplane ticket."

Esmond poured forth torrents of arguments to demolish each objection I raised to the scheme. I knew he was really only practicing on me, glad of the opportunity to clarify his thoughts in preparation for laying siege to Mr. Meyer, for he never doubted that in the long run I would support anything he wanted to do.

The interview with Mr. Meyer proved extremely brief. As Esmond described it on his return, two days later, Mr. Meyer had leaned back, a fairy-godfatherly twinkle in his eye, and said, "A thousand dollars? Yes, I think I can lend you a thousand dollars." Esmond, expecting long resistance, was so completely taken aback that the only rejoinder he could think of was, "Oh! Well, I hope it won't leave you short." Mr. Meyer was exceedingly tickled by this remark, and the discussion ended in gales of hilarity, with Esmond in possession of the magic paper saying "pay to bearer . . ."

32

The Chizzola brothers put on a magnificent feast to celebrate the new partnership. The maître d'hôtel climbed one of the trees in the patio out of sheer joy that the bar had been salvaged, and jumped from branch to branch, pretending alternately to be a parrot and a monkey. John put on a very creditable imitation of Esmond being a handyman: "Where's the mop? Where's the mop?" Crash! Bang! Slosh! I proudly assisted Tony, who was preparing mountains of spaghetti in the kitchen: "Decca! Quick! Where's that thing, the spaghetti he stop, the water he go through?" I loved them on sight, they were so completely different from the depressing, hard-faced Anglo-Saxons who were my daily companions at the drugstore.

It was a merry occasion indeed, and we ate and drank far into the night, the party ending with a magnificent concert of anti-fascist Italian songs by the brothers.

I threw up the drugstore job to assume my new duties at the Roma, where I was to be buyer of supplies, bookkeeper, and bouncer. "We need a nice young woman to take care of some of the ladies who have passed out," John explained seriously. "The maître d'hôtel will be pleased; he doesn't like having to go and drag them out of the ladies' rest room." ("What *would* Muv say?" was still a theme that ran through my mind on occasions like this.)

Life in the Roma bar had much to recommend it. Our agreement with the Chizzolas included meals with the family, and now, for the first and only time during our marriage, we ate three regular and delicious meals a day. A novelty much to Esmond's liking; he prospered and grew fat. The old regime of feast and famine, hastily gulped snacks at the nearest hash house interspersed with occasional glorious Meyer or equivalent banquets, faded into memory.

The customers were a constant source of amusement. For the most part they were middle-aged businessmen on vacation, or traveling salesmen. Once the restaurant and bar was taken over for the evening by American Federation of Labor officials, meeting in convention in Miami. To our amazement, these representatives of millions of American workers were indistinguishable from the midwestern businessmen who usually crowded the bar. "Aren't you going to sing the 'Red Flag' after the banquet?" I asked one of them, but he looked completely mystified, as though I must have lost my mind. I gathered that, like Mr. Meyer, he was "in favor of capitalism." We eagerly quizzed them about what stand the unions would take on foreign policy, only to be met with blank, uncomprehending stares.

Esmond made a study of the habits of the American drunk. He found that after two or three drinks, the customer would invariably produce his wallet and fumble through it for photos of "the wife and kids, she's the grandest little woman in all the world, and our Junior can lick any punk on the block you betcha." A few more cocktails, and the customer was crashing his fist on the bar: "Yessir, the U.S.A., best little old country you'll find; and Kansas just about the finest state in the Union, you can say what you like about these furrin parts, we've got the lot of them beat . . ." and on and on. With the tenth drink, the customer began to feel a curious, but apparently universal, need to assert and prove his own identity. "Robert G. McKinley, G. for George, that's me. Bob, they call me. Vice-president of the Smith-Alford Tractor Company, Kansas City, Kansas. You don't believe me, do you? Huh? Well, I'll *prove* it to you." Out would come the business card, driver's license, social security card. "See? Right there. Robert George McKinley, but they call me Bob. Robert G. McKinley of Kansas City, Kansas, finest li'l old city you'll find, and they *all* call me Bob at home . . ." By this time the bar would be littered with a horrid assortment of identification cards, permits of one kind or another, various Kiwanis and Rotary membership cards, and the pictures of the Little Woman and Kids, their round and guileless faces incongruously splotched with spilled whiskey. This stage would signal the need for me to swing into action in my capacity as bouncer, which I performed by scooping the customer's squalid belongings back into his wallet and gently leading him to a waiting cab. "Robert George McKinley's the name, Bob everyone back home calls me . . . finest little old home in all the dang blasted world . . ." we'd hear as he stumbled into the taxi. Esmond soon learned to judge just when the bouncing stage had been reached. "Decca, he's getting out the driver's license: would you run out and call a cab?"

Esmond applied himself with great concentration to making the business a going concern. It was as though he was deliberately trying to shut out, for the time being, the realities of life and politics. He was in rather a unique position to accomplish this, being physically unavailable for English conscription and, as a foreigner, not subject to the American draft if one should be announced. He even wrote to tell Philip that we had a "Talk Neutral" sign in the bar. No such sign in fact existed; Esmond elaborately invented it as a way of notifying our friends at home that he was not about to be drawn in as part of a war machine whose purpose was as yet indistinct. The major headlines of that winter dealt with the mobilization of troops at Southampton for possible use against the Soviet Union, and there were indications that highly placed individuals in the British Government were giving full encouragement to the Germans to intensify their feverish war preparations against the day when at last we should be happily allied with them in the crusade against Communism. It was an atmosphere of plots within plots, the final outcome of which remained most unclear.

Perhaps because of the unsettling quality of the news, perhaps because I had taken such a dislike to Miami, at times I felt that something unpleasant would spring out at us from behind the garish façade of that horrible tinselly town with its maddening eternal sunshine pouring incessantly down on white stucco, its hideous sham-looking poinsettias, like cheap Christmas tree ornaments, advertising their scarlet presence from every garden.

Esmond was impervious to such imaginings; he radiated warmth and life, developed all sorts of wild plans for the future of the bar, set to work doggedly to learn the ins and outs of liquor merchandising, the ways and means of attracting and keeping customers. As usual, he was the center of a whirlpool of activity of his own making, into which he drew everyone around him. The Chizzola brothers regarded him with affection and ever-growing amazement. They had never quite got over the shock of their first acquaintance with him, his gall in posing as a trained waiter on their opening night, the fact that he had successfully hypnotized them into giving him a job as a busboy in spite of his obvious incompetence, and above all his successful quest of the $1000, which they seemed to view as some sort of hilarious conjuring trick.

Now Esmond was actually "admitted to practice at the bar," as he said, we found there was a lot more to running the business than the mere mixing of *pousse cafés* and Horse's Necks. There were puzzling matters of cash discounts and long- and short-term credit to be mastered, strange terms like Bill of Lading and Daily Ledger to be learned.

The days developed their own rhythm. Mornings were devoted to doing accounts and cleaning up from the night before, and to earnest consultation with the brothers about supplies followed by more earnest consultations with the liquor wholesalers. About noon came the exciting moment of opening, with its attendant conjecture about what odd specimens of humanity might fetch up at the Roma this time. After that, the fun began in earnest. Esmond developed several alternative personalities which he tried out on the customers: The Damon Runyon "tough guy," the courtly old-fashioned English servitor, the sophisticated Ernest Hemingway self-made-world-traveler-at-home-in-five-continents type. I was always afraid that he would get them mixed up, and that a customer who had been given the Damon Runyon treatment (complete with American accent) might return a few days later to find himself being served apparently by the identical twin of the previous bartender — a twin of somber demeanor, addicted to bowing gravely in stiff English fashion, who spoke only when addressed, and then in monosyllables delivered in Esmond's BBC voice — Cockney, with a heavy veneer of Oxford accent.

Esmond's most successful act was that of Homely Philosopher. It consisted of getting a conversation going with a customer, then capping every trite remark with a triter one: "*I* always say young people have too few responsibilities/ too many responsibilities/ too much freedom/ too little initiative these days." "*I* always say what this country needs is a firm hand/ a free rein/ a return to the good old principles of our fathers/ to look forward instead of backward . . ." Almost anything would do, if delivered in ponderous enough manner and preceded by the words "*I* always say." His audience was merely impressed by such depths of wisdom in one so young. As the customer downed more and more drinks, Esmond would dexterously lead him round in circles for my amusement, and would soon have him agreeing with platitudes the sense of which was exactly opposite to those with which he had started out. I watched the show from my vantage point at the cash register, occasionally volunteering a Homely Philosopher's Wife's remark: "*I* always say that if more of us women were more like our mothers, this little old world would be a better place," or, "*I* always say it's up to us womenfolk to keep our menfolk away from the race track and bars." The latter remark could only be safely delivered if the customer was thoroughly drunk, and therefore in a mood to polemicize against the evils of liquor, specially when consumed by the younger generation.

At Christmas, the serene, escapist fun of the bar was shattered. There were a couple of days of newspaper rumor to the effect that Boud had been badly wounded by a gunshot and was being returned home by ambulance, to be accorded the extraordinary measure of safe-conduct through enemy lines. There was the usual wild conjecture, then news that she had arrived in England. A journalistic storm of huge proportions broke over us. The telephone rang continually with calls from newspapers all over the country demanding to know the "inside story": was it true that Unity had been shot by the

S.S.? That she had had a violent quarrel with Hitler just after the outbreak of war? Where had she been for the last few months?

"I don't know ... I don't know ... I don't know."

I was terrified for Boud, and grieved over the accounts of her final homecoming, the endless flow of photographs in the papers showing her so changed and ill-looking. The simple truth of what had happened was plain to me. Boud had always said she would kill herself if war should break out between England and Germany; she had tried, but somehow failed. Although a bullet had entered her brain, her enormously strong physique pulled her back to life.

I pondered over the unsolvable riddle: why had she, to those of us who knew her the most human of people, turned her back on humanity and allied herself with those grinning beasts and their armies of robot goose-steppers? The cry of the old Basque woman in Bayonne, *"Alemanes! Criminales! Bestiales! Animales!"* still rang in my ears. How could Boud, a person of enormous natural taste, an artist and poet from childhood, have embraced their crude philistinism? She had been an eccentric all her life, completely outside the bounds of normal behavior, uncontrollable by governesses, parents and the headmistress of her boarding school (who had diplomatically informed my mother that, since many girls leave school at sixteen she saw no reason why Unity shouldn't be one of them); yet she had enthusiastically adopted the most deadeningly conformist of all philosophies. She was always a terrific hater — so were all of us, except possibly Tom — but I had always thought she hated intelligently, and admired her ability to reduce the more unpleasant of the grown-up relations to a state of acute nervous discomfort with one of her smoldering looks of loathing. But when she wrote gaily off to *Der Stürmer*, "I want everybody to know I am a Jew-hater," I felt

forgotten the whole point of hating, and had once
all put herself on the side of the hateful.
erhaps futile to try to interpret the actions of another
nay be so completely wrong; but it always seemed to
this last really conscious act of her life, the attempt
lestruction, was a sort of recognition of the extra-
contradictions in which she found herself, that the
ion of war merely served as the occasion for her
which would in any case have been inevitable sooner

urned my Boud of Boudledidge days, my huge, bright
ry of the D.F.D., when we used to fight — only three
years ago, but it seemed a lifetime — under the banners
tika and hammer and sickle. I knew I couldn't expect
l, who had never met her, to feel anything but disgust
, so by tacit understanding we avoided discussing her.

33

Usually the events which make history seem to take an interminable time when one is living through them. Only years later do the essentials appear in perspective, telescoped and summarized in glib phrases for the history books: "the Thirty Years War," "the Restoration," "the Industrial Revolution." In real life, the maturing of the crisis that leads up to a change in government, the course of international negotiations and conferences that shape the destiny of a generation, the ebb and flow of battles that decide the outcome of a war unroll in maddening slow-motion fashion, the decisive meaning of each stage often obscured and buried under mountains of newsprint, speculation, rumor, interpretation, "inspired" stories, comment pro and con.

Not so the German offensive against Western Europe, when it was finally unleashed. On the 9th of May, a month after Chamberlain had looked into his clouded crystal ball, there to find that Hitler had "missed the bus" and was no longer capable of waging aggressive war, the Germans struck. The offensive moved with such speed that no newspaper could keep up with it; "extras" were out of date before they appeared on the streets. Once more we stayed glued to the radio. Each hourly news broadcast announced new tragedies, and the regular programs were peppered with special bulletins from the front. Within hours the Germans had swept through Holland, whose much vaunted system of dykes had proved about as effective a defensive weapon as a child's sand-castle moat, and the French front was reported to be in mortal danger, perhaps already lost.

Out of the wild confusion of those first few days of the attack, one fact emerged; the German rain of fire against these ill-prepared, disunited countries had illuminated in one vast flash the real nature of the danger confronting Europe, had exposed for all to see and understand the criminal stupidity of the years of shabby deals and accommodation to Hitler's ambitions. Overnight, the appeasement policy was buried forever. The day after the offensive began to roll, Chamberlain announced his resignation, and Churchill was summoned to form a national government.

To Esmond, this was the turning point, the moment when all doubts as to whether or not the war would be fully prosecuted were at an end, and the course of English policy was once and for all clear. As he saw it, Churchill's advent to power, accompanied as it was by an unparalleled display of support from labor, had set the seal on this policy. The fiddling about with civilian gas masks that didn't work, the ill-conceived leaflets for airplane distribution behind German lines which had marked the first five months after the declaration of hostilities, were at last done with.

In deciding to go back and fight — a decision that was inevitable from the moment the course of the war became clear in those first days of the offensive — Esmond was ruefully conscious of just what he was heading into. This would be no replica of Spain, no thrilling adventure of self-propelled action directed against the oppressors. The machine was roll-

ing, a machine whose every cog was cluttered up with Wellington prefects grown older, dominated at every point by the Old
School Tie enemies of *Out of Bounds* days. The upper classes,
even the most pro-Hitler of them, would now swing into line
to do their duty to King and Empire, and would no doubt
find themselves in their ordained role of leadership in all
phases of the war. "I'll probably find myself being commanded
by one of your ghastly relations," Esmond commented glumly.

There was no doubt it was going to be a dull war, and
the absence of the Communists, who announced they were
sticking by their characterization of it as an "imperialist war,"
would make it even duller. Fighting in such a war would
be an irksome task, dogged by boredom every step of the way,
but nonetheless essential.

Characteristically, while analyzing and expatiating at length
on all the drawbacks and drearier aspects of the war, Esmond
was full of optimism. He predicted that the necessary clearing
away of the Nazi rubble would open up the way to enormous
social change everywhere, that in the course of the war the
"spirit of Madrid" would once more emerge.

He was exultant at being in a position to arrange the
details of his own participation in the war. Had he been
caught up in the English conscription he would have found
himself at the mercy of officialdom, with nothing whatsoever
to say about what branch of the services he would join. As
things stood, he was free to steer as clear as possible of the
more tradition-bound centers of the armed forces. He
decided to leave immediately for Canada, there to volunteer
for the Air Force.

Esmond was of the opinion that the only thing which really
mattered in life now was the defeat of the Axis powers. The
horrors they were visiting on Europe made it unthinkable to
stand aside from the war. If Hitler should win, he reasoned

— and, as the days passed, news from the front began to make this look quite probable — it would be unlikely that we or any of our friends would survive. Therefore, in view of all that was involved, it was pointless to dwell on the drabber and more distasteful aspects, the interminable drilling, mastery of neatness, submission to all kinds of meaningless routines administered by a legion of Officer Class petty tyrants that he anticipated in a war which was basically being run by English Tories. Overriding all this were the issues at stake; exactly the same issues, he felt, as in Spain, only on a much larger scale, for now the survival of the whole of Europe was in the balance.

His attitude toward his own prospects was serious and practical. He was prepared to submit wholeheartedly to whatever lay in store for him in Canada, to suppress for now any temptation that might arise to torment, bait, or in any way harass his superiors in the Air Force. He would, of course, have to overcome the habits of a lifetime in order to carry out this resolution; but he was convinced that it could be done.

Esmond was a complicated and many-sided person, with an enormous capacity for change and almost none for self-analysis. His reversal of mood at this time was one that he would, no doubt, had he given it any thought, have put down entirely to the practical needs, as he saw them, of the existing situation; just as he would have defended any of his past attitudes on the grounds of necessity in the particular circumstances in which he had found himself at any given time. It would have seemed to him merely logical that his entire outlook should now be colored by a single-minded devotion to the problem of winning the war; for he was above all a person of political action, and this quality, dormant when no action seemed called for, now came to the fore in full force.

Perhaps it is inevitable that, to those who came into his orbit, Esmond appeared in so many different guises, for the personality of a fifteen- to twenty-one year-old, no matter how strong, is still in a state of flux and development, now one trait and now another emerging as the dominant one. I always thought that my family looked on him as a sort of Struwwelpeter ("There he stands! With his nasty hair and hands!"), a youthful ruffian of uncouth appearance and even less couth ways; in fact, a cousin once remarked, "It seems so strange that you and Esmond should have managed to have such a sweet little baby, I was quite sure it would turn out to be a baby dragon." To his friends among his contemporaries, he appeared as a delightful but formidable figure, always excellent company because so predictably unpredictable, at times a leader, but more often too dangerous to follow. To the Durrs and others who got to know him best after he joined the Air Force, during his frequent visits to the States, he seemed to epitomize all that was best and most hopeful of his generation: "though there's nothing *sweet* about Esmond," Virginia used to say regretfully — for she rather liked sweetness, a quality much cultivated by her fellow Southerners.

Whichever of these contrasting views of Esmond may have been closest to the objective truth, to me he was my whole world, my rescuer, the translator of all my dreams into reality, the fascinating companion of my whole adult life — three years, already — and the center of all happiness.

Both Esmond and I would have scouted the idea that anything in our conduct was remotely attributable either to heredity or to upbringing, for, like most people, we regarded ourselves as "self-made," free agents in every respect, the products of our own actions and decisions. Yet our style of behavior during much of our life together, the strong streak of delinquency which I found so attractive in Esmond and which struck such a responsive chord in me, his carefree intransigence, even his supreme self-confidence — a feeling of being able to walk unscathed through any flame — are not hard to trace to an English upper class ancestry and upbringing.

The qualities of patience, modesty, forbearance and natural self-discipline that the worker brings to his struggle for a better life, the instinctive respect for the fundamental dignity of every other human being — even his enemy — so often displayed by the Negro or Jew in his own fight for equality, were on the whole conspicuously lacking in us, or only present in the most undeveloped form.

Esmond's strong and perfectly genuine love for his fellow man was hardly of the St. Francis of Assisi type, his hatred of war hardly that of a Gandhi. His brand of socialism was uncluttered by fine Christian sentiments, for like Boud he was a gifted hater, although unlike her he directed his venom against the enemies of humanity, peace and freedom.

Our childhood surroundings, through which ran a rich vein of lunacy, and in Esmond's case of brutality, were hardly calculated to endow us with an instinct for the highest in humanity and culture. No wonder that much of our rebellion against this past took at times a highly personal turn. "Comrades, Oi bring a message from the grive!" we once heard a Hyde Park Sunday speaker declare. "From the grive of Lenin, Marx and Nietzsche! You see them things be'oind them plite glass winders in Selfridge's. Brike them winders! Tike them things!" We never did find out just what Nietzsche was doing in such company, and although we chortled at this odd speech, we did feel a certain sympathy for the point of view it expressed. "Tike that car! Pocket them cigars!" we might have paraphrased from time to time as these opportunities presented themselves.

In other generations the same heritage no doubt produced its quota of gentleman racers of horses or cars, gentleman gamblers with love or money, who so often managed to die eventually horseless, carless, penniless and unloved. Such pursuits held no interest for our generation. The drama that attracted us and so many of our contemporaries was the real-life drama of politics, the vision of organizing a world of plenty and a good life for all. To the diversity of banners offering to lead the way to the new life flocked a tremendous variety of people from all kinds of different backgrounds.

While almost all of them, I think it can truthfully be said, joined the struggle from the highest motives, and would have gone to any lengths of personal sacrifice to further whatever cause they followed, some, like us, had a number of old scores to settle along the way. Too much security as children, coupled with too much discipline imposed on us from above by force or threat of force, had developed in us a high degree of wickedness, a sort of extension of childhood naughtiness. We not only egged each other on to ever greater baiting and acts of outrage against the class we had left, but delighted in matching wits with the world generally; in fact, it was our way of life. Years later, Philip Toynbee reminded me of the time we had stolen a carload of top hats from the cloakroom of the Eton chapel, and of the time we had pilfered the curtains at a rich country house where we were staying to embellish the Rotherhithe Street windows. "Don't you *remember?*" he kept saying. When I confessed that I remembered only the barest outlines of these particular incidents, Philip rejoined sadly, "It all made an enormous impression on me, but I suppose that to you and Esmond it was just another day's work."

Yet by the end of his short life * Esmond had almost com-

* He was killed in action in November, 1941, at the age of 23.

pletely outgrown the violence and automatic rebellion against authority of his adolescence, had replaced these qualities with a most serious devotion to the cause which to him was the all-important goal, without the realization of which life would no longer be worth living: the defeat of fascism. "Your buccaneering days are over now, Esmond," Virginia Durr used to say teasingly. "My Lord! How neat and respectable you look in your uniform!"

The winding up of our affairs in Miami was a simple matter, for by the sort of coincidence which so often seemed to regulate our lives the six months' bar license was just expiring and we had saved almost enough to repay the $1000 loan. Less simple was the prospect of having to learn to live apart for any length of time — at least for a matter of months, perhaps for as long as a year, depending on how long the Air Force training course should turn out to be. The unutterable blankness of such a separation loomed menacingly for both of us, and we each tried rather unsuccessfully to reassure the other that it wouldn't really be for very long, that soon we should be together again in England.

On the long drive up from Miami to Washington, which was to be Esmond's taking-off point, we discussed the future. We decided to have a baby right away, a friend and companion for me during the next few years. By the end of the war it would be just the right age — three? four? five? — to appreciate the new postwar social order that we were convinced was on the way.

Meanwhile, I would get a job in Washington, and perhaps enroll in some sort of training course — journalism? stenography? — which would come in useful both during and after the war. Plans, plans, plans; Esmond was a master planner, and he managed to infuse these discussions with so much life, make it all sound such fun and so constructive, that it was impossible to take too gloomy a view of the months ahead.

Esmond urged me to look into the possibility of living with the Durrs, pointing out that the bustling atmosphere of a large family, and Virginia's inexhaustible energy, would greatly reduce the danger of loneliness. I was delighted with this idea. Not only were the Durrs a center of all that was fascinating in Washington life, but they radiated warmth and affection — qualities that seemed very important just then. Living in the midst of such a family would undoubtedly be the perfect arrangement, something completely new to look forward to, an adventure in itself.

We dropped in on them as soon as we arrived in Washington to see if they were really as wonderful as we remembered. Esmond pointed out that, in spite of Virginia's rather casual treatment of Baby Sister the night we had dined there, she must have had considerable experience in looking after babies, which would be invaluable when ours was born. Virginia has often told me later that she sensed Esmond had preselected her for this task. There was an appraising look in his eyes, she recalls, as he glanced round her house. She felt there was nothing haphazard or unplanned in the fact that, when she subsequently invited me to stay for a weekend, I remained for two and a half years, adding yet another member to her bulging household during that time.

In Washington, there were a thousand details to attend to, inquiries about how to volunteer to be made at the Canadian legation, maps of the route to Canada to be studied, the car to be made ready for the trip. Esmond, solicitous that I might suffer unnecessarily if inaction should follow his departure, arranged for me to accompany Virginia Durr on a motor trip to the Democratic Convention in Chicago, which was to take place shortly after he left. The baby, already uncomfortably making its presence felt, was promptly nicknamed the Donk, after the Democratic Donkey.

At last all was attended to; there was no reason for further delay. Esmond's peculiar-looking luggage was stuffed about the car, a last fire in the engine doused with the contents of the cocktail shaker, "goodbyes" and "see you soons" ("not if I see you first!") said all round, and he drove slowly off down the Durr's drive. I watched the car turn the corner, feeling dimly that a chunk of my life was now over for good, rounded off and put behind.